# Moments of Peace for Moms

365 Daily Devotions from

## Our Daily Bread

## Our Daily Bread
### Publishing™

*Moments of Peace for Moms: 365 Daily Devotions
from Our Daily Bread*
© 2019 by Our Daily Bread Publishing
All rights reserved.

Requests for permission to quote from this book should be
directed to: Permissions Department, Our Daily Bread Publishing,
PO Box 3566, Grand Rapids, MI 49501,
or contact us by email at permissionsdept@odb.org.

All Scripture quotations, unless otherwise indicated, are
taken from the Holy Bible, New International Version®,
NIV®. Copyright © 1973, 1978, 1984, 2011 by Biblica,
Inc.™ Used by permission of Zondervan. All rights reserved
worldwide. www.zondervan.com. The "NIV" and "New
International Version" are trademarks registered in the United
States Patent and Trademark Office by Biblica, Inc.™

Scripture quotations marked KJV are
from the King James Version.

Scripture quotations marked NASB are from the New American
Standard Bible®, copyright © 1960, 1962, 1963, 1968, 1971,
1972, 1973, 1975, 1977, 1995 by the Lockman Foundation.
Used by permission. (Lockman.org)

Scripture quotations marked NKJV are from the New King James
Version®. Copyright © 1982 by Thomas Nelson.
Used by permission. All rights reserved.

Scripture quotations marked NLT are taken from the Holy
Bible, New Living Translation, copyright ©1996, 2004, 2015
by Tyndale House Foundation. Used by permission of Tyndale
House Publishers, Inc., Carol Stream, Illinois 60188.
All rights reserved.

Interior design by Sherri L. Hoffman

Printed in the United States of America

20  21  22  23  24  25  26  /  8  7  6  5  4  3  2

# A Break for Mom

$\mathcal{M}$oms deserve their very own devotional book. Of course, if you are a mom, you may not feel that you have time to read it—what with the thousand-and-one things that occupy your time.

But maybe, just maybe, the people you work so hard to guide and help and serve and love and encourage through life can band together to give you a break each day so you can replenish and renew your relationship with God. After all, what is better for the whole family than a mom who has a strong relationship with Jesus after spending quality time reading His Word and talking to Him in prayer?

We've strived to put together a collection of articles that you as a mother can use in those moments of peace and solitude to draw closer to your strength and your comfort—the God who made you, the Savior who redeemed you, and the Holy Spirit who energizes you.

We've selected a range of subjects in the articles, because no two moms need the same thing to reinvigorate their spiritual walk each day. Many of the articles have fun Mom stories—stories about kids and their mothers interacting in the course of real life. We've also chosen a number of articles that focus on achieving peace and calm by trusting our great God, because the whirlwind that is life sometimes calls for a reminder that our Savior is the Prince of Peace.

Also, we've chosen articles that were written both by current *Our Daily Bread* writers and by some of our "classic" writers—voices of wisdom from the past that can bring valuable insights into our lives as the often hectic twenty-first century approaches its second quarter. You'll find strength in the wisdom of writers from an earlier era, such as Julie Ackerman Link and Joanie Yoder. We think you'll be challenged and encouraged by all of the writers—new and old—as they dig into Scripture to pass along to you hope and inspiration from God's holy Word.

So, take a break from the hubbub that is the life of a mom. Sit down with your favorite cup of coffee, open up the Bible, and discover moments of peace that can bring calm to your heart and courage to your life.

## Influence of Godly Mothers

*Listen, my son, to your father's
instruction and do not forsake your
mother's teaching.* —PROVERBS 1:8

Many godly men of the past were richly blessed by what they learned from their mothers. Consider biblical characters Moses, Samuel, and Timothy, who had strong maternal influence. Or men like Augustine, John Newton, and the zealous Wesley brothers. Their names would probably never have graced the pages of history if it hadn't been for the godly women who raised them in Christ-honoring homes.

Susannah Wesley, the mother of preachers John and Charles, spent an hour each day praying for her seventeen children. She also took each child aside for an hour every week to discuss spiritual matters. Here are a few of her training rules: (1) Subdue self-will in a child and thus work together with God to save his soul. (2) Teach him to pray as soon as he can speak. (3) Give him nothing he cries for and only what is good for him if he asks politely. (4) To prevent lying, punish no fault that is freely confessed, but never allow a rebellious, sinful act to go unnoticed. (5) Commend and reward good behavior. (6) Strictly observe all promises you have made to your child.

Godly mothers can change the world!          —HB

# A Prayer Challenge

*Then people brought little children to
Jesus for him to place his hands on them
and pray for them. But the disciples
rebuked them.* —MATTHEW 19:13

A young mother once said, "I wish I could wrap my children in bubble wrap to protect them from the big, bad world outside."

Author Stormie Omartian understands how that mother feels. In her book *The Power of a Praying Parent*, she writes, "One day I cried out to God, saying, 'Lord, this is too much for me. I can't keep a twenty-four-hours-a-day, moment-by-moment watch on my son. How can I ever have peace?'"

God responded by leading Stormie and her husband to become praying parents. They began to intercede for their son daily, mentioning the details of his life in prayer.

The desire to wrap our children in bubble wrap to protect them is rooted in fear. Wrapping children in prayer, as Jesus did (Matthew 19:13–15), is a powerful alternative. God cares more about our children than we do, so we can release them into His hands by praying for them. As we pray, He will give us the peace we long for (Philippians 4:6–7).

This challenge is for all parents—even those whose children have grown up: Don't ever stop wrapping your children in prayer!         —JY

## Safe and Still

*Whoever dwells in the shelter of the*
*Most High will rest in the shadow*
*of the Almighty.* —PSALM 91:1

As a full-of-energy preschooler, my son Xavier avoided afternoon quiet time. Being still often resulted in an unwanted, though much-needed, nap. He did everything possible to evade the quiet. "Mom, I'm hungry . . . I'm thirsty . . . I have to go to the bathroom . . . I want a hug."

Understanding the benefits of stillness, I'd help Xavier settle down by inviting him to snuggle. Leaning into my side, he'd give in to sleep.

Early in my spiritual life, I mirrored my son's desire to remain active. Busyness made me feel accepted, important, and in control. Surrendering to rest only affirmed my frail humanity. So I avoided stillness and silence, doubting the Lord could handle things without my help.

But God is our refuge, no matter what lies ahead. The path may seem long, scary, or overwhelming, but His love envelops us. He hears us, answers us, and stays with us . . . now and forever, into eternity (Psalm 91:1–16).

We can embrace the quiet and lean into God's unfailing love and constant presence. We can be still, because we're safe under the shelter of His unchanging faithfulness (v. 4).                              —XD

## Comforted by God

*When anxiety was great within me, your*
*consolation brought me joy.* —PSALM 94:19

A mother was trying to calm her fretful little daughter. Soon her loving embrace and tender caresses quieted the four-year-old's uneasiness. But the mother herself was grieving because of the recent death of her own mother.

Looking up, the little girl saw her moist eyes and asked sweetly, "Mama, do you want to be holded too?" The mother's tears began to flow freely, and the child hugged her and whispered, "Mama, God will hold you, won't He?" Those words consoled her.

How reassuring to know that our Lord is the "God of all comfort" (2 Corinthians 1:3). Although we may sorrow greatly, God is good, and heaven will one day reveal that His purpose was never to hurt us but to bless us. So we cast all our care upon the Lord, believing that He is holding us even when we do not feel it. There is solid comfort in that reality.

As we turn our problems over to the loving Savior, we will be able to say with the psalmist, "When anxiety was great within me, your consolation brought me joy" (Psalm 94:19).　　　　　　—HB

## He Carries Us

*"As a mother comforts her child, so will I comfort you; and you will be comforted over Jerusalem."* —ISAIAH 66:13

My friend entrusted me with the privilege of holding her precious, four-day-old daughter. Not long after I took the baby into my arms, she started to fuss. Despite my best attempts and my decade and a half of parenting experience, I couldn't pacify her. She became increasingly upset until I placed her back into the crook of her mother's eager arm. Peace washed over her almost instantaneously. My friend knew precisely how to hold and pat her daughter to alleviate her distress.

God extends comfort to His children like a mother: tender, trustworthy, and diligent in her efforts to calm her child. When we are weary or upset, He carries us affectionately in His arms. As our Father and Creator, He knows us intimately. He "will keep in perfect peace all who trust in [him], all whose thoughts are fixed on [him]" (Isaiah 26:3 NLT).

When the troubles of this world weigh heavy on our hearts, we can find comfort in the knowledge that He protects and fights for us, His children, as a loving parent.                                    —KH

## Don't Forget Yourself!

*"Father, glorify me in your presence
with the glory I had with you before
the world began."* —JOHN 17:5

Are you surprised that Christ's high-priestly prayer in John 17 began with a petition for himself? He was at the most crucial moment of His earthly life; soon He would take up the cross and bear the punishment for the sins of the world. His concern for others was obvious. He would specifically mention His disciples. Then He would intercede for His church, which would endure great persecution through the centuries. But first He prayed for himself.

Some Christians think it's wrong to pray for themselves. However, we shouldn't feel guilty about bringing our own needs and concerns to the Lord. A girl listened carefully to her mother's prayers and said, "Mom, you're always praying for somebody else. You never pray for yourself, but I think you should." She was right, for we do need to ask the Lord for His guidance, forgiveness, patience, and grace.

When you spend time in God's presence, tell Him about your hopes, your worries, your desires, and your needs. He'll help you see things more clearly and give you the needed direction. As you go to the Lord in prayer, pray for others. But don't forget yourself.                                                   —DE

## Be Still, My Soul

*But I have calmed and quieted myself, I am*
*like a weaned child with its mother; like a*
*weaned child I am content.* —PSALM 131:2

Picture a mother poised lovingly over her child, gently patting, softly speaking—"Hush now. Shhh." The demeanor and simple words are meant to comfort and quiet anxious little ones in the midst of disappointment, discomfort, or pain. When I ponder Psalm 131:2, this is the picture that comes to mind.

The language and flow of this psalm suggest that the writer, David, had experienced something that provoked serious reflection. Have you experienced a disappointment, defeat, or failure that prompted thoughtful, reflective prayer? When you lose a friendship or lose your composure with your family? David poured out his heart to the Lord and in the process did a bit of honest soul-searching and inventory (Psalm 131:1). In making peace with his circumstances, he found contentment like that of a young child who was satisfied with simply being with his or her mother (v. 2).

Life's circumstances change, and sometimes we are humbled. Yet we can be hopeful and content knowing that there is One who has promised to never leave or forsake us. We can trust Him fully.          —AJ

## Sharing Is Hard

*Do not forget to do good and to share
with others, for with such sacrifices
God is pleased.* —HEBREWS 13:16

On the way home from church, my daughter sat in the backseat enjoying Goldfish crackers as my other children implored her to share. Trying to redirect the conversation, I asked the hoarder of snacks, "What did you do in class today?" She said they made a basket of bread and fish because a child gave Jesus five loaves and two fish that Jesus used to feed more than 5,000 people (John 6:1–13).

"That was very kind of the little boy to share. Do you think maybe God is asking you to share your fish?" I asked. "No, Momma," she replied.

I tried to encourage her to share. She was unconvinced. "There's not enough for everyone!"

Sharing is hard. And the assumption is that if I give, I will be left wanting.

Paul reminds us that all we have comes from God, who wants to enrich us so He can "produce a great harvest of generosity" in us (2 Corinthians 9:10–11 NLT). We can share joyfully because God promises to care for us even as we are generous to others.   —LS

## Spiritual Jotting

*Pray continually.*
—1 THESSALONIANS 5:17

I have met many young mothers who are discouraged by their inadequate devotional life. The term "quiet time" only reminds them how little "quiet" or "time" they have for Bible reading, prayer, and meditation.

When my children were young, a speaker shared how she overcame this dilemma during her childrearing years. Throughout her house she placed pencils and notepads. During the day, wherever she was, she would jot down insights, prayer needs, or Bible verses as they came to mind. Each evening she would gather up her jottings—the ingredients of a spiritual feast she had been preparing all day. How eagerly she welcomed the opportunity to nourish her hungry spirit with her Bible and her jottings! I put her method to the test, and my daily devotions became what they needed to be—a workable vehicle for strengthening my devotion to Christ.

If you're an overworked mother, I recommend "spiritual jotting," both now and as a lifelong habit. Not only will it put more devotion into your devotions, but it will also bring you closer to fulfilling Paul's admonition to "pray continually" (1 Thessalonians 5:17).

—JY

# God Arranged Their Seating

*In their hearts humans plan their course, but the
L*ORD* establishes their steps.* —PROVERBS 16:9

As Pastor John Aker boarded a plane in Newark, he discovered that he had been assigned a seat next to a man named Richard. Once airborne, the two began talking. Richard had come from the Memorial Sloan Kettering Cancer Center. His condition: skin cancer. Doctors gave him ten months at best. He was going home to Nebraska. "May I tell you about something that changed my life?" asked John. Richard nodded. John explained the way of salvation, and Richard was interested. Right there, 20,000 feet over Chicago, he gave his heart to Christ.

Months later, John again boarded a plane at Newark. This time he sat next to an elderly woman headed for Beatrice, Nebraska. Amazingly, this was Richard's mother. She told him her son was growing in the Lord. "I'm so encouraged," said Richard's mother. John replied, "I'm inspired that Richard has followed through and that God arranged for us to sit together." The woman replied, "Just before you came on the plane a woman asked me to change seats with her."

God does direct our steps! If we are yielded to Him, He will use us. Let's trust God to "arrange the seating" in our lives.                                    —DD

# The Freedom of Boundaries

*Direct me in the path of your commands,*
*for there I find delight.* —PSALM 119:35

The temperature outside hovered near zero, but my children begged to go sledding. I thought it over and said yes, but I asked them to bundle up, stay together, and come inside after fifteen minutes.

I lovingly created those rules so my children could play freely without suffering frostbite. I think the author of Psalm 119 recognized the same good intent in God as he penned two verses that might seem contradictory: "I will always obey your law" and "I will walk about in freedom, for I have sought out your precepts" (vv. 44–45). The psalmist associated freedom with a spiritually law-abiding life.

Following God's wise, loving instruction allows us to escape the consequences of bad choices. Without the weight of guilt or pain, we are freer to enjoy our lives.

While my kids were sledding, I watched them blast down the hill—smiling at the sound of their laughter. They were free within the boundaries I'd given them. This compelling paradox is present in our relationship with God—and we say, "Direct me in the path of your commands, for there I find delight" (v. 35).

—JBS

## Faces

*We all, who with unveiled faces contemplate the Lord's glory, are being transformed into his image with ever-increasing glory, which comes from the Lord, who is the Spirit.* —2 CORINTHIANS 3:18

When our granddaughter Sarah was young, she explained to me what happens when you die: "Only your face goes to heaven, not your body. You get a new body but keep the same face."

Sarah's concept of our eternal state was a child's understanding, of course, but she did grasp an essential truth. In a sense, our faces are a visible reflection of the invisible soul.

My mother used to say that an angry look might someday freeze on my face. She was wiser than she knew. A worried brow, an angry set to our mouths, a sly look in our eyes may reveal a miserable soul. On the other hand, kind eyes, a gentle look, a warm and welcoming smile—despite wrinkles, blemishes, and other disfigurements—become the marks of inner transformation.

We can't do much about our faces, but we can do something about the kind of person we're growing into. We can pray for humility, patience, kindness, tolerance, gratefulness, forgiveness, peace, and love (Galatians 5:22–26).

By God's grace, may you and I grow toward an inner resemblance to our Lord.             —DR

## "Peace, Be Still!"

*He got up, rebuked the wind and said to the waves, "Quiet! Be still!" Then the wind died down and it was completely calm.* —MARK 4:39

The account of the storm-tossed disciples and their deliverance still has significance for us today. We are adrift on the sea of life, but all is well if Jesus is in the boat with us.

To our faithless eyes, God often appears detached and unconcerned, as though He were asleep. Yet His constant watchfulness is our guarantee of safety. To the frantic inquiry, "Teacher, don't you care?" He answers, "Why are you so afraid? Do you still have no faith?" (Mark 4:38, 40). As long as we insist on looking at circumstances, there will be unrest in our hearts. But as soon as we fix our eyes on the Almighty One, there will come a restfulness and peace that only His grace can impart.

In time of trouble, all our resources may be cut off. Therefore, our peace must not be dependent on our surroundings. The peace that Jesus gives (John 14:27) continues to satisfy us in our times of need and produces a great calm.                    —HB

## A Gift from God

*Lord our God, all this abundance that we
have provided for building you a temple for
your Holy Name comes from your hand, and
all of it belongs to you.* —1 CHRONICLES 29:16

When I was eighteen, I worked and saved until I
had enough money for a year of school. Then my
mom had emergency surgery, and I realized I had the
money in the bank to pay for her operation.

My love for my mother suddenly took precedence
over my plans. These words from *Passion and Purity*
by Elisabeth Elliot took on new meaning: "If we hold
tightly to anything given to us, unwilling to let it go
when the time comes to let it go . . . , we stunt the
growth of the soul. . . . 'If God gave it to me,' we say,
'it's mine. I can do what I want with it.' No. The truth
is that it is ours to thank Him for and ours to offer
back to Him."

I saw my savings as gift from God! I could give
to my family because I was sure God could get me
through school another way, and He did.

Today, think about David's prayer from 1 Chronicles 29:14, "Everything we have has come from you,
and we give you only what you first gave us" (NLT).

—KO

## "Go Away, Satan"

*Submit yourselves, then, to God. Resist the
devil, and he will flee from you.* —JAMES 4:7

A mother was resting on the couch after placing a
dish of fruit on a nearby table. As she lay there with
her eyes half closed, she saw her little daughter tip-
toe into the room. Thinking her mom was asleep,
she took some grapes and sneaked off. Five minutes
passed; then the child crept back into the room and
returned all of the grapes. She whispered, "This time
I beat you, Mr. Devil. Now go away!" The mother
was glad her young daughter recognized the enemy
of her soul and had decided to resist him.

That little girl's experience may not seem very serious to us, but to her the grapes were a real enticement
to evil. The tactics of the evil one are always the same.
He is constantly stalking the sheep of God's pasture
to ensnare them in a subtle trap. If we don't resist
when he tests us with trivial things, the next time he
will shift his attack to a more critical area.

Are you facing a great temptation? Don't waver.
By God's grace resist the devil. With the Spirit's help,
exclaim victoriously, "Go away, Satan!"          —HB

## Carried through Our Pain

*You will not abandon me to the realm
of the dead, . . . You make known to me
the path of life; you will fill me with joy
in your presence.* —PSALM 16:10–11

Have you noticed how peace—powerful, unexplain-
able peace (Philippians 4:7)—can somehow fill our
hearts even in our deepest grief? I experienced this
at my father's memorial service. As a long line of
sympathetic acquaintances passed by offering their
condolences, I was relieved to see a good high school
friend. Without a word, he wrapped me in a long bear
hug. His quiet understanding flooded me with the
first feelings of peace within grief that difficult day,
a powerful reminder that I wasn't as alone as I felt.

The kind of peace and joy God brings into our
lives isn't caused by a choice to stoically stomp down
the pain during hard times. David implies that it's
more like a gift we can't help but experience when we
take refuge in our good God (Psalm 16:1–2).

The life God has given us—even in its pain—is still
beautiful and good (vv. 6–8). And we can surrender
to His loving arms that tenderly carry us through our
pain into a peace and joy that even death can never
quench (v. 11).                                   —MB

## With and Without Words

*"So you became a model to all the believers in Macedonia and Achaia."* —1 THESSALONIANS 1:7

Jay Kesler told of a sailor who committed immoral acts while on leave in Tokyo. That night as he lay in his bunk, sleep would not come to his eyes. His thoughts kept going back to his godly mother. He could see her kneeling beside her bed, praying for him. He recalled too the warm and loving life she had lived over the years. These vivid mental images pressed heavily upon his conscience. Finally, he could resist the Holy Spirit's urging no longer. Getting out of his bunk, he kneeled and prayed, "God of my mother, forgive me." Right there he became a Christian, and he went on to serve the Lord as a pastor.

Helping others find the joy of forgiveness in Christ is a challenging and rewarding task. It's one reason God saved us and left us on this earth. Living for Him by showing kindness, being thoughtful, and doing good through the power of the Spirit is imperative. Such a testimony—personified by this sailor's mother—will leave an unforgettable impression for Christ on others. This kind of witness without words gives the greatest impact to our witness with words.

—DD

## He Understands

*Because he himself suffered when he was*
*tempted, he is able to help those who*
*are being tempted.* —HEBREWS 2:18

How comforting it is to know that we have a Savior who can identify with our trials, suffering, and sorrow! Our Lord knew both physical and mental anguish.

Jesus knew the suffering caused by being misunderstood. Members of His own family did not understand that He had come to die. He experienced the pain of poverty. He faced strong temptations. He felt the sorrow of losing a good friend to death (John 11).

Gordon Chilvers tells of a grief-stricken mother. The death of a wayward daughter had left her crushed with sorrow. Her grief was so heavy that she couldn't cry. Then a woman came to see her who had experienced an identical loss. She sat down beside the sorrowing mother and lovingly placed an arm around her waist. With her face close to the face of the grieving woman, she wept. Soon the bereaved mother began to weep and relief came at last. That woman could sympathize because she had known the same sorrow.

We have One who has experienced deep suffering. Tell Him about your pain and draw on His strength. He understands and cares.                    —PVG

## The Snake and the Tricycle

*I too decided to write an orderly account for*
*you, most excellent Theophilus.* —LUKE 1:3

For years, I retold a story from a time in Ghana when my brother and I were toddlers. As I recalled it, he had parked our old iron tricycle on a small cobra. The trike was too heavy for the snake, which remained trapped under the front wheel.

But after our mother had passed away, we discovered a long-lost letter Mom wrote recounting the incident. In reality, I had parked the tricycle on the snake, and my brother had run to tell Mom. Her eyewitness account, written close to the actual event, revealed the reality.

The historian Luke understood the importance of accurate records. He explained how the story of Jesus was "handed down to us by those who from the first were eyewitnesses" (Luke 1:2). The result was the gospel of Luke.

Our faith is not based on hearsay or wishful thinking. It is rooted in the well-documented life of Jesus, who came to give us peace with God. His story stands.

—TG

## Our Central Focus

*He must become greater;*
*I must become less.*
—JOHN 3:30

Krista stood in the freezing cold, looking at the beautiful snow-encased lighthouse along the lake. As she pulled out her phone to take pictures, her glasses fogged over. She couldn't see a thing, so she pointed her camera toward the lighthouse and snapped three pictures. Looking at them later, she realized the camera had been set to take "selfies." She laughed as she said, "My focus was me, me, and me. All I saw was me." This got me thinking of a similar mistake—becoming so self-focused we lose sight of the bigger picture of God's plan.

Jesus's cousin John clearly knew his focus wasn't himself. From the start, he recognized that his calling was to point others to Jesus. "Look, the Lamb of God!" he said when he saw Jesus coming toward him (John 1:29). Later, John said, "'I am not the Messiah but am sent ahead of him.' . . . He must become greater; I must become less" (3:28–30).

May the central focus of our lives be Jesus and loving Him with our whole heart.                —AC

## Horsepower

*Ask for the ancient paths, ask where the
good way is, and walk in it, and you will
find rest for your souls.* —JEREMIAH 6:16

On a cold Michigan winter day, a woman in labor
was being rushed to the hospital. But the ambulance
slid off an icy road into a ditch. A four-wheel drive
truck stopped, and the driver tried unsuccessfully to
haul the emergency vehicle out.

That's when help arrived. An Amish man driving
a two-horse team stopped. He told the ambulance
driver that the horses' shoes had been sharpened so
they would bite into the ice. He hooked up the horses
to the ambulance, and they walked it right out of
the ditch.

This young mother received help from an old-
fashioned source of strength. On that day, old ways
helped to ensure the safe arrival of new life into the
world.

More than 2,500 years ago, Jeremiah reminded
us that there is nothing more relevant than the truth
of the past. He urged his neighbors to walk in the
old paths of truth so they would find peace and rest
for their souls (Jeremiah 6:16). Today, we can still
find rest and peace in the old but ever new story of
Jesus—our eternal source of truth (Matthew 11:28).

—MD

## We Belong Together

*All the believers were together and had
everything in common.* —ACTS 2:44

My friend Carrie's five-year-old daughter, Maija, has
an interesting approach to playtime. She loves mixing
together dolls from different playsets to come up with
a new community. She believes her people are happiest when they're together, despite being different
sizes and shapes.

This reminds me of God's purpose for the church.
On the day of Pentecost, "there were staying in Jerusalem God-fearing Jews from every nation under
heaven" (Acts 2:5). Though these people were from
different cultures and spoke different languages, the
Holy Spirit's arrival made them a new community: the
church. From then on, they would be considered one
body, unified by the death and resurrection of Jesus.

The leaders of this new body were Jesus's disciples. If Jesus hadn't united them, more than likely
they would never have come together. And now
more people—"about three thousand" (2:41)—had
become Christ-followers. Thanks to the Holy Spirit,
this once divided group "had everything in common"
(v. 44). They were willing to share what they had
with each other.

The Holy Spirit continues to bridge the gaps between people groups of various origins and languages.
As believers in Christ, we belong together.     —LW

## Unknown Riches

*Oh, the depth of the riches of the wisdom
and knowledge of God!* —ROMANS 11:33

Many years ago, as the story goes, an elderly woman
in Scotland lived in poverty. Her son had moved to
America and had not returned to his native land. One
day a friend visited the mother and asked, "Does your
son ever help you?" "No," she said reluctantly, "but
he writes me nice long letters and sends me interesting pictures of famous people." The visitor asked,
"May I see the pictures?" When the aged mother
took them out of a drawer, the friend was amazed
to see that they were all sizable banknotes. She had
been needlessly living in poverty.

Do we ever do that by failing to see the treasures
found in Scripture? Bishop Perowne wrote, "Of all
books in the world, the Bible is one which will not
yield up its riches and its sweetness except to the
diligent and faithful and earnest student."

It's fine to believe the Book "from cover to cover,"
but we must apply its truths to our everyday lives.
Let's cash in on all our "banknotes"!          —PVG

## Someone Special

*"There are those who curse their fathers and
do not bless their mothers."* —PROVERBS 30:11

A postcard arrived in the mail. Then another. And a
third. They were unsigned, but I could tell they came
from the same person—an elderly mother who had
given her all for her son but was getting only cruel
abuse in return.

She wrote, "Will you please print some articles on
how Christian people should treat their elderly parents and widows? I have been physically and verbally
abused by a son who professes to be a Christian."

To think about such a tragedy reminds us that we
need to think often about the goodness of motherhood—to say thank you to the one who has nursed
our pains and cheered our gains. We must honor
Mother for being a guiding light, a calming sight,
and a warrior for right. And we must help any moms
who are like the one who wrote those cards.

Mothers cherish daily praise and offers of help.
They enjoy frequent phone calls and visits. They need
love and appreciation. Their needs should be met.

From all of us, we say thank you to our mothers.

—DB

# Peace of Mind

*Trust in the LORD forever, for the LORD, the LORD himself, is the Rock eternal.* —ISAIAH 26:4

A contest was held in which artists were invited to paint a picture of perfect peace. The judges eventually narrowed the number of competitors to two. The first had created a scene of a quiet mountain lake. The second depicted a thundering waterfall with the branch of a birch tree bending over the foam. On the fork of that limb, wet with spray, a robin sat undisturbed on her nest. The first picture spoke of tranquility, but the second won the prize because it showed in dramatic detail that absolute calmness can be found in the midst of turbulent surroundings. Yes, it is easy to remain unruffled when everything is quiet and serene. But to rest while the storm is raging—that is "perfect peace."

A. B. Simpson, commenting on Isaiah 26:3–4, remarked, "The Christian's rest is not the result of passive inaction. Rather, it is an active reliance on the mighty and everlasting arms of God."

As you face the trials and testings of life, turn all your anxieties over to the Lord. Center your thoughts on Him and the precious promises of His Word, and you'll experience a peace that passes all understanding.                                    —HB

## Shine Through

*"In the same way, let your light shine before
others, that they may see your good deeds and
glorify your Father in heaven."* —MATTHEW 5:16

A little girl wondered what a saint might be. One day
her mother took her to a great cathedral to see the
gorgeous stained-glass windows with scenes from the
Bible. When she saw the beauty of it all she cried out
loud, "Now I know what saints are. They are people
who let the light shine through!"

When a translation of Scripture uses the word
*saint*, it is actually referring to anyone who belongs
to God through faith in Christ. Saints are people like
us who have the high calling of serving God while
reflecting our relationship with Him wherever we
are and in whatever we do. That is why the apostle
Paul prayed that the eyes and understanding of his
readers would be opened to think of themselves as
the treasured inheritance of Christ and saints of God
(Ephesians 1:18).

So what then do we see in the mirror? If we are
fulfilling our calling, we will look like people who,
maybe even without realizing it, are letting the rich
colors of the love, joy, peace, patience, kindness,
gentleness, faithfulness, and self-control of God shine
through.        —KO

## Good Medicine

*A cheerful heart is good medicine.*
—PROVERBS 17:22

My wise Christian mother often quoted Proverbs 17:22 to me: "A merry heart doeth good like a medicine" (KJV). Usually she did this when I needed to change my attitude. Would I allow a negative spirit to poison my thinking, or would I embrace an outlook of thankfulness and its resulting joy?

She would smile at me and quote that verse. That was it. No sermon, no lecture, just eight words about the phenomenal value of God-produced happiness that springs from deep inside.

In Proverbs 15 we read, "A happy heart makes the face cheerful" (v. 13). The state of my heart determines the look on my face.

Next we read, "All the days of the oppressed are wretched, but the cheerful heart has a continual feast" (v. 15). When circumstances yield discouragement, I can still eat from God's rich banquet table of love. That's because no matter what life gives me, God can "fill my heart with joy" (Psalm 4:7).

My mother believed that if I stopped complaining and began thanking God for the possibilities at hand, I could have the powerful medicine of a merry heart.

I think she was right.                    —DM

## An Open Book

*And whatever you do, whether in word*
*or deed, do it all in the name of the*
*Lord Jesus.* —COLOSSIANS 3:17

The Christian's life should be an open book, inscribed on every page with good works that reveal a vital relationship with the Lord. For instance, believers must do more than merely encourage those in need; they should help them in tangible ways in the name of the Savior (James 2:14–17). Their lives should be in harmony with His will so their walk can be consistent with their talk.

A Christian girl was giving her testimony and telling of her love for the Savior. Just before she sat down, a man stood up in the back row and asked this question, "What you're saying is all right, but tell me, how do you behave at home?" Graciously, she responded, "Sir, my mother is sitting just in front of you. Why don't you ask her?" The mother arose and said, "I can truthfully say that at home my daughter lives just the way she talks here." The man was silent, seemingly convicted by the reality of the girl's witness.

May our love for the Lord lead us to be Christlike in both our actions and our words.          —HB

## Resurrection Power

*When Mary reached the place where Jesus*
*was and saw him, she fell at his feet and said,*
*"Lord, if you had been here, my brother*
*would not have died." —*JOHN 11:32

Audrey, who just the day before had been dangling
from the monkey bars, was listless with a 105-degree
fever. I quickly took her to the pediatrician, expect-
ing a diagnosis and some antibiotics. But the diagnosis wasn't clear, and we went home. But when the
fever persisted, we bee-lined to the ER, and an X-ray
revealed severe pneumonia. The doctor's tone was
serious. "We need to admit her to the ICU. She's a
very sick little girl."

*Was I too late? Why didn't the experts catch it?* In
a sudden crisis, it can be tempting to blame self, others, and even God. Fear wants to devour our faith,
"Lord, if you have all this power, why are You holding out on us?"

Mary reacted similarly to Jesus's delay. When Jesus
finally came, Lazarus was four days dead. Mary's
unhinged, raw emotions spilled out: "Lord, if you
had been here, my brother would not have died"
(John 11:32). But this situation was not a surprise to
Jesus; in fact, He designed it to show His resurrection
power.

The Lord chose to heal Audrey. As mothers, we
can trust Jesus's presence as we "wait and watch" in
prayer.                                    —LR

## Love Hurts!

*"My command is this: Love each other
as I have loved you."* —JOHN 15:12

"Sometimes love sure hurts!" The mother and father were expressing the difficulties and heartaches of guiding their children through their teen years. "Maybe if we didn't love them quite so much it wouldn't be so hard," the husband added.

Even though love brings pain and sorrow, what would life be without it? In his book *The Four Loves*, C. S. Lewis wrote:

> To love at all is to be vulnerable. Love anything and your heart will be wrung and possibly be broken. If you want to make sure of keeping it intact, you must give your heart to no one, not even an animal. Wrap it carefully around with hobbies and little luxuries; avoid all entanglements; lock it up safe in the casket or coffin of your selfishness.

To love is to take risks, to expose our hearts. Sometimes it hurts! It hurt Christ, but He kept on loving, even at the cost of His life. He commanded us, "Love each other as I have loved you" (John 15:12).

We must keep loving that spouse, that teenager, that neighbor, that coworker. It is Christlike—and it's better than locking your heart in a coffin of self-centeredness.                    —DE

## Forgiven

*Blessed is the one whose transgressions are
forgiven, whose sins are covered.* —PSALM 32:1

A little boy had just been tucked into bed by his
mother, who was waiting to hear his prayers. But he
had been naughty that day, and now it was bothering
him. So he said, "Mama, I wish you'd go now and
leave me alone. I want to pray by myself."

She asked, "Bobby, is there anything you ought to
tell me?" "No, Mommy," he replied. "You would just
scold me, but God will forgive me and forget about it."

That little boy understood one of the greatest
salvation benefits of all—sins forgiven. The Bible
indicates that in Christ "we have redemption, the
forgiveness of sins" (Colossians 1:14). We who have
received Jesus as Savior enjoy freedom from sin's
eternal condemnation (Romans 8:1), and we can also
have daily forgiveness and cleansing (1 John 1:9).

We should never get the idea that our sins are
taken lightly by the Lord. But when we acknowledge our guilt with true repentance, God is ready to
forgive because of what Jesus did on the cross. It's up
to us to accept it.                              —RD

## Appreciated

*"Truly I tell you, wherever this gospel is preached
throughout the world, what she has done will
also be told, in memory of her."* —MATTHEW 26:13

The heroes and heroines of the Bible often take us by surprise. The woman in today's Scripture reading is a prime example. She was singled out by Jesus to be mentioned wherever the gospel is preached. She had scandalized some of those dining with Jesus by her breathtaking generosity. In anticipating Jesus's death, she had anointed Him with costly perfume that was worth more than a year's wages.

"Why this waste?" asked those at the table who expressed a concern for the poor. Had these same people been attending Jesus's funeral rather than a dinner with Him, I believe they would have reacted differently. Yet, when this woman showed Him her lavish love while He was alive, she was severely criticized for such waste.

We can learn a valuable lesson from the devotion of this woman. We need to break out our best perfumes for the living. Yet all too often we wait until someone dies to show the appreciation that we are reluctant to show in life.

Is there someone you know who would be honored and encouraged by an expression of your love and appreciation? Now is the time to open your heart to that person.                              —HR

## Real Love

*[Love] always protects, always trusts,*
*always hopes, always perseveres. Love*
*never fails.* —1 CORINTHIANS 13:7–8

A few years ago, my friend's mother was diagnosed with Alzheimer's disease. Since then, Beth has been forced to make tough decisions about her mom's care, and her heart has often been broken as she watched her vibrant and fun-loving mom slowly slipping away. In the process, my friend has learned that real love is not always easy or convenient.

After her mom was hospitalized for a couple of days, Beth wrote these words to some of her friends: "As backwards as it may seem, I'm very thankful for the journey I am on with my mom. Behind the memory loss, confusion, and utter helplessness is a beautiful person who loves life and is at complete peace. I am learning so much about what real love is."

The Bible reminds us that love is patient and kind. It is not self-seeking or easily angered. It "bears all things, believes all things, hopes all things, endures all things" (1 Corinthians 13:7 NKJV).

As we seek to show God's love to others, we can follow the example of Christ, who laid down His life for us (1 John 3:16–18).                    —CHK

## Three Keys to Peace

*Blessed is the people of whom this
is true; blessed is the people whose
God is the LORD.* —PSALM 144:15

In a story from a different era, a young boy was walking with his father three miles from his rural home to his grandmother's house. While they were visiting, the sun set. The boy recalls, "Between our home and grandmother's house was a swamp. The croaking of the frogs, the chirping of the crickets, and the shadows of the trees frightened me. I asked my father if there was any danger, but he assured me that there was nothing to dread. Taking me by the hand, he said, 'I will not allow anything to harm you.' Immediately my fears passed away and I was ready to face the world."

Someone has said that the three keys to real peace are: fret not, faint not, fear not.

1. Fret not—because God loves you
   (1 John 4:16).
2. Faint not—because God holds you
   (Psalm 139:10).
3. Fear not—because God keeps you
   (Psalm 121:5).

As we rest in the love of Christ and recognize that God holds our hand, we too shall be at peace and unafraid. Let's step out into the full joy and liberty of the children of God!                    —HB

## Praying or Packing?

*Show me the way I should go, for to
you I entrust my life.* —PSALM 143:8

I read an amusing story about a minister who received a call from a church that offered him a salary four times bigger than what he was then receiving. Being a devout man, he spent much time in prayer trying to discern what God wanted him to do.

One day a friend met the minister's young son on the street. "Do you know what your dad is going to do?" he asked.

"Well," replied the youngster, "Dad's praying, but Mom's packing!"

Sometimes we do that—instead of earnestly seeking God's design and plan, we move ahead of Him and suggest, "This is what I'm going to do."

Before we can go forward with confidence, we must resolve this basic issue: Do I really want to know what God wants me to do? Am I willing to do it? Or am I merely seeking His blessing on my own plans? If we truly desire what He wants, we will never be caught packing when we should be praying.

—DD

## Out of Context

*She turned around and saw Jesus
standing there, but she did not realize
that it was Jesus.* —JOHN 20:14

As I queued up to board my flight, someone tapped my shoulder. I turned and received a warm greeting. "Elisa! Do you remember me? It's Joan!" My mind flipped through various "Joans" I'd known, but I couldn't place her.

Sensing my struggle, Joan responded, "Elisa, we knew each other in high school." A memory rose: Friday night football games, cheering from the stands. Once the context was clarified, I recognized Joan.

After Jesus's death, Mary Magdalene went to the tomb early in the morning and found the stone rolled away and His body gone (John 20:12). She ran to get Peter and John, who returned with her to find the tomb empty (vv. 3–10). But Mary lingered outside in her grief (v. 11). When Jesus appeared there, "she did not realize that it was Jesus" (v. 14).

How could she have not recognized Jesus? Perhaps, like me, because Jesus was "out of context," alive in the garden instead of dead in the tomb, she didn't recognize Him.

How might we too miss Jesus when He comes into our days—during prayer or Bible reading, or by simply whispering in our hearts?　　　　　—EM

# God Is at Work

*"The L*ORD *is my strength and my defense; he has become my salvation."* —EXODUS 15:2

Jack and Trisha were driving to the hospital late one night for the birth of their second child when the unexpected happened. Trisha began to deliver the baby! Jack called 911 and Cherie White, an emergency dispatcher, was able to talk Jack through the delivery. But the baby wouldn't breathe. Cherie then instructed Jack how to give emergency breathing, which he had to do for six anxious minutes. Finally, the newborn took a breath and cried. When asked later how they all got through the ordeal and remained calm, Cherie responded, "I'm glad God works midnights!"

In the Bible reading for today, it's obvious that God should get the credit for parting the Red Sea to help His people escape from Pharaoh, even though Moses was the one who raised his staff (Exodus 14:21–27). All the Israelites and Moses gathered together and sang the Lord's praises: "Who among the gods is like you, LORD? Who is like you—majestic in holiness, awesome in glory, working wonders?" (15:11).

When something good happens, the Lord deserves the credit, for He is the source of all that is good. Give Him the glory. Aren't you glad He works midnights?

—AC

## It's Sally!

*Fathers, do not exasperate your children;
instead, bring them up in the training and
instruction of the Lord.* —EPHESIANS 6:4

Benjamin West was just trying to be a good baby-sitter for his little sister Sally. While his mother was out, Benjamin found some colored ink and painted Sally's portrait. When Mrs. West returned, ink blots stained the table, chairs, and floor. Benjamin's mother surveyed the mess without a word until she saw the picture. Picking it up she exclaimed, "Why, it's Sally!" And she bent down and kissed her young son.

In 1772, when he was thirty-four, Benjamin West was selected as history painter to England's King George III. He became one of the most celebrated artists of his day. Commenting on his start as an artist, he said, "My mother's kiss made me a painter." Her encouragement was just what he needed.

The apostle Paul instructed parents not to exasperate their children but to "bring them up in the training and instruction of the Lord" (Ephesians 6:4).

It's easy to notice the wrong in a child but difficult to look beyond an innocent offense to see an act of creativity and love. What a challenge to raise our children according to God's standards, knowing when to say, "It's a mess!" and when to say, "Why, it's Sally!"
—DM

## Safe in His Arms

*"As a mother comforts her child, so will I comfort you; and you will be comforted over Jerusalem."* — ISAIAH 66:13

I sat next to my daughter's bed in a recovery room after she had undergone surgery. When her eyes fluttered open, she realized she was uncomfortable and started to cry. I tried to reassure her by stroking her arm, but she only became more upset. With help from a nurse, I moved her from the bed and onto my lap. I brushed tears from her cheeks and reminded her that she would eventually feel better.

Through Isaiah, God told the Israelites, "As a mother comforts her child, so will I comfort you" (Isaiah 66:13). God promised to give His children peace and to carry them the way a mother totes a child around on her side. This tender message was for the people who had a reverence for God—those who "tremble at his word" (v. 5).

God is gentle and sympathetic with us when we are in trouble.

One day all suffering will end. Our tears will dry up permanently, and we will be safe in God's arms forever (Revelation 21:4). Until then, we can depend on God's love to support us when we suffer.   —JBS

## Surprising Circumstances

*A happy heart makes the face cheerful, but heartache crushes the spirit.* —PROVERBS 15:13

I piled groceries in my car and carefully exited my parking spot. Suddenly a man darted across the pavement just in front of me, not noticing my approach. I slammed on my brakes, just missing him. Startled, he looked up and met my gaze. In that moment, I knew I had a choice: respond with rolled-eye frustration or offer a smiling forgiveness. I smiled.

Relief flickered across his face, raising the edges of his own lips in gratefulness.

Proverbs 15:13 says, "A happy heart makes the face cheerful, but heartache crushes the spirit." Indeed, there are times for genuine mourning, despair, and even anger at injustice. But in our everyday moments, a smile can offer relief, hope, and the grace needed to continue.

Perhaps the point of the proverb is that a smile naturally results from the condition of our inner beings. A "happy heart" is at peace, content, and yielded to God's best. With such a heart, happy from the inside out, we can respond to surprising circumstances with a genuine smile, inviting others to embrace the hope and peace they too can experience with God.  —EM

## Helpful Love

*The Word became flesh and made his*
*dwelling among us.* —JOHN 1:14

At the end of my mother's earthly journey, she and Dad were still very much in love and shared a strong faith in Christ. My mother had developed dementia and began to lose memories of even her family. Yet Dad would regularly visit her at the assisted living home and find ways to accommodate her diminished capacities.

For instance, he would take her some saltwater taffy, unwrap a piece, and place it in her mouth—something she could not do for herself. Then as she slowly chewed the candy, Dad would quietly sit with her and hold her hand. When their time together was over, Dad, beaming with a wide smile, would say, "I feel such peace and joy spending time with her."

He was depicting God's grace. Jesus was willing to humble himself to connect with us in our weaknesses. In reflecting on Christ's incarnation, John wrote, "The Word became flesh and made his dwelling among us" (1:14). Taking on human limitations, He did countless acts of compassion to accommodate us in our weakness.

Do you know anyone who might benefit from Jesus's helpful, accommodating love that could flow through you to them today?                    —DF

## Joy and Peace

*Therefore, since we have been justified through
faith, we have peace with God through
our Lord Jesus Christ.* —ROMANS 5:1

Lucky Lawrence thought he had it all. He sought
fulfillment in fame, money, and success, but he struggled to find real joy. His real name was Larry Wright,
and he was at one time the number-one rock-and-roll
radio personality in Phoenix. But his family life was a
mess, and he was fast becoming an alcoholic.

As Mike Yorkey tells it in his book *Touched by the
Savior*, the solution came when his wife Sue trusted
Jesus as her Savior. Larry noticed her peace and joy
and the obvious change in her attitude toward him.
Soon he too asked Jesus to forgive him and be his
Savior.

Gone was the frustrating search for peace. In its
place was the joy and peace of God. Larry and Sue
went on to serve the Lord for more than thirty years.

In Romans we see the contrast between two kinds
of existence. Romans 1:18–32 tells about the sad,
frightening, troubled life of those who refuse to live
for God. But in Romans 5:1–11, we see what happens when a person trusts Christ. Peace, hope, love,
salvation. What a contrast!

Which of these two worlds are you living in?

—DB

## Say It with Love

*My beloved spoke and said to me, "Arise,
my darling, my beautiful one, come
with me."* —SONG OF SONGS 2:10

Often we take for granted the ones we love. Perhaps we get caught up in the day-to-day process of living and working, and we neglect to share our true inner feelings. "She knows I love her," we tell ourselves. But we never tell our spouse.

Maybe you grew up in a family where positive, loving feelings were never expressed in words, so you don't know what to say. Perhaps you're afraid you'll say the wrong thing, or that if you try to express your feelings you won't be able to control them. That's okay, even if you cry a little.

A familiar ad reads, "Say it with flowers!" Maybe that's how you tell that special someone of your love. Or perhaps you say it with a well-chosen card. My wife, Shirley, loves dark chocolates, so I often give her candy and a card on special occasions. She appreciates these tokens of love, but I also need to say the words, "I love you."

Everyone needs to hear words of love. In the Song of Solomon, the lovers frequently used endearing terms when speaking to each other.

Today, tell that special person "I love you." With words.                                    —DE

# The Test of Love

*"If you love me, keep my commands."* —JOHN 14:15

When I was little, my mother often recited to me Joy Allison's simple yet profound poem. Although a bit old-fashioned, it captures the heart of today's text about the true test of love.

> "I love you, Mother," said little John;
>     Then, forgetting his work, his cap went on,
> And he was off to the garden swing,
>     Leaving his mother the wood to bring.
> "I love you, Mother," said little Nell;
>     "I love you better than tongue can tell!"
> Then she teased and pouted half the day,
>     Till Mother rejoiced when she went to play.
> "I love you, Mother," said little Fran;
>     "Today I'll help you all I can."
> Then stepping softly, she took the broom
>     And swept the floor and dusted the room;
> Busy and happy all day was she,
>     Helpful and cheerful as she could be.
> "I love you, Mother," again they said,
>     Three little children going to bed.
> How do you think that Mother guessed
>     Which of them really loved her best?

Neither is it difficult to discern who really loves the Lord. Actions will always speak louder than words! What have you done out of love for Jesus today?

—HB

## Who Gets the Love?

*"'My son,' the father said, 'you are always with me, and everything I have is yours.'"* —LUKE 15:31

A sociologist was writing a book about the difficulties of growing up in a large family, so he interviewed the mother of thirteen children. He asked her, "Do you think all children deserve the full, impartial love and attention of a mother?"

"Of course," she responded.

"Well, which of your children do you love the most?" he asked.

She answered, "The one who is sick until he gets well, and the one who is away until he gets home."

That mother's response reminds me of the shepherd who left ninety-nine sheep to seek the one that was lost (Luke 15:4).

The religious leaders of Jesus's day resented the way He gave so much attention to sinners (vv. 1–2). So He told those stories to emphasize God's love for people who are lost in sin. God has more than enough love to go around. Besides, those who are not "lost" experience the Father's love as fully as those to whom He gives special attention (v. 31).

*Father, forgive us for feeling slighted when you shower your love on needy sinners. Help us abide in your boundless love.*                              —MD

## Always Awake

*In peace I will lie down and sleep, for you alone,*
*Lord, make me dwell in safety.* —PSALM 4:8

A mother and her four-year-old daughter were preparing for bed. The child was afraid of the dark. The girl noticed the moon shining through the window. "Mommy," she asked, "is that God's light up there?" "Yes, it is," came the reply. "Will He put it out and go to sleep too?" "Oh no, He never goes to sleep." The little girl decided, "As long as God is awake, I'm not scared." Realizing that the Lord would be watching over her, the reassured child soon fell into a peaceful sleep.

As Christians, we may confidently commit both the night and the day to our ever-faithful God. He is aware of our fears in the dark as well as our frustrations in the light. We can be assured of His constant care. His loving eye and protecting hand are always upon us.

Perhaps you face lonely hours because of illness or the loss of a loved one. Trust our heavenly Father, and with the psalmist say, "In peace I will lie down and sleep, for you alone, Lord, make me dwell in safety" (Psalm 4:8). Remember, God is always awake.

—PVG

## Parent's Ten Suggestions

*The father of a righteous child has great joy; a man who fathers a wise son rejoices in him.* —PROVERBS 23:24

Children come without guarantees.

But this doesn't mean we as parents are without responsibility. We must help our children grow into godly people. David Wilkerson, author of *The Cross and the Switchblade*, said, "Devoted, dedicated, hardworking mothers and fathers can weigh the balance in favor of decency and moral character."

Here are ten suggestions for guiding your children.

1. Teach them, using God's Word (Deuteronomy 6:4–9).
2. Tell them what's right and wrong (1 Kings 1:6).
3. See them as gifts from God (Psalm 127:3).
4. Guide them in godly ways (Proverbs 22:6).
5. Discipline them (Proverbs 29:17).
6. Love them unconditionally (Luke 15:11–32).
7. Do not provoke them to wrath (Ephesians 6:4).
8. Earn their respect by example (1 Timothy 3:4).
9. Provide for their physical needs (1 Timothy 5:8).
10. Pass your faith along to them (2 Timothy 1:5).

There are no guarantees. But we can have an edge in trying to "weigh the balance."                    —DB

## Perfect Vision

*From his dwelling place he watches all
who live on earth.* —PSALM 33:14

I was as mischievous as any other child in my early years. I hid my misdeeds to avoid getting into trouble. Yet my mother usually found out what I'd done. When I asked how she knew, she always replied, "I have eyes in the back of my head." This, of course, led me to study her head whenever she'd turn her back—were the eyes invisible or merely cloaked by her red hair? As I grew, I gave up looking for those extra eyes and realized I just wasn't quite as sneaky as I'd supposed. Her watchful gaze was evidence of her loving concern for her children.

As grateful as I am for my mother's attentive care, I'm even more grateful that God "sees all mankind" as He looks upon us from heaven (Psalm 33:13). He sees so much more than we do; He sees our sadness, our delights, and our love for one another.

God sees our true character and always knows exactly what we need. With perfect vision He watches over those who love and put their hope in Him (v. 18). He is our attentive, loving Father.                    —KH

## Living Peaceably

*If it is possible, as far as it depends on you,
live at peace with everyone.* —ROMANS 12:18

A man who had been having problems with an unreasonable neighbor finally had to defend himself legally against unwarranted and dishonest actions. He commented, "I have tried to follow Romans 12:18, but in a case like this I thank the Lord for the 'escape clause' He put in this text. It does not say that we have to live peaceably with all men under every circumstance—for even the Lord recognizes that with some people this is not possible."

I am reminded of a story about a boy who asked his dad, "How do wars begin?" The father replied, "Well, World War I began because Germany invaded Belgium." At this point his wife interrupted, "Tell the boy the truth. It began because somebody was murdered." The husband quickly retorted, "Are you answering the question, or am I?" The wife stormed out of the room and slammed the door. When the room stopped vibrating, an uneasy silence followed. The son then said, "Daddy, you don't need to tell me how wars begin. Now I know!"

Are you quick to retaliate, or have you cultivated a peaceable spirit? Let's do all we possibly can to live peaceably.                                        —HB

## I See You

*She gave this name to the LORD who*
*spoke to her: "You are the God who sees*
*me," for she said, "I have now seen the*
*One who sees me."* —GENESIS 16:13

"I see you," a friend said in an online writers' group where we support and encourage each other. Having felt stressed and anxious, I experienced a sense of peace and well-being with her words. She "saw" me—my hopes, fears, struggles, and dreams—and loved me.

When I heard my friend's simple but powerful encouragement, I thought of Hagar, a servant in Abram's household. After many years of Sarai and Abram longing for an heir, Sarai followed the custom of the culture and told her husband to conceive through Hagar. But when Hagar became pregnant, she treated Sarai with contempt. When Sarai mistreated her in return, Hagar fled far away to the desert.

The Lord saw Hagar in her pain and confusion, and He blessed her with the promise that she would be the mother of many descendants.

As Hagar was seen—and loved—so are we. We might feel ignored or rejected by friends or family, yet we know that our Father sees not only the face we present to the world but all of our secret feelings and fears as well. —ABP

## The Peacemaker

*Blessed are the peacemakers, for they will
be called children of God.* —MATTHEW 5:9

Abigail was a remarkable woman! She was a true
peacemaker whose courage spared the future king
of Israel from committing a terrible sin.

Here's her story:

David had been forced to live in the countryside
to escape King Saul's jealous wrath. Six hundred men
and their families had gathered around him. They
camped near Carmel where the flocks of Nabal (Abigail's husband) were grazing. David's men had helped
Nabal's shepherds protect the sheep from robbers.
Now the shearing time had come, and David sent
messengers to request compensation from Nabal,
who was a wealthy man. But he refused and treated
David's men with disdain.

In anger David rashly decided to kill Nabal and all
the men in his household. When Abigail heard about
this, she quickly gathered a large supply of food,
intercepted David and his fighting men, and humbly
apologized for her husband's surly behavior. David
immediately realized that she had prevented him from
carrying out a vengeful decision, and he praised God
(1 Samuel 25:32).

Are we as quick to resolve a conflict? Jesus said,
"Blessed are the peacemakers, for they will be called
children of God" (Matthew 5:9).              —HVL

## Still Small Voice

*And after the earthquake a fire, but the*
*LORD was not in the fire; and after the fire*
*a still small voice.* —1 KINGS 19:12 NKJV

When God spoke to Elijah on Mount Horeb, He could have done so in the wind, earthquake, or fire. But He didn't. He spoke with a "still small voice" (1 Kings 19:12 NKJV). God asked, "What are you doing here, Elijah?" (v. 13), as he hid from Jezebel who had threatened to kill him.

Elijah's reply revealed what God already knew— the depth of his fear and discouragement. He said, in effect, "Lord, I have been most zealous when others have forsaken you. What do I get for being the only one standing up for you?" (see v. 14).

In the depths of our fear or despair, we too may think we're the only one serving God. Psalm 46:10 reminds us to "be still, and know" that He is God. The sooner we focus on Him and His power, the quicker we will see relief from our fear and self-pity.

Both the clashing cymbals of our failures and the loud trumpeting of our successes can drown out God's still small voice. Perhaps it's time for us to quiet our hearts to listen for Him as we meditate on His Word.                                    —AL

## The Rewards of Grace

*At that time each will receive their praise
from God.* —1 CORINTHIANS 4:5

A young child by the name of Frances loved her mother deeply and wanted to please her. One day she picked up a linen handkerchief her mother had been embroidering. Hoping to help her mom, she eagerly made some stitches. When her mother saw her "handiwork," her eyes filled with tears. Although the stitching was awkward and uneven, she appreciated the love that prompted her daughter to "help" her.

A teenage Christian girl lay dying. She asked a visitor, "What shall I say to Jesus when I meet Him? I haven't really done anything for Him like some people. You see, Mother died when I was eight. While Daddy worked, I tried to take care of the four little ones, kept the house tidy, and then I was too tired to do more." Taking the rough little hand in her own, the woman said tenderly, "Don't say anything, dear. Just show Him your hands!"

No matter how insignificant the deed may appear, we must do what we can for Jesus. God will reward us for every good motive and faithful endeavor.

—HB

## Handling Conflict

*A gentle answer turns away wrath, but a
harsh word stirs up anger.* —PROVERBS 15:1

Eric Liddell, the Scottish runner whose life was portrayed in the movie *Chariots of Fire*, served as a missionary in China for twenty years—the last two in a Japanese internment camp during World War II. He was known as a peacemaker among individuals and groups whenever anger flared in the stressful environment of the camp. Liddell's life left a deep impression on everyone.

When a Japanese guard asked why Liddell was not at roll call one day, a man told him that Eric had died unexpectedly a few hours earlier. The guard paused, then replied, "Liddell was a Christian, wasn't he?"

Liddell spoke no Japanese; the guard spoke no English. Their only direct contact was at the required roll calls, twice a day. How did the guard know that Liddell was a Christian? He must have seen Christ in Eric as he resolved conflicts in the camp.

"Blessed are the peacemakers," said Jesus, "for they will be called children of God" (Matthew 5:9). More than solving arguments, peacemakers are living evidence of God's reconciling love in Christ.

We can show Jesus Christ to others by the way we handle conflict.                          —DM

# Something about Babies

*For you created my inmost being; you knit me together in my mother's womb.* —PSALM 139:13

What is it about babies that makes us smile? Many people will stop everything at the sight or sound of a baby and will flock to gaze at the little one. I noticed this when I visited my dad at a nursing home. Though most of the residents were wheelchair-bound and suffered from dementia, the visit of a family with a baby almost unfailingly brought a spark of joy to their eyes that—tentatively at first but then undoubtedly—became a smile. It was amazing to watch.

Perhaps babies bring a smile because of the wonder of a new life—so precious, tiny, and full of promise. Seeing a baby can remind us of our awesome God and the great love He has for us. He loved us so much that He gave us life and formed us in our mother's womb (See Psalm 139:13).

Not only does He give us physical life but He also offers us spiritual rebirth through Jesus (John 3:3–8). God promises believers new bodies and life eternal when Jesus returns (1 Corinthians 15:50–52).

Physical life and spiritual rebirth—gifts to celebrate from our Father's hand.                    —AK

## Silence, Please!

*Do not be anxious about
anything.* —PHILIPPIANS 4:6

According to a news report, science has found a way to achieve absolute silence: "Scientists have shown off the blueprint for an 'acoustic cloak,' which could make objects impervious to sound waves. The technology, outlined in the *New Journal of Physics*, could be used to build sound-proof homes, advanced concert halls, or stealth warships."

When we seek out a quiet place for devotional time with God, we may wish we had an "acoustic cloak." But even if we could silence all external sound, the internal noises of worry would still reverberate in our minds.

God understands our dilemma and has provided His own "acoustic cloak" to quiet our hearts. It involves exchanging our cares for His peace. "Do not be anxious about anything, but in every situation by prayer and petition, with thanksgiving, present your requests to God. And the peace of God, which transcends all understanding, will guard your hearts and your minds in Christ Jesus" (Philippians 4:6–7).

As we place our concerns in God's capable hands, we find a quietness that only He can provide. —DF

## An Ever-Present Protector

*The LORD will watch over your*
*coming and going both now and*
*forevermore.* —PSALM 121:8

While I shopped for shoes, our two-year-old Xavier and my husband Alan played hide-and-seek behind stacks of shoeboxes. Suddenly, I saw Alan dash frantically from aisle to aisle, calling Xavier's name. We raced to the front of the store. Our child, still laughing, ran toward the open door leading to a busy street. Within seconds, Alan scooped him up. We embraced as I thanked God, sobbed, and kissed our toddler's chubby cheeks.

A year before I became pregnant with Xavier, I'd lost our first child during the pregnancy. When God blessed us with our son, I became a fearful parent. I knew I couldn't always protect him, but I discovered peace as I learned to turn to my only sure source of help—God—when I struggled with worry and fear.

Our heavenly Father never takes His eyes off us (Psalm 121:1–4). While we can't prevent trials, heartache, or loss, we can live with confident faith, relying on an ever-present Protector (vv. 5–8).

Our all-knowing God never loses sight of us—His beloved children.                                    —XD

## Silent Witness

*Whatever happens, conduct yourselves
in a manner worthy of the gospel
of Christ.* —PHILIPPIANS 1:27

On a beautiful, warm January morning, a colleague and I were having breakfast in an outdoor coffee shop at MacRitchie Reservoir Park in Singapore. With a beautiful lake and immaculate gardens surrounding us, the setting was quiet, calm, and lovely with a light breeze blowing across the water.

At a nearby table, a young woman sat quietly reading her Bible. She was absorbed in the text, occasionally looking up to consider what she had read. She never said a word, but her heart and priorities were visible to everyone at that coffee shop. It was a gentle, positive, silent witness.

She was not ashamed of Christ or His Book. She neither preached a sermon nor sang a song. She was willing to be identified with the Savior, yet she did not need to announce that allegiance.

There are times when the quietness of our everyday actions speak loudly, revealing our love for the Lord. In our desire to share Christ with a broken world, let's not ignore the power of our silent witness.

—BC

## Perfect Peace Is Possible

*You will keep in perfect peace those whose minds are steadfast, because they trust in you.* —ISAIAH 26:3

Few things (if anything at all) in this fallen world can be called perfect. But God promises to keep us in "perfect peace" if we keep our minds focused on Him and continue trusting Him (Isaiah 26:3).

So why do we find it so difficult to trust Him? Often, it's because we're afraid that things won't go as we want them to unless we control them ourselves. The less we are in control, the more anxious and worried we become.

We often think our situation is too difficult for God. If we can't solve things ourselves, we doubt that He can. We have our Christian beliefs, yes—but that isn't the same as believing God. Believing God is a personal response that grows out of our Christian faith and is expressed by our increasing trust in Him and His promises.

As our mind remains on Him, He keeps us in perfect peace. This has been the experience of countless believers, and you can experience it too.　　　—JY

## Held by Love

*Jesus knew that the hour had come for him
to leave this world and go to the Father.
Having loved his own who were in the world,
he loved them to the end.* —JOHN 13:1

In a cemetery in New Orleans stands a monument that was designed to represent a great ship at sea in the midst of a storm. A mother and her daughter cling to each other as they stand in the sinking vessel. The bronze plate on the monument says that the mother and the daughter, sole survivors of a large estate, both drowned. Upon their deaths, lawyers were faced with the question of who died first in the shipwreck. The court decided that the estate should be administered in the name of the daughter, figuring that she went down last. They reasoned that the mother would have sacrificed her own life for her daughter. Those officials recognized the strength of a mother's love.

Even more powerful and beautiful is God's love for us. In sending His Son Jesus, He sacrificed himself for us. Because of Calvary, all who trust Jesus can rest in the assurance that we will never enter into condemnation.

God's love is supernatural. It will hold us for all eternity.                                   —PVG

## Peaceless in Pittsburgh

*"Do not worry about tomorrow, for tomorrow will worry about itself. Each day has enough trouble of its own."* —MATTHEW 6:34

A follower of Christ can find a lot to worry about these days—the moral degeneration of society, political instability, anti-Christian sentiment, and on and on. Often we are troubled about what could happen in the future, or we spend way too much time dwelling on the past. Our minds whirl and emotions rise because of some sin we committed or a sad event that occurred years ago.

Because we can neither change the past nor manipulate the future, we are peaceless in Pittsburgh, fretful in Fresno, or worried in Washington.

Author Jean-Pierre de Caussade said that we can experience the peace of God when we stop worrying about *what might be* and focus on *what is*. He wrote, "It is necessary to be disengaged from all we feel and do, in order to walk with God in the duty of the present moment."

But how can we walk with the Lord and experience His peace when we're paralyzed with worry about the past or the future? We can't! No wonder Jesus told us, "Do not worry" (Matthew 6:34).                     —DE

## Jesus Makes It Heaven

*They will see his face, and his name will be
on their foreheads.* —REVELATION 22:4

A little boy came running into his house one day
and said to his mother, "I love my house so much!"
A neighbor lady who was visiting responded, "Reid,
why don't you come over and see me sometime?
Our house is built just like yours. What makes your
house so enjoyable?" The youngster thought for a
moment, then went over to his mother and put his
arms around her neck: "I guess it's Mom!"

Commenting on this story, Pastor Paul S. Rees
said, "We talk about gates of pearl and streets of gold
and walls of jasper, and we are thrilled. But those
beauties would not be attractive if Jesus were not in
Glory. His presence is what makes it so grand."

When a believer is "away from the body" he is
"at home with the Lord" (2 Corinthians 5:8). There
we will sing this song: "Worthy is the Lamb, who
was slain to receive . . . honor and glory and praise!"
(Revelation 5:12).

Moms make home a great place, but heaven is
even better. We will be with Jesus!          —HB

## Hold Fast

*We do not know what we ought to pray*
*for, but the Spirit himself intercedes for us*
*through wordless groans.* —ROMANS 8:26

There are times when life seems unbearable. Physical pain, difficult decisions, financial hardships, the death of a loved one, or shattered dreams threaten to engulf us. We become fearful and perplexed. Plagued by doubts, we may even find it difficult to pray.

Those of us who know the Lord through personal faith in Christ have in Him a calm retreat in the storms of life, even while the howling winds of trial are sweeping over us. We can experience peace of mind and calmness of spirit.

Richard Fuller, a nineteenth-century Baptist preacher, told of an old seaman who said, "In fierce storms, we must put the ship in a certain position and keep her there." Said Fuller, "This, Christian, is what you must do. . . . Only a single course is left. You must put your soul in one position and keep it there. You must stay upon the Lord. You must hold fast your confidence in God's faithfulness."

Do you feel overwhelmed by life? Fix your mind on the Lord. Ask for His help. Trust Him. Let Him give you peace in your storm (Philippians 4:6, 7).

—RD

## Is God Too Busy?

*As a father has compassion on his*
*children, so the LORD has compassion on*
*those who fear him.* —PSALM 103:13

Several mothers of small children were sharing encouraging answers to prayer. One woman admitted that she felt selfish when she troubled God with her personal needs. "Compared with the huge global needs God faces," she explained, "my circumstances must seem trivial to Him."

Moments later, her little son pinched his fingers in a door and ran screaming to his mother. She didn't say, "How selfish of you to bother me with your throbbing fingers when I'm busy!" No, she showed him great compassion and tenderness.

As Psalm 103:13 reminds us, this is the response of love, both human and divine. In Isaiah 49, God assured His people that He had inscribed them on the palms of His hands (v. 16).

Such intimacy with God belongs to those who fear Him and rely on Him rather than on themselves. As that child with throbbing fingers ran freely to his mother, so may we run to God with our daily problems.

Our almighty God never has to neglect others to respond to your concerns. He has limitless time and love for each of His children. No need is too trivial for Him.                                    —JY

## Drop Your Hands

*He says, "Be still, and know that I am God;*
*I will be exalted among the nations, I will*
*be exalted in the earth." —*PSALM 46:10

You'd think I would have my mother's fingerprints embedded in my knee from all the times she squeezed my leg in church and whispered in no uncertain terms, "Be still." Like any child, I had a bad case of the wiggles in places like church. So for years, when I read, "Be still, and know that I am God" (Psalm 46:10), I thought of it in terms of not being antsy.

But the Hebrew word for *still* means "to cease striving." It's the concept of putting your hands down and letting God intervene in your situation without your interference. In other words, stop struggling and wait on God to do His work!

In the face of all of life's circumstances, we can know the peace of trusting the presence and power of God in the midst of trouble as we wait patiently and prayerfully for His deliverance. So, drop your hands, for God's hands are busy on your behalf!          —JS

## Friends Showed Up

*Share with the Lord's people who are in
need. Practice hospitality.* —ROMANS 12:13

My husband left for a month-long trip, and almost immediately I was overwhelmed by the needs of my job, our house, and our children. A writing deadline loomed. The lawn mower broke. My children were on school break and bored. How would I take care of all of these things on my own?

I soon realized I wasn't on my own. Friends from church showed up to help. Josh fixed my lawn mower. John brought me lunch. Cassidy helped with the laundry. Abi invited my kids over to play with hers so I could get my work done. God worked through these friends to provide for me. They were a living picture of the kind of community Paul describes in Romans 12. They loved sincerely (v. 9), considered the needs of others (v. 10), shared with me when I was in need, and showed hospitality (v. 13).

Because of their love, I was "joyful in hope" and remained "patient in affliction" (v. 12), even the mild affliction of solo parenting for a month. My brothers and sisters in Christ became what one friend calls "God with skin on" for me. I hope to be more like them. —AP

## Peaceful Anxiety

*And the peace of God, which transcends all*
*understanding, will guard your hearts and*
*your minds in Christ Jesus.* —PHILIPPIANS 4:7

I was scheduled to teach at a Bible conference outside the US and was waiting for my visa to be approved. It had been rejected once, and time was slipping away. Without the visa, I would lose an opportunity for ministry.

A coworker asked how I felt about it all. I told him I was experiencing "peaceful anxiety." When he looked at me rather quizzically, I explained: "I have had anxiety because I need the visa and there is nothing I can do about it. But I have great peace because I know that, after all, there is nothing I can do about it!"

It's comforting to know that such things are in our Father's hands. My inability to do anything about the problem was more than matched by my confidence in God, for whom all things are possible. As I prayed about the situation, my anxiety was replaced by His peace (Philippians 4:6–7).

As we learn to trust in the Father's care, we can have the peace that overcomes our anxiety. We can be at rest, for we are in God's hands.              —BC

## The Power of Ritual

*When he had given thanks, he broke it and said,
"This is my body, which is for you; do this in
remembrance of me."* —1 CORINTHIANS 11:24

When I was growing up, one of the rules in our house was that we weren't allowed to go to bed angry (Ephesians 4:26). All our fights and disagreements had to be resolved. The companion to that rule was this bedtime ritual: Mom and Dad would say to my brother and me, "Good night. I love you." And we would respond, "Good night. I love you too."

As my mother lay in a hospice bed dying of lung cancer, she became less and less responsive. But each night when I left her bedside I would say, "I love you, Mom." Though she could say little else, she would respond, "I love you too." How meaningful this ritual had become!

Time and repetition can rob our rituals of meaning. But some are important reminders of vital spiritual truths. First-century believers misused the practice of the Lord's Supper, but the apostle Paul didn't tell them to stop celebrating it. Instead he told them, "For whenever you eat this bread and drink this cup, you proclaim the Lord's death until he comes" (1 Corinthians 11:26).

Rather than give up the ritual, perhaps we need to restore the meaning.                              —JAL

## A Commitment to Care

*Carry each other's burdens, and in this way you
will fulfill the law of Christ.* —GALATIANS 6:2

During the months following the death of my wife's
mother, we received a number of cards and letters
from the hospice team who had so lovingly cared for
Mom and walked with our family along the path-
way of loss. One letter offered thoughts on dealing
constructively with grief. Another said, "As the date
of your mother's birthday approaches, we remember
her, and our prayers and thoughts are with you and
your family." These wonderful caregivers knew that
grieving is an ongoing process that requires continuing help and support.

Paul's words "Carry each other's burdens" (Galatians 6:2) come as an exclamation point to his description of life in the Spirit. In contrast to the destructive
acts of the sinful nature (Galatians 5:19–21), the fruit
of the Holy Spirit in and through us is "love, joy,
peace, longsuffering, kindness, goodness, faithfulness,
gentleness, self-control" (vv. 22–23 NKJV). The freedom we have in Christ allows us to serve each other
in love (v. 13).

A word of encouragement to a hurting friend is
like a refreshing rain. When we care in tangible ways,
it grows into a life-giving stream of healing and love.

—DM

## Brownies and Gleaning

*"She said, 'Please let me glean and gather*
*among the sheaves behind the harvesters.'*
*She came into the field and has remained*
*here from morning till now, except for a*
*short rest in the shelter." —*RUTH 2:7

My daughter and I consider brownies to be one of the seven wonders of the culinary world. One day, as we were mixing the ingredients of our favorite chocolate treat, my daughter asked if I would leave some batter in the bowl after pouring most of it into the baking pan. She wanted to enjoy what was left over. I smiled and agreed. Then I told her, "That's called gleaning, you know, and it didn't start with brownies."

As we enjoyed the remnants of our baking project, I explained that Ruth had gathered leftover grain in order to feed herself and her mother-in-law Naomi (Ruth 2:2–3). Because both of their husbands had died, the women had returned to Naomi's home-land. There Ruth met a wealthy landowner named Boaz. She asked him, "Please let me glean and gather among the sheaves" (v. 7). He willingly consented and instructed his workers to purposely let grain fall for her (v. 16).

God provides for us out of His abundance. His resources are infinite, and He lets blessings fall for our benefit. He willingly provides us with physical and spiritual nourishment. Every good gift we receive comes from Him.                                    —JBS

## Facing Death

*If I go and prepare a place for you, I will
come back and take you to be with me that
you also may be where I am.* —JOHN 14:3

One evening when a mother was tucking her young
daughter into bed, the child pleaded, "Mother, stay
with me while I go to sleep." Remembering all the
tasks that still awaited her, she hesitated. But she
knew of the child's dread of the darkness, so she sat
beside the bed and took her daughter's hand in her
own. Soon the child was asleep.

As the mother sat there, she bowed her head and
prayed, "O Lord, when life's evening shall come, stay
with me while I go to sleep, guide me safely in the
valley, and receive me when I awaken in Glory!"

David expressed this confidence in Psalm 23:4,
"Even though I walk through the darkest valley, I
will fear no evil, for you are with me." Dying may be
sudden or prolonged, but the Lord will be there just
as that loving mother was with her child. He will stay
by our side.

Death is an enemy, but it is our last enemy. Yet
we can face it without fear because Jesus is with us
and will usher us into the glorious mansions He has
prepared for us.                                        —HB

## As Strong as Ever

*So do not fear, for I am with you; do not be
dismayed, for I am your God. I will strengthen
you and help you; I will uphold you with
my righteous right hand.* —ISAIAH 41:10

On the day before my mother died, my brother and I
were called to her bedside. She sensed that she would
soon be with her Lord. She was too weak for extended
conversation, but she did quote two verses—Isaiah
41:10 and John 10:29. She wasn't simply trying to
console us but was reinforcing her own faith. She was
holding fast to what God had said—and what God
had said was holding her fast.

It reminded me of what Jesus did when He was
tempted. He overcame the enemy's suggestions by
quoting Scripture. Why did He do this? Because the
Word held Him steady. Jesus was not quoting verses
to Satan as if they contained some magical power.
Rather, He was calling them to mind to guide and
reinforce himself as He remained true to God's will.

Whatever your test, child of God, be it a severe
temptation, an overwhelming fear, or the specter of
death itself, you can rest with confidence on God's
sure and abiding Word. It's as strong as ever! —DD

## Inner Peace

*Be compassionate and humble. Do not repay evil
with evil or insult with insult. On the contrary,
repay evil with blessing.* —1 PETER 3:8–9

How do we react to hostile criticism? If it causes us to
strike back angrily at our critics, we need to learn from
colonial preacher Jonathan Edwards (1703–1758).

Regarded by scholars as an insightful philosopher,
Edwards was vindictively attacked by the ruling body
of his church in Northampton, Massachusetts. They
felt he was wrong to teach that a person needed to be
born again before taking part in the Lord's Supper.

Although he was dismissed from his church, Edwards still maintained a loving and forgiving attitude.
One supportive member wrote of him, "I never saw
the least symptoms of displeasure in his countenance
. . . , but he appeared like a man of God, whose happiness was out of the reach of his enemies."

Edwards was simply copying the example of the
Lord Jesus. When the Savior was insulted, He did not
repay with an insult (see Isaiah 53:7).

Do you have an inner peace even when criticized?
As you ask the Holy Spirit for His help, you can, as
Edwards did, respond in a Christlike way to false
accusations or gossip.                               —VG

## The Joy of Waiting

*I prayed for this child, and the LORD has granted me what I asked of him.* —1 SAMUEL 1:27

Nine months can seem like forever for a mother-to-be. In the first trimester, hormonal changes sometimes cause lingering morning sickness. Emotions rise to the surface, prolonging afternoon blues. Then a changing appetite stretches out evening hours with late-night cravings.

During the next three months, Mom outgrows her clothes and spends long hours looking for a new wardrobe. The last trimester turns normal activity into a chore as the final watch begins.

Then suddenly the endless waiting is over. Nine months become like yesterday's news. They're gone. A faint memory—overcome by joy. Ask the new mom if she regrets enduring her pregnancy. Never!

Hannah's wait began even more slowly. For years she was unable to have a child. She felt so unfulfilled, so dishonored (1 Samuel 1). But the Lord remembered her, and she conceived. Her joy was complete.

Hannah waited patiently and saw the Lord turn her sorrow into overflowing joy. Her song (2:1–10) is a reminder that disappointment and the most bitter distress can lead to fulfillment and delight. For those who wait on the Lord, long hours of enduring will one day give way to rejoicing.          —MD

## The Peace-Filled Life

*"Do not let your hearts be troubled
and do not be afraid."* —JOHN 14:27

When H. B. Macartney, an Australian pastor, visited Hudson Taylor (1832–1905) in China, he was amazed at the missionary's serenity in spite of his many burdens and his busy schedule. Macartney finally mustered up the courage to say, "You are occupied with millions, I with tens. Your letters are pressingly important, mine of comparatively little value. Yet I am worried and distressed while you are always calm. Tell me, what makes the difference?" Taylor replied, "I could not possibly get through the work I have to do without the peace of God, which passes all understanding keeping my heart and mind." Macartney later wrote, "He was in God all the time, and God was in him. It was the true abiding spoken of in John 15."

Do you feel as if your life is more like Macartney's than Taylor's? Are you tense, troubled, anxious, fearful?

The path to abiding in Him is that of confessing and rejecting all known sin, surrendering completely, and looking trustfully to the Lord Jesus for strength. It's a continual depending on Him. You too can enjoy the serenity of a peace-filled life as you abide in Christ.                              —HVL

## Greater Compassion

*"Can a mother forget the baby at her*
*breast and have no compassion on the child*
*she has borne? Though she may forget,*
*I will not forget you!"* —ISAIAH 49:15

The first time I saw my wife, Marlene, working with children, I knew what a natural fit this was for her. She loved children. It became even more obvious when we got married and had children of our own. Seeing her with them was a lesson in unconditional love and acceptance. It was clear to me that there is nothing in all the world like the tender love and compassion of a mother for her newborn child.

That's what makes Isaiah 49:15 so remarkable. It's here that God told His people, who were feeling forsaken and forgotten (v. 14), that His compassion is even greater than a mother's: "Can a mother forget her nursing child? Can she feel no love for the child she has borne? But even if that were possible, I would not forget you" (v. 15 NLT).

God's love for us is as expansive as the open arms of Christ on the cross. And the tender compassion of our heavenly Father is more dependable and more enduring than the love of a nursing mother for her infant. Be comforted—His love never fails.      —BC

## Side by Side

*Impress them on your children. Talk about
them when you sit at home and when you
walk along the road, when you lie down and
when you get up.* —DEUTERONOMY 6:7

In my family scrapbook is a picture of my daughter
at age four working next to me, using a toy hammer
to repair the siding on the house. Side by side we
worked that day; she imitated my every action, absolutely convinced that she too was fixing the house.
Rarely have I enjoyed a chore more. In the picture,
it's obvious that she's enjoying it too.

That photo reminds me that our children mimic
most of what they see in us—words and deeds. They
also form their images of God from the images they
have of us as parents. If we're stern and unmerciful,
they're likely to see God that way too. It is one of our
most important duties as parents to help our children
see God clearly, especially the unconditional nature
of His love.

I can imagine the family scrapbook of my relationship with God having a similar picture. I'm learning
from Him how to live life and how to love. He then
teaches me how to teach others (Deuteronomy 6:1–7).

May the Lord grant us an understanding of Him
and the wisdom to pass it on.                    —RK

# The Look of Compassion

*Jesus, when He came out, saw a great
multitude and was moved with compassion
for them, because they were like sheep not
having a shepherd.* —MARK 6:34 NKJV

Time after time the New Testament tells us that Jesus
met the needs of suffering people. Luke 7:11–18 tells
us that when He saw the widow stricken with grief
over the death of her son, He had compassion on
her and healed the boy. Earlier when He saw a man
who was full of leprosy—despised, ostracized, and no
doubt terribly disfigured—He made him whole (Luke
5:12–15). Still today, Jesus looks upon human need
with compassion.

A little girl's mother had been taken to the hospital, and she was spending the night alone with her
father for the first time. Soon after the lights were
turned out, the girl asked quietly, "Daddy, are you
there?" "Yes," he assured her. A moment later she
asked, "Daddy, are you looking at me?" When he
said yes, she fell asleep.

Likewise, every child of God can depend on the
Savior's look of love. No matter how painful the
problem or how deep the sorrow, we know that His
eye is fixed on us. While the world may turn its eye
from suffering, we are always under the watchful
gaze of our compassionate Savior.          —DE

## Velvet's Predicament

*"In my distress I called to the Lord, and
he answered me. From deep in the realm
of the dead I called for help, and you
listened to my cry."* —JONAH 2:2

When my mother discovered my kitten Velvet devouring her homemade bread, she scooted the feline out the door. Later, as we searched for the missing cat, a faint meow whistled on the wind. I looked up to the peak of a poplar tree where a black smudge tilted a branch.

In her haste to flee my mother's frustration, Velvet chose a more precarious predicament. Is it possible that we sometimes do something similar—running from our errors and putting ourselves in danger? Even then, God comes to our rescue.

The prophet Jonah fled in disobedience from God's call to preach to Nineveh, and he was swallowed up by a great fish. "From inside the fish Jonah prayed to the Lord his God" (Jonah 2:1). God heard Jonah's plea, and the fish expelled the prophet (v. 10). Then God gave Jonah another chance (3:1).

After we failed to woo Velvet down, we summoned the fire department. A kind man climbed a ladder, plucked my kitten from her perch, and returned her safely to my arms.

Oh, the heights—and the depths—God goes to in rescuing us from our disobedience with His redeeming love!                                              —EM

## God's Quieting Peace

*"Why are you so afraid?"*
—MATTHEW 8:26

I heard about a submarine that was on patrol during wartime and had to remain submerged overnight. When it resurfaced the next day, a friend on another ship radioed the captain, "How did you fare in that terrible storm last night?" Surprised, the officer exclaimed, "What storm? We didn't know there was one!"

Although the ocean's surface had been whipped into huge waves by high winds, the vessel was not affected because the waters below remained calm and tranquil.

Likewise, the Christian's mind can be protected from the distracting waves of worry caused by troubling circumstances. American pastor and author A. T. Pierson (1837–1911) described the peace of God as "that eternal calm which lies far too deep in the praying, trusting soul to be reached by any external disturbances."

Someone once outlined the words of Isaiah 26:3 this way: "You—a precious God. Perfect peace—a priceless possession. Whose mind is stayed on you—a present focus. Because he trusts in you—a powerful faith."

The believer who rests in God's grace and who relies on His Holy Spirit will experience the miracle of His quieting peace.                              —HB

# A Lingering Afterglow

*All the widows stood around [Peter],*
*crying and showing . . . clothing that*
*Dorcas had made.* —ACTS 9:39

Only a few people become so famous that their life stories are recorded for future generations. But all of us can leave a lingering afterglow when we depart this earth. For example, Dorcas was not a great leader remembered by secular history, but when she went to heaven, her good deeds remained behind as an eloquent testimony to the spiritual quality of her life.

This godly first-century Christian came to mind when I read a moving poem by Joy Jacobs. In it she expressed her reflections while her mother was in surgery. She recalled that her mother went to the operating room without fear, "thinking only of something she could say to turn the minds of those around her to her living Lord." She wrote, "I would not trade her for a queen." She closed with a prayer: "O Father, if it be Your will, spare her. I need to learn so many things—kindness, patience, love—and her life teaches me so well."

As we touch the lives of others, we should pray, "Lord, help me to be the kind of person who leaves behind a lovely, lingering afterglow."          —HVL

## Our Singing Father

*The LORD your God is with you. . . . He will
take great delight in you; in his love he will
no longer rebuke you, but will rejoice over
you with singing." —ZEPHANIAH 3:17*

No one told us before we had children how important singing would be. All three had problems sleeping
early on. Each night, we took turns rocking our little
ones, praying they'd nod off quickly. I spent hundreds of hours rocking them, crooning lullabies to
(hopefully!) speed up the process. But as I sang over
our children night after night, it deepened my bond
of love and delight for them.

Did you know Scripture describes our heavenly
Father singing over His children? Just as I sought to
soothe my children with song, so Zephaniah concludes with a portrait of our heavenly Father singing
over His people: "He will take delight in you. . . . [He]
will rejoice over you with singing" (3:17).

Much of Zephaniah's prophetic book warns of a
coming time of judgment for those who'd rejected
God's teachings. But Zephaniah concludes with a description of God rescuing His people (vv. 19–20) and
tenderly loving and rejoicing over them with song
(v. 17).

Our God is not only a "mighty savior" who restores
(v. 17 NLT) but also a loving Father who tenderly sings
songs of love over us.                              —AH

## Grace, Mercy, and Peace

*Praise the LORD, my soul; all my inmost
being, praise his holy name.* —PSALM 103:1

The words *grace* and *peace* are found in all of Paul's
greetings in his New Testament letters to the churches.
In his letters to Timothy and Titus, he also includes
mercy: "Grace, mercy and peace from God the Father
and Christ Jesus our Lord" (2 Timothy 1:2).

*Grace* is what our holy God gives that we don't
deserve. In Acts 17:25, we learn that He "himself gives
everyone life and breath and everything else." His gifts
include our very next breath. Even in our darkest
hour, strength is given by God so we can endure.

*Mercy* is what God withholds that we do deserve.
In Lamentations 3:22, we read, "Because of the
LORD's great love we are not consumed." Even when
we're wayward, God helps us turn back to Him.

*Peace* is what God brings to His people. Jesus said:
"Peace I leave with you; my peace I give you" (John
14:27). Even in the worst of times, we have inner
tranquility because our God is in control.

We can be encouraged that throughout our lives
the Lord will give us the grace, mercy, and peace we
need to live for Him.                    —AL

## Incomplete

*Being confident of this, that he who began a*
*good work in you will carry it on to completion*
*until the day of Christ Jesus.* —PHILIPPIANS 1:6

When I was a little girl, my parents bought their first
house. One afternoon, the family hopped into the
car and drove to see where we soon would be living.

I couldn't believe it. The house had no windows or
doors, and there was a strange odor. The basement
was clearly visible through big gaps in the floor and
we had to climb a ladder to get down there.

That night when I asked my mother why they
wanted to live in a house like that, she explained that
the builder wasn't finished with it yet. "Just wait and
see," she said. "I think you'll like it when it's done."

Soon we began to see changes as the house was finished. The incomplete house had been transformed.
It had taken some time, but finally it was finished.

As Christians, we need "finishing" too. Although
the groundwork is laid at our conversion, the growing
process continues throughout our life. As we obedi-
ently follow Jesus, "the pioneer and perfecter of faith"
(Hebrews 12:2), one day we too will be complete.

—CHK

# Celebrate Beginnings

*You will conceive and give birth to a son,
and you are to call him Jesus.* —LUKE 1:31

Many churches observe March 25 as Annunciation Day. It commemorates the angel's announcement to Mary that she would be the mother of Jesus, the Messiah. In our success-oriented society, this festival is a needed reminder to recognize and rejoice at the beginning of God's work in a person's life rather than holding our applause for the accomplishments.

Because we often read Luke's gospel at Christmas, we may forget that nine months of trust and waiting separated Mary's response to Gabriel from the birth of Jesus. When we read her words of surrender in light of this timespan, they take on added meaning: "I am the Lord's servant. . . . May your word to me be fulfilled" (Luke 1:38). Mary must have received great encouragement when her cousin Elizabeth told her, "Blessed is she who has believed that the Lord would fulfill his promises to her" (v. 45).

We can celebrate beginnings by giving a hug or handshake to a new believer who professes faith in Christ. We can write a note of encouragement to a friend who has chosen to obey God's Word.

Let's grasp every opportunity to celebrate the beginnings of God's work in the lives of others.

—DM

## Mom's Dream Home

*A wise son brings joy to his father, but a foolish man despises his mother.* —PROVERBS 15:20

What is a mother's idea of a dream home? A one-story, ranch-style house with a fenced-in yard for the children? Three bedrooms, a big family room, and a modern kitchen? Or maybe her dream home would have a beautiful garden overlooking a quiet lake.

Most mothers know it takes more than that to make a house a home. The most important characteristics of a home are the spiritual qualities and the love between father, mother, and children.

In Proverbs 15, Solomon said that it is better to live in poverty while fearing the Lord than to possess great treasure and have trouble because of it (v. 16). And a dream home is a place where children obey their father and honor their mother (v. 20). A loving, spiritual atmosphere is the feature most desired in a home, and that can be found in a simple one-room house or in a spacious mansion.

Yes, I think we would all agree that love for our family and the fear of the Lord can turn any house into a dream home. It's a place where Mom—and the rest of the family—will find true joy.          —MD

# For Example

*Eager to serve . . . being examples
to the flock.* —1 PETER 5:2–3

I remember when the principle of modeling was used by a life insurance salesman. After telling me about the strengths of his company and the benefits of a particular policy, he shared with me how much coverage he had for his own family. Suddenly, I began paying more attention to what he was saying. His words took on new meaning because he was showing me by his own example the value of being adequately insured.

If we want to teach others the art of knowing God and walking with Him, we can't overemphasize the importance and the power of example. That, after all, is how Christ and His apostles undertook the job of communicating the same message. They demonstrated that they were passing along a message they themselves were first willing to accept and obey.

The power of example makes leadership more than something that automatically goes with an official title like Mom. It's a law of nature, a principle of salesmanship, and the pattern called for by the heavenly Father himself. Parents who want to lead must first be examples. —MD

## Shared Tears

*Mourn with those who mourn.*
—ROMANS 12:15

A story is told about a little boy with a big heart. His next-door neighbor was an older gentleman whose wife had recently died. When the youngster saw him crying, he climbed onto his lap and simply sat there.

Later, his mother asked the boy what he had said to their saddened neighbor. "Nothing," the child replied. "I just helped him cry."

Sometimes that's the best thing we can do for people who are facing profound sorrow. Often, our attempts to say something wise are far less valuable than just sitting next to the bereaved ones, holding their hand, and crying with them.

One of the ways we can help our fellow believers is to "mourn with those who mourn" (Romans 12:15). Jesus demonstrated that principle when He visited Mary and Martha after Lazarus died. Sensing the depths of Mary's despair over her brother Lazarus's death, Jesus shared her grief by weeping (John 11:35). Bystanders remarked, "See how he loved him!" (v. 36).

Sometimes the best thing we can do for those who are traveling life's sad and lonely road is to "help them cry." Is there anyone who needs your tears today?
—DB

## "Jesus Loves You, Baby Boy"

*"But now that he is dead, why should
I go on fasting? Can I bring him back
again? I will go to him, but he will not
return to me." —2 SAMUEL 12:23*

Some years ago, an abandoned baby died in the cold
of a Minnesota night. Carol Hamline, a mother of
three, was so touched about this incident that she
arranged for a funeral and bought a small monument
for the grave. Another person donated space in her
family plot, and someone else provided a tiny casket. The next day only a few attended the memorial
service. Mrs. Hamline said, "That incident broke my
heart. I couldn't get that little child out of my mind.
I felt he should have a decent burial. We're having
these words put on his marker: 'Jesus Loves You,
Baby Boy.'"

Dr. M. R. DeHaan once wrote: "If children die, it's
due to Adam's sin, but our Lord's atoning sacrifice
took care of that. What condemns us is the rejection
of Christ. Since babies cannot be guilty of this, they
go straight to heaven if they die."

If children die before they're accountable, they're
saved because Jesus's merits are applied to them and
they are taken to heaven. The Savior won't let any
little one perish.                                    —HB

## Magnets and Mothers

*"Honor your father and your mother, as*
*the LORD your God has commanded you,*
*so that you may live long and that it may*
*go well with you."* —DEUTERONOMY 5:16

A teacher gave her class of second-graders a lesson on the magnet and what it does. The next day, in a written test, she included this question: "My name has six letters. The first one is 'm.' I pick up things. What am I?" When the test papers were turned in, the teacher was astonished to find that almost fifty percent of the students answered the question with the word *mother*.

Yes, mothers do pick up things. But they are much more than "magnets," gathering up clothes and picking up toys around the house. As willing as many mothers are to do such chores, they have a higher calling than that.

A good mother loves her family and provides an atmosphere where each member can find acceptance, security, and understanding. She is there when the children need a listening ear, a comforting word, a warm hug, or a loving touch. And for the Christian mother, her greatest joy is in teaching her children to trust and to love Jesus as their Savior.

Mothers like that deserve to be honored through respect and thoughtfulness and loving deeds.  —RD

## Making Faces at a Bulldog

*Do not repay anyone evil for evil.*
—ROMANS 12:17

I read a humorous story about a little girl who was making angry faces at a bulldog. Her mother noticed and asked her to stop. The girl said, "But Mom, he started it!"

In one sense, the girl was right. A bulldog naturally looks tough and mean. But the girl gained nothing by competing with him in making faces.

So too, the person who thinks he must return every angry look he sees or repay any hurtful deed that is directed toward him will have a never-ending and profitless job. In fact, in the end he's the one who will suffer the most.

As heirs of the grace of God, we should be gracious toward others. The Spirit of Christ says, "Love your enemies and pray for those who persecute you" (Matthew 5:44).

If you want to know how spiritual you are, ask yourself, "What is my attitude toward those who mistreat me? Am I kind, considerate, and loving in my words and actions toward them?"

To live like Christ is not natural; it's supernatural. Only as we yield to the Holy Spirit can we ever hope to exhibit the life of Christ.                              —HB

## Are You Listening?

*The LORD came and stood there, calling
as at the other times, "Samuel! Samuel!"
Then Samuel said, "Speak, for your
servant is listening." —1 SAMUEL 3:10*

One of the happiest memories of my childhood is that of my mother reading bedtime Bible stories to me. They made a great impression on me, especially the incident in the life of Samuel described in 1 Samuel 3. I can still hear my mother reciting the young boy's response to the call of God: "Speak, for your servant is listening" (v. 10).

We need to be like Samuel, willing to pause in the midst of life's turmoil to hear the voice of the Lord. And we have this opportunity if we prayerfully read and study the Bible regularly. You see, God's Spirit communicates to us through the Word.

Thomas à Kempis (1379–1471) summed it up well when he wrote: "Blessed indeed are those ears which listen not for the voice sounding without, but for the truth teaching inwardly. Blessed are they who are glad to have time to spare for God, and who shake off all worldly hindrances. Hear what the Lord your God speaks."

How long has it been since you've asked the Lord to make your heart receptive to His Word? He wants to hear you say, "Speak, Lord, I'm listening." —RD

# A Prize for Peace

*"I have told you these things, so that in
me you may have peace. In this world you
will have trouble. But take heart! I have
overcome the world."* —JOHN 16:33

Alfred Nobel made a fortune from the invention of dynamite, which changed the course of warfare. Perhaps because of the horrors that wars inflicted with the use of dynamite, he made a provision in his will for a prize to be given annually to those who work to promote peace. Today it's called the Nobel Peace Prize.

God's expression of peace to the world was His Son. When Jesus was born, the angels' clear, unmistakable message to the shepherds was "on earth peace to those on whom his favor rests" (Luke 2:14).

The biblical definition of peace is, first of all, peace with God (Romans 5:1). Sin makes us enemies with God (v. 10), but Jesus's coming to this earth and dying on the cross turned away God's wrath. We can now be reconciled with Him. Having put right our relationship with God, Jesus now enables us to work at breaking down the barriers between us and others.

Having brought peace, Jesus is now seated at the right hand of the Father (Hebrews 12:2). Today, we can have peace with God and the peace of God.

—CPH

# School of Hard Knocks

*No discipline seems pleasant at the time,
but painful. Later on, however, it produces a
harvest of righteousness and peace for those
who have been trained by it.* —HEBREWS 12:11

It happened in kindergarten. I'm not sure of the details, but I clearly remember telling my teacher to "shut up." She sent me home, so I got up and began to walk the half-block home, which was not a safety issue in those days. Walking down the sidewalk, I saw my mother weeding in our garden. I was faced with a strategic decision—continue on my way and tell my mother why I was home early, or turn around and go back to face my teacher.

I returned to the classroom, where I was escorted to the restroom so my teacher could wash my mouth out with soap. That probably wouldn't happen today, but take it from me, it was effective! To this day I am acutely sensitive about the impact of my words.

God is passionately interested in our positive growth as His children. At times He needs to confront us to catch our attention and reorient our lives to more consistently produce "a harvest of righteousness and peace" (Hebrews 12:11).

He loves us enough to care about what kind of a person we are becoming.       —JS

# "Behold Your Mother!"

*Her children arise and call her blessed; her husband also, and he praises her.* —PROVERBS 31:28

The Son of God was hanging on a Roman cross. His body had been brutally beaten, and He was spiritually separated from the Father. Yet He remembered His mother! His concern for her welfare was not lost amid the agonies of that crisis. With the words, "Behold your mother" (John 19:27 NKJV), He commended her into the care of His beloved disciple John. His example shows us the importance of honoring and caring for our own mother.

Behold your mother! Remember the look in those loving eyes, the sweetness in that tender voice, the feeling of even a single touch of that gentle hand. Recall the concern that clouded her face when troubles came your way. Cherish your mother while you still have that most precious of all good gifts.

Behold your mother! Learn from her blessed example. Her teaching and guidance in the home help mold and shape the character of her children.

Behold your mother! Look to her for the same reason that Jesus told John to look—to give her the special care she needs. Today, with praise and thankfulness to God, "Behold your mother."          —HB

## His Calming Presence

*But he said to them, "It is I;*
*don't be afraid."* —JOHN 6:20

For as long as I can remember, I've wanted to be a mother. I dreamed about holding my baby in my arms for the first time. When I got married, my husband and I never even considered waiting to have children. But with each negative pregnancy test, we were buried deeper into infertility. Months of doctors' visits, tests, and tears followed. Infertility was a bitter reality, and it left me wondering about God's goodness and faithfulness.

When I reflect on our journey, I think about the story of the disciples caught in the storm on the sea in John 6. As they struggled against the waves in the dark of the storm, Jesus unexpectedly came to them walking on the stormy waves. He calmed them with His presence, saying, "It is I; don't be afraid" (v. 20).

My husband and I had no idea what was coming in our storm, but we found comfort in knowing our faithful and true God more deeply. Although we would not have the child we had dreamed of, we learned that we can experience the power of His calming presence. He is there—powerfully working in our lives.                                    —KW

## Cross and Crown

*"Just as Moses lifted up the snake in the wilderness, so the Son of Man must be lifted up, that everyone who believes may have eternal life in him."* —JOHN 3:14–15

In April 2002, along with thousands of others in London, I filed past the casket of Britain's Queen Mother as her body lay in state. In the muffled silence of Westminster Hall, I was struck by the sight of the magnificent crown resting on top of the coffin, and the cross standing nearby—symbols of her life and faith. We had come to pay our respects to a much-loved member of the royal family. But on that night, it was clear to me that the cross of the Lord Jesus Christ matters far more than any crown.

For all who trust in Christ, the cross symbolizes our hope both in life and in death. No positions of power we may inherit or achieve will follow us beyond the grave. But Christ is the giver of abundant life now and forever.

The cross speaks of forgiveness and of peace with God. It points to the merits of Christ and not our own. As we step through the doorway of death, we must lay aside our "earthly crowns." Our only hope is to cling to our Savior, who died so we could have everlasting life.                    —DM

## Our Living Hope

*Praise be to the God and Father of our
Lord Jesus Christ! In his great mercy
he has given us new birth into a living
hope through the resurrection of Jesus
Christ from the dead.* —1 PETER 1:3

The morning after my mother died, I was reading the
Bible and talking to the Lord about my sadness. My
Bible reading for that day was John 6.

When I came to verse 39, the Lord whispered comfort to my sad heart: "This is the will of him who sent
me, that I shall lose none of all those he has given me,
but raise them up at the last day."

As I continued reading, I noticed three other times
in John 6 that Jesus said He will raise His people
from the dead at the last day. He was repeating this
truth to those who were listening long ago as well as
to my heart.

Our hope of resurrection will be realized when
Jesus returns. "In a flash, in the twinkling of an eye,
at the last trumpet. For the trumpet will sound, the
dead will be raised imperishable, and we will be
changed" (1 Corinthians 15:52). After the resurrection, believers in Jesus will receive their new bodies
and rewards for their faithful service (1 Corinthians
3:12–15; 2 Corinthians 5:9–11).

The resurrection is the living hope of the Christian.
Do you have that hope?                        —AC

## Encouraging Words

*And let us consider how we may spur one
another on toward love and good deeds,
not giving up meeting together, as some
are in the habit of doing, but encouraging
one another.* —HEBREWS 10:24–25

Amy had just about had it with her lively two-year-old. The week had been difficult as she tried to stay ahead of her little tornado. She had to give constant reminders about correct behavior. It required vast amounts of emotional energy.

Then came the Sunday evening service. Her little girl was at her wiggly, loud-whisper, constant-motion best. At one point all that could be seen was her feet sticking straight up in the air as she lay on the seat. Amy was frustrated and embarrassed. What must the older couple sitting right behind her be thinking?

As she came into the church the next week, she ran into the older gentleman. *Uh-oh,* she thought, *Here it comes.* She was surprised by what he said. "What a great little girl you have. She's a special gift from God to you." It was just the kind of understanding and encouragement she needed to make the task of mothering her active little girl easier.

We go to church for a lot of reasons—worship, giving, learning. According to Hebrews 10:24–25, we are also there to encourage one another. Let's find a way to offer the kind of encouraging word that lifted Amy.                                    —DE

## Peace and Reconciliation

*"Shouldn't you have had mercy
on your fellow servant just as I had
on you?"* —MATTHEW 18:33

When the US Civil War ended in 1865, more than half a million soldiers lay dead, the economy was shattered, and people remained deeply divided politically. The observance of Mother's Day in the United States began with two women's efforts for peace and reconciliation. In 1870, Julia Ward Howe called for an International Mother's Day on which women would unite in opposing war. A few years later, Anna Reeves Jarvis began her annual Mother's Friendship Day in an effort to reunite families and neighbors alienated by the war. Both were efforts at peace and reconciliation.

The gospel of Jesus Christ brings the promise of peace and reconciliation with God and with each other. When Peter asked Jesus how often he should forgive a brother who sinned against him (Matthew 18:21), the Lord surprised everyone with His answer of "seventy-seven times" (v. 22). Then He told an unforgettable story about a servant who had received forgiveness and failed to pass it on (vv. 23–35). As God freely forgives us, He requires that we extend what we have received to others.

With God's love and power, forgiveness is always possible.                                      —DM

## Two Sides of Work

*May the LORD repay you for what you have done. May you be richly rewarded by the LORD, the God of Israel, under whose wings you have come to take refuge."* —RUTH 2:12

Ruth was facing serious problems. Her husband had died, and she had come to a foreign land with her widowed mother-in-law.

Many women find themselves in similar situations today. For various reasons, they must care for a family without the assistance of a husband.

So what did Ruth do? She went to work. She walked the barley fields, picking up grain the reapers left behind. And she met the landowner, Boaz, who would become her husband.

What happened with Ruth points out two important principles. First, God wants us to be compassionate. The needs of Ruth and Naomi were met because landowners left excess grain in the fields for the poor and the widows.

Second, the Lord rewards those who work (Genesis 1:28–30; 2:15; Proverbs 22:29; 2 Thessalonians 3:10–12). In this case, Ruth received a special blessing from the Lord (Ruth 2:12).

Both laborers and those who are in positions of authority have obligations to each other and to the Lord. No matter what our situation is, we need to follow godly principles. Any other approach to labor doesn't work.                                —DB

## Inspired by a Child's Giving

*Each of you should give what you have
decided in your heart to give, not reluctantly
or under compulsion, for God loves a
cheerful giver.* —2 CORINTHIANS 9:7

Pastor Larry Browning told his small Mississippi congregation that the church faced an urgent $1,000 missionary offering. He put no pressure on his parishioners but merely said that if they'd give cheerfully as the Lord directed, the need would be met.

Six-year-old John Jordan whispered to his mother, "Mom, I feel God wants me to give $100." Surprised, she didn't know what to say. That's so much for a young boy.

Realizing that the youngster was not about to change his mind, she asked if she could say something. Standing, she told the congregation what her son wanted to do. The announcement electrified the audience. John's father quickly offered to provide the $100, but the boy shook his head. He said he had saved that exact amount and wanted to help the missionaries tell people about Jesus.

Billfolds and purses were reopened. When the offering was finally received, the goal of $1,000 was easily surpassed. The young lad's generous spirit had inspired the people to new heights of Christian stewardship.

Open-hearted financial support of the church and its outreach honors the Lord. He loves sacrificial cheerful givers.                              —HB

## Satisfied with the Best

*Consider it pure joy, my brothers
and sisters, whenever you face trials
of many kinds.* —JAMES 1:2

A woman was overwhelmed with grief as she approached the church on the Sunday morning after her mother died. Just outside the door a seven-year-old boy met her. He stopped and with tearful eyes looked up at her. "I prayed for your mother," he said, "but she died."

For a moment the sorrowing woman wanted to scoop him up in her arms and cry with him, but she could see he was upset because he thought his prayers had not been answered. She said to the boy, "You wanted God to do His best for my mother, didn't you?" He nodded slowly. "Son, He answered your prayer. His best for her was to take her home to live with Him." The lad's eyes lit up as he replied, "That's right, He did." Off he ran, content that God had taken her to heaven.

Do the events in your life appear contrary to everything you think is good? Is it hard to understand why circumstances haven't fallen into place like you prayed? Don't be dismayed. Trust God and ask Him to help you learn the difficult but rewarding lesson of being satisfied with His best.          —DD

## "Did You Find Me?"

*I write these things to you who believe in the
name of the Son of God so that you may know
that you have eternal life.* —1 JOHN 5:13

Sadly, many true Christians are plagued with doubt about their salvation. Even though they have come in repentance and faith to Jesus as their Savior, they still wonder, "Am I really saved?"

My late husband Bill often told about something that happened to him when he was two years old. One day he strayed from home and got lost. When his parents realized he was missing, they went searching for him. Finally, to everyone's immense relief, they spotted their tearful boy and took him safely home.

Days later, Billy overheard his mother relate this incident to a visitor. When she reached the part where they went out searching for him, Billy began to relive the story. "Mommy, Mommy!" he sobbed. "Did you ever find me?" She embraced him and said, "Of course, my child! Don't you remember that happy moment? See, you're with us now." That settled it for Billy. He simply believed her word.

First John was written to give believers the assurance of salvation. That assurance can be yours as you take God at His word.                    —JY

## "He Left the Lights On"

*By faith Abel brought God a better offering*
*than Cain did. By faith he was commended*
*as righteous, when God spoke well of his*
*offerings. And by faith Abel still speaks,*
*even though he is dead.* —HEBREWS 11:4

A mother and her young daughter were walking past the house in Springfield, Illinois, where Abraham Lincoln once lived. The lights were burning inside, making the home seem warm and inviting. They paused for a few minutes as the mother told the girl what a great president Mr. Lincoln had been and how the whole nation mourned when he died. Then, noticing the glow coming from the windows, she said, "Look, Momma. When Mr. Lincoln went away, he left the lights on."

That little girl's response, though mistaken, unwittingly suggests an important truth: The influence of our lives continues even after we die. Notice what the writer of Hebrews said of Abel: "[he] still speaks, even though he is dead" (Hebrews 11:4). And John recorded this message from heaven: "Blessed are the dead who die in the Lord from now on. . . . They will rest from their labor, for their deeds will follow them" (Revelation 14:13).

Let's ask God to help us be faithful to Him so that it can be said of us that we "left the lights on." —RD

## Chapel of Silence

*Therefore, since we have been justified through*
*faith, we have peace with God through*
*our Lord Jesus Christ.* —ROMANS 5:1

The Kamppi Chapel of Silence in Helsinki, Finland, stands out in its urban setting. The curved wooden structure buffers the noise from the busy city outside. Designers created the chapel as a quiet space and a "calm environment for visitors to compose themselves." It's a welcome escape from the hustle and bustle of the city.

Many people long for peace, and a few minutes of silence may soothe our minds. But the Bible teaches that real peace—peace with God—comes from His Son. The apostle Paul said, "Therefore, since we have been justified through faith, we have peace with God through our Lord Jesus Christ" (Romans 5:1). Without Christ, we are enemies of God because of our sin. Thankfully, accepting Jesus's sacrifice reconciles us to God and ends the hostility that existed between us (Colossians 1:19–21).

Having peace with God does not ensure problem-free living. However, it does steady us during difficult times. Jesus told His followers, "In this world you will have trouble," but He also said, "In me you may have peace" (John 16:33). Because of Christ, the true peace of God can fill our hearts (Colossians 3:15).

—JBS

## The Gift behind the Gift

*I am amply supplied, now that I have received
from Epaphroditus the gifts you sent. They
are a fragrant offering, an acceptable sacrifice,
pleasing to God.* —PHILIPPIANS 4:18

The love behind a gift is more important than the gift
itself. At least that's what the husband who wrote the
following lament to his wife hoped was true:

M is for the mink coat you want, dear,
O is for the opal ring you crave,
T is for the tiny car you'd love, sweet
H is for the hat that makes you rave,
E is for the earrings you'd admire, love
R is for the rug on which you'd tread;
Put them all together, they spell bankrupt
So I'm giving you this handkerchief instead.

Once, my nine-year-old grandson asked me what
he should get Grandma for her birthday. Kiddingly I
told him, "A mink coat or a Mercedes." He grinned
and said he had only about five dollars. I assured him
that she would be happier with a small gift from him
than she would be with a mink coat from someone
she didn't know.

With the Philippian believers' gifts to Paul or with
generosity to our loved ones, it's the gift behind the
gift that counts—our caring, our thoughtfulness, our
love.                                                          —HVL

## Proper Casting

*Cast all your anxiety on him because
he cares for you.* —1 PETER 5:7

When I was young, my mother was deeply concerned about my future. Although I had survived two bouts with tuberculosis, I had been left weak and crippled. When she privately expressed her anxiety to an acquaintance, he gave her good advice. "Mrs. Bosch," he said, "you must stop worrying about your boy and cast all your care upon the Lord. I am sure He has the answer to all these problems. Somehow He will make it possible for Henry to support himself."

How right that person was! Later, strengthened in body, I was able to go through college, get into Christian broadcasting, and finally work as editor of *Our Daily Bread*. Not only did I take care of my own needs but after my father's death I also provided for my mother, my wife, and our three children! Mother realized then that her concern about me, while natural, was a needless worry. That's why we need the reminder of 1 Peter 5:7 to cast our care on the Lord.

In times of trial, we can have victory if we do the proper kind of casting!                    —HB

## Be Still

*Trust in the* LORD *with all your heart and lean not on your own understanding.* —PROVERBS 3:5

As I sat in the dentist's chair, I braced myself for the drilling that would begin my root canal. I was ready for the worst, and my body language and facial expression exposed my sense of dread. The dentist looked at me and smiled, saying, "It's okay, my friend. Try to relax."

That isn't easy to do. The words *try* and *relax* just don't seem to fit together—not only in the dentist's chair but in the spiritual realm as well.

In my relationship with Christ, I find myself not pressing for God's purposes but for my own interests. In those moments, the hardest thing for me to do is "try to relax" and genuinely trust God for the outcome of life's trials.

In Psalm 46:10, we read, "Be still, and know that I am God; I will be exalted among the nations, I will be exalted in the earth"! In the moments when my heart is anxious, this verse reminds me to "be still, and know." Now, if I can only put that into practice and rest confidently in His care, I'll be at peace.      —BC

## The Time to Obey Is Now

*Still another said, "I will follow you,*
*Lord; but first let me go back and say*
*goodbye to my family." —LUKE 9:61*

Most parents are familiar with the words: "I'll do it in a minute, but first . . ." Our heavenly Father often receives a similar response from us.

I'll never forget my inner battle one morning as I scrubbed the kitchen floor. It began with a strong impression from the Lord that I should visit a young mother named Carol. So I decided to do it later. "But first I must finish this floor," I said to myself.

Then the prompting began to feel more urgent. "As soon as I finish the floor, I'll go straight over to Carol's," I promised the Lord. But deep inside, I knew He meant now, before the floor was finished!

Finally, I said, "Okay, Lord, I'll go now!" When Carol opened her door, she said tearfully, "How did you know I needed you right now?" I didn't, but God did. My surrender to Him played a part in Carol's eventual surrender to Christ as her Savior.

In Luke 9, Jesus taught that some things can wait. That includes half-scrubbed floors—and a host of other things. But a ripe harvest can't wait!        —JY

## A Notable Habit

*We always thank God, the Father
of our Lord Jesus Christ, when we
pray for you.* —COLOSSIANS 1:3

It was a letter from a soldier during World War II, and it was delivered to a West Virginia farmhouse. The soldier had received the address of a young woman and had written to her, not realizing she was married. When the letter arrived, the addressee showed it to her unmarried sister-in-law, who decided that with a war raging the least she could do would be to write an encouraging note to this Second Lieutenant.

One letter led to another and soon a romance had started. Within a year of that first letter, the soldier and the farm girl were married.

Not all notes of encouragement lead to long-term relationships, as did this exchange between the people who became my parents. But their story of long-distance love, sparked by my mother's sense of duty, reminds us that writing to those in need can be very rewarding.

Just as the apostle Paul gave the churches uplifting messages of hope, we too can serve Christ and bring joy to others through thoughtful messages.

Think of someone in need of a lift, and send that person a card with a word of encouragement. It is a notable habit.                    —DB

## If You Criticize, Be Wise!

*Wounds from a friend can be trusted, but an enemy multiplies kisses.* —PROVERBS 27:6

In an interview for a Christian magazine, longtime pastor Dave Burnham and his wife Sue were asked about criticism. Sue said, "I think Christ's example in John 1:14 is a helpful one. The passage describes Jesus as being 'full of grace and truth.' When I read this verse, I think of a mother with her child. If the child has a dirty face, the mother doesn't scold her for having a dirty face. She does the loving thing. She gently washes the child's face, perhaps saying, 'Tell me how you got your face so dirty.' If I'm going to be honest with Dave, I need to be sure that I'm acting in loving ways—in a sense, getting out the washcloth—even while I'm talking about the dirt."

Let's speak the truth in love. Think of how Christ has been dealing with us through the indwelling Holy Spirit. He is grieved when we fail Him, but He is never bitter. And He is always lavish in His love and forgiveness. If we imitate the way Jesus treats us, we will be wise when it becomes necessary to criticize.

—DD

## Thank You for Not Squawking

*Do everything without grumbling
or arguing.* —PHILIPPIANS 2:14

On a recent flight, I was seated behind two small children who were not happy about being on a plane. Their cries of complaint filled the cabin.

Just before takeoff, a flight attendant stopped next to them and said with a big smile, "What is all this squawking up here?" After charming the fussy three-year-old and his younger sister for a few minutes, the flight attendant bent down and whispered very seriously, "I must remind you, this is a nonsquawking flight."

The little ones became unbelievably quiet. That made everyone feel better. It's a long journey when you have to sit in the squawking section.

I'm sure God would like to remind me every morning that He wants this day to be a nonsquawking flight. Philippians 2:14 says to "do everything without grumbling or arguing." While my natural tendency is to complain, God has another approach in mind—one that lets His light shine through me and encourages others (v. 15).

If we went through each day without complaining, how would it affect our family and friends? What about our ability to share the Word of life with others? (vv. 15–16).

Squawking or nonsquawking? The choice is ours.

—DM

## The Laws of a Godly Mother

*My son, keep your father's command
and do not forsake your mother's
teaching.* —PROVERBS 6:20

The righteous parents in Proverbs 6:20 were good examples to their sons because they obeyed the will of God as set forth in the commandments.

As I thought about this, I recalled some unique, helpful "laws" of my own mother. First, "the law of the warm kitchen." When we got home from school on a cold winter's day or when the holidays rolled around, the kitchen was always so warm from baking and cooking that the windows were steamed. It was also warm with a mother's love. Second, "the law of a mother's perspective." When I'd come to her all upset over some childish matter, she'd often say, "Ten years from now you'll have forgotten all about it." That helped me put things into perspective. Above all was Mother's "law of faith." Like Lois and Eunice in 2 Timothy 1:5, she had an unswerving trust in God that kept her strong and gentle amid the fears, pressures, and sacrifices of my growing up years.

I'm still grateful for Mom's "laws," because they have helped me through many difficult days. All mothers are writing "laws" for their children. Are they worth remembering?                              —DE

## Flowing Peace

*"Peace I leave with you; my peace
I give you."* —JOHN 14:27

"I'm not surprised you lead retreats," said an acquaintance in my exercise class. "You have a good aura." I was jolted but pleased by her comment, because I realized that what she saw as an "aura" in me, I understood to be the peace of Christ. As we follow Jesus, He gives us the peace that transcends understanding (Philippians 4:7) and radiates from within—though we may not even be aware of it.

Jesus promised His followers this peace when, after their last supper together, He prepared them for His death and resurrection. He told them that though they would have trouble in the world, the Father would send them the Spirit of truth to live with them, be in them, and teach them (John 14:16–17). Though soon they would face trials—including fierce opposition from the religious leaders and seeing Jesus executed—He told them not to be afraid. The Holy Spirit's presence would never leave them.

Although as God's children we experience hardship, we too have His Spirit living within and flowing out of us. God's peace can be His witness to everyone we meet.                                    —ABP

## Times of Refreshing

*Repent, then, and turn to God, so that your*
*sins may be wiped out, that times of refreshing*
*may come from the Lord.* —ACTS 3:19

What do you find most refreshing? A cold drink on a hot day? An afternoon nap? Listening to praise and worship music?

The biblical theme of refreshing has a variety of physical and spiritual meanings. In Scripture we read of refreshment by resting on the Sabbath (Exodus 23:12), with cool water after physical activity (Judges 15:18–19), by soothing music (1 Samuel 16:23), and with encouraging fellowship (2 Timothy 1:16).

The apostle Peter describes a time of spiritual refreshment that took place on the Day of Pentecost. He exhorted his listeners to repent and respond to the gospel "that times of refreshing may come from the Lord" (Acts 3:19).

Even now as believers we can experience a time of refreshing by quieting our hearts in a devotional time of prayer and Bible reading. When we spend time alone with the Lord, we can experience His peace and joy which renew us in spirit. Aren't you thankful for these times of spiritual refreshment?                —DF

## Welcome Wings

*How priceless is your unfailing love, O
God! People take refuge in the shadow
of your wings.* —PSALM 36:7

One spring a pair of blue jays built a nest in the per-
simmon tree in our backyard. I enjoyed watching
the mother bird as she sat patiently on her eggs. After the eggs hatched, I would edge closer to the tree
to get a better look. When I got too close, however,
Mama Blue Jay would spread her wings over her little
brood. She was always on guard, protecting her little
ones with her wings.

This beautiful picture of protection reminds me of
David's words in Psalm 36:7. When he said that we
can find safety "in the shadow of [God's] wings," he
may have been referring to the words of his ancestor
Boaz (Ruth 2:12). Boaz had said to Ruth, "May the
LORD repay you for what you have done. May you
be richly rewarded by the LORD, the God of Israel,
under whose wings you have come to take refuge."

Surely that's a promise we still need. Life is filled
with dangers! Yet, we can rest securely because we
know that God is aware of them all. What better
refuge could we have than to live under the shadow
of His wings!                                   —PVG

## A Mother's Love

*He will call on me, and I will answer him; I*
*will be with him in trouble, I will deliver*
*him and honor him.* —PSALM 91:15

Because of a divorce and other issues, Sue was sent
to a children's home for a while. She felt lonely and
abandoned because she rarely saw her parents. Years
later, her mother told her that although the home's
rules prevented her from visiting often, she had
stood at the fence every single day, hoping to catch
a glimpse of her daughter. "Sometimes," she said, "I
would just watch you playing in the garden, just to
check if you were okay."

When Sue shared this story, it gave me a glimpse of
God's love. Sometimes we may feel abandoned and
alone in our struggles, but in fact God is watching
over us all the time! (Psalm 33:18). Like a loving
parent, His eyes and His heart are constantly on us
wherever we go. Yet, unlike Sue's mom, He can act
on our behalf at any time.

Psalm 91 describes God delivering, protecting,
and lifting up His children. As we navigate the dark
valleys of life, we can take comfort in the knowledge
that the all-powerful Lord is watching over us and is
active in our lives.                                  —LK

## The Comfort of a Queen

*Then they sat on the ground with him*
*for seven days and seven nights. No one*
*said a word to him, because they saw*
*how great his suffering was.* —JOB 2:13

Once during Queen Victoria's reign, she heard that the wife of a common laborer had lost her baby. Having experienced deep sorrow herself, she felt moved to express her sympathy. So she called on the bereaved woman one day and spent some time with her. After she left, the neighbors asked what the queen had said. "Nothing," replied the grieving mother. "She simply put her hands on mine, and we silently wept together."

In Scripture we read that Job's friends came to "sympathize with him and comfort him" in his trouble (Job 2:11). Although they wept, they recognized that his suffering was so overwhelming that words seemed inappropriate. The Bible says that "no one said a word to him, because they saw how great his suffering was" (v. 13). Silent empathy was the best comfort they could give.

In my times of grief, the most comforting people were those who expressed their love by just gripping my hand. They didn't say much, but their presence spoke volumes.

If you care for people who are sorrowing, a warm handclasp or an embrace of loving compassion will convey to them your strengthening fellowship and Christian love.                                      —HB

## Little Lies and Kittens

*God's wonderful grace rules . . . ,
giving us right standing with God and
resulting in eternal life through Jesus
Christ our Lord.* —ROMANS 5:21 NLT

Mom noticed four-year-old Elias scurrying away from the newborn kittens. She had told him not to touch them. "Did you touch the kitties?" she asked.

"No!" he said earnestly. So Mom had another question: "Were they soft?"

"Yes," he volunteered, "and the black one mewed."

With a toddler, we smile at such duplicity. But Elias's disobedience underscores our human condition. No one has to teach a four-year-old to lie. The apostle Paul said: "When Adam sinned, sin entered the world. Adam's sin brought death, so death spread to everyone, for everyone sinned" (Romans 5:12 NLT). That depressing news applies equally to kings, four-year-olds, and you and me.

But there's plenty of hope! "God's law was given so that all people could see how sinful they were," wrote Paul. "But as people sinned more and more, God's wonderful grace became more abundant" (Romans 5:20 NLT).

God is not waiting for us to blow it so He can pounce on us. He is in the business of grace, forgiveness, and restoration. We need only recognize that our sin is neither cute nor excusable and come to Him in faith and repentance.                              —TG

## Learning to Trust

*Trust in the* LORD *and do good; dwell in the land and enjoy safe pasture.* —PSALM 37:3

When I stuck my camera into the bush to take a picture of the baby robins, they opened their mouths without opening their eyes. They were so used to having mama robin feed them whenever the branches moved that they didn't even look to see who (or what) was causing the disturbance.

That is the kind of trust that loving mothers instill in their children. That is the kind of mom I was blessed to have. Growing up, I could eat whatever food she put on the table without fear that it would harm me. Although she made me eat things I didn't like, I knew she did so because they were good for me. No matter what Mom told me to do, or not to do, I knew she had my best interest in mind.

That is the kind of relationship we have with God, who compared himself to a mother: "As a mother comforts her child, so will I comfort you" (Isaiah 66:13). As His children, we have no reason to fear what happens to us nor to envy what happens to others. When we trust His goodness, we are fed by His faithfulness.                              —JAL

## Peace and Comfort

*On the evening of that first day of the week,*
*when the disciples were together, with the*
*doors locked for fear of the Jewish leaders,*
*Jesus came and stood among them and*
*said, "Peace be with you!"* —JOHN 20:19

A friend shared with me that for years she searched for peace and contentment. She and her husband built up a successful business, so she was able to buy a big house, fancy clothes, and expensive jewelry. But these possessions didn't satisfy her inner longings for peace, nor did her friendships with influential people. Then one day, when she was feeling low and desperate, a friend told her about the good news of Jesus. There she found the Prince of Peace, and her understanding of true peace and contentment was forever changed.

Jesus spoke words of peace to His friends after their last supper together (John 14), when He prepared them for the events that would soon follow: His death, resurrection, and the coming of the Holy Spirit. Describing a peace unlike anything the world can give He wanted them to learn how to find a sense of well-being even in the midst of hardship.

Later, when the resurrected Jesus appeared to the frightened disciples after His death, He greeted them, saying, "Peace be with you!" (John 20:19). What a comfort—to rest in what He has done for us!

—ABP

## Someone to Touch

*Jesus reached out his hand and touched the*
*man. "I am willing," he said. "Be clean!" And*
*immediately the leprosy left him.* —LUKE 5:13

Commuters on a Canadian Metro train witnessed a heart-moving conclusion to a tense moment. They watched as a seventy-year-old woman gently reached out and offered her hand to a young man whose loud voice and disturbing words were scaring other passengers. The lady's kindness calmed the man, who sank to the floor of the train with tears in his eyes. The woman later admitted to being afraid. But she said, "I'm a mother, and he needed someone to touch." While better judgment might have given her reason to keep her distance, she took a risk of love.

Jesus understands such compassion. He didn't side with the fears of unnerved onlookers when a desperate man, full of leprosy, showed up begging to be healed. Neither was He helpless as other religious leaders were—men who could only have condemned the man for bringing his leprosy into the village (Leviticus 13:45–46). Instead, Jesus reached out to someone who probably hadn't been touched by anyone for years, and healed him.

Thankfully, for that man and for us, Jesus came to offer what no law could ever offer—the touch of His hand and heart.                                    —MD

## A Gift of Hope

*"You will become pregnant and have a son*
*whose head is never to be touched by a razor*
*because the boy is to be a Nazirite, dedicated*
*to God from the womb."* —JUDGES 13:5

When a powerful typhoon swept through the city of
Tacloban, Philippines, in 2013, an estimated 10,000
people died. Necessities became scarce. Three months
later, while the town was still struggling, a baby was
born on a roadside near Tacloban amid torrents of
rain and strong wind. Although the weather brought
back painful memories, residents worked together
to find a midwife and transport the mother and
newborn to a clinic. The baby survived, thrived, and
became a symbol of hope during a time of despair.

Forty years of Philistine oppression marked a grim
period in Israel's national history. During this time,
an angel informed an Israelite woman that she would
give birth to Samson, a special son (Judges 13:3). According to the angel, Samson would become a man
set apart to God and would "take the lead in delivering Israel from the hands of the Philistines" (v. 5). He
was a gift of hope born in a troubled time.

Trouble is unavoidable, yet Jesus has the power to
rescue us from despair. Christ was born "to shine on
those living in darkness" (Luke 1:79).          —JBS

## Picking Daisies

*See what great love the Father has
lavished on us, that we should be called
children of God!* —1 JOHN 3:1

I recall when in grade school my eyes first met those of a brown-eyed girl in my classroom. It was my first case of "puppy love." Those were the days when we'd take a daisy and pluck off its petals one by one while saying, "She loves me, she loves me not." It hurt when the daisy's last petal was "she loves me not."

This reminds me of a little girl who came running into the house, sobbing. "What's wrong, dear?" her mother asked. She cried, "God doesn't love me anymore." "Of course He does," the mother said reassuringly. "No, He doesn't," the child sobbed. "I know He doesn't because I tried Him with a daisy."

One way to know that God loves us is to consider everything He does for us each day. If there's still any doubt, think of what He did to save us! The Bible says, "God demonstrates his own love for us in this: While we were still sinners, Christ died for us" (Romans 5:8).

We can be confident of God's unfailing love. He has proven it beyond all question. His love is a sure thing!                                                   —RD

## Signs of Love

*"If you love me, keep my commands."* —JOHN 14:15

School was over, and fourteen-year-old Sandy couldn't wait to get home. Bursting into the kitchen, she exclaimed, "Mother, Steve gave me his ring. I'm in love!" Sandy's mother responded, "I can see you're on cloud nine. Tell me about it." Mother listened as Sandy bubbled over about the wonders of being in love, but she wasn't unduly alarmed. She expected the "romance" to end soon. And it did. Sandy didn't understand that there's much more to true love than a tingling sensation.

Likewise, the signs of a genuine love for Jesus must be more than good feelings gained from enthusiastic singing and exciting experiences. I heard of a lady who exuberantly enjoyed her church and exclaimed, "O how I love Jesus!" Yet she disliked her mother-in-law, fought with her sisters, and was mean to her husband. If she couldn't show her devotion to Jesus by obeying His command to love others, the happiness she felt at church meant nothing. Proof of her love for Christ would be loving attitudes toward others.

When Jesus said, "If you love me, keep my commands" (John 14:15), He was giving us the supreme test of our devotion to Him.                    —HVL

## Unconventional Tactics

*"Our God, will you not judge them? For we
have no power to face this vast army that is
attacking us. We do not know what to do, but
our eyes are on you."* —2 CHRONICLES 20:12

In 1980, a woman who started running the Boston
Marathon took a little detour on the subway. She
finished well ahead of all the other female runners,
and oddly, she wasn't winded or even sweating much.
For a brief time she looked like the winner—until her
ruse was discovered.

In a conflict long ago, a people who were losing
a battle found a more honorable way to win. When
messengers told King Jehoshaphat, "A vast army is
coming against you from Edom," he was terrified
(2 Chronicles 20:2–3). But instead of turning to typical military tactics, Jehoshaphat turned to God. He
prayed, "We do not know what to do, but our eyes
are on you" (v. 12). Then the king chose singers to
lead the army into battle. Instead of a war cry, they
sang of God's love (v. 21). Surprisingly, their enemies
turned on each other (vv. 22–24). In the end, "The
kingdom of Jehoshaphat was at peace, for his God
had given him rest on every side" (v. 30).

Life can ambush us with overwhelming challenges. Yet that gives us the opportunity to turn to
our all-powerful God. He specializes in the uncon-
ventional.                                          —TG

# Pleasing God

*So that you may live a life worthy of the Lord and please him in every way: bearing fruit in every good work, growing in the knowledge of God.* —COLOSSIANS 1:10

A minister was the commencement speaker at a small midwestern college. During the ceremony a medal was awarded to the student with the highest grade-point average throughout his college career. After the program, the minister walked behind the winning senior in the recessional. As they came to a row of seats near the back, the graduate stopped briefly by a middle-aged couple who were seated by the aisle. They appeared to be quite poor.

The young man bent down, placed the medal in his mother's hands, and kissed her on the cheek. As he stepped back in line, the preacher saw the mother place her small hand upon the hand of her husband and squeeze it. The minister heard her say, "It's worth all it cost, isn't it?" Their radiant faces reflected the joy their son's success had brought them. He had wanted to please the ones who had sacrificed so much to help him gain an education.

In much the same way, Christians should "live a life worthy of the Lord" because of all He has done for us. In view of Christ's sacrifice at Calvary, pleasing Him should be our highest motivation. —PVG

## The Widow's Faith

*"For the pagans run after all these things,
and your heavenly Father knows that
you need them."* —MATTHEW 6:32

It is pitch dark when Ah-pi starts her day. She makes her way to the rubber plantation where she works to harvest latex from the trees there. But first she will spend time communing with God.

Ah-pi's father, husband, and only son have passed away, and she—with her daughter-in-law—is providing for an elderly mother and two young grandsons. Her story reminds me of another widow in the Bible who trusted God.

The widow's husband had died and left her in debt (2 Kings 4:1). In her distress, she looked to God for help by turning to His servant Elisha. She believed that God cared and that He could do something about her situation. And God did. He provided miraculously for the dire needs of this widow (vv. 5–6). This same God also provided for Ah-pi—though less miraculously—through the toil of her hands, the produce from the ground, and gifts from His people.

Though life can make various demands on us, we can always draw strength from God. We can entrust our cares to Him, do all we can, and let Him amaze us with what He can do with our situation.   —PFC

## In Word and Deed

*Her children arise and call her blessed; her husband also, and he praises her.* —PROVERBS 31:28

A man decided to make Mother's Day special for his wife. He bought her presents. He took her out to eat. He made life easy for her around the house.

But what she appreciated more than anything was something he did during church. When the men in the church were told they could have the microphone to say something about a special woman in their life, he hesitated. But when the last call was given, he spoke ever so briefly about his wife—telling how thankful he was for her godly example. She was moved as he honored her before others. Those eighteen seconds were the highlight of her weekend. She even requested a tape of the service to savor his thoughtful words.

It's admirable when a man does kind things for his wife, but if he compliments her publicly by saying, "You are special to me, and I appreciate you," he demonstrates wisdom.

The husband in Proverbs 31 praised his wife by saying, "Many women do noble things, but you surpass them all" (v. 29). Nothing a man can do is more honoring than speaking words like those.     —DB

## The Best Mum

*Her children arise and call her
blessed; her husband also, and he
praises her.* —PROVERBS 31:28

On Mother's Day one year, British national television ran an intriguing story. Peggy Bush's daughter had died, so Peggy absorbed the responsibility of caring for her daughter's three children while her son-in-law worked. Then, tragically, her son-in-law also died. With both parents gone, Peggy took her three grandchildren in and raised them as her own.

This woman's love and sacrifice were recognized, acknowledged, and honored as the nation took note of her as Britain's "Best Mum" for 2007.

Most of the efforts, sacrifices, and expressions of love our mothers have given us will not be the lead story on the news. Their recognition will be more personal. But what matters is not the scope of the appreciation but its genuineness.

May we thank God for the mothers who have molded our own hearts. As we honor them, we fulfill the truth of Proverbs 31:28, "Her children arise and call her blessed; her husband also, and he praises her."

—BC

## A Good Mother's Influence

*The sayings of King Lemuel—*
*an inspired utterance his mother*
*taught him.* —PROVERBS 31:1

King Lemuel had a good mother. Her words to her son, recorded in Proverbs 31, urged him to be a pure, sober, honest, and compassionate king.

How fortunate for King Lemuel that he had a mother who taught him well! Some children and young people today don't receive this kind of teaching from their mom. That idea and Lemuel's mother's good words should challenge moms everywhere to be the best they can be for their kids.

Abraham Lincoln declared, "No man is poor who has had a godly mother." A Spanish proverb reads, "An ounce of mother is worth a ton of priest." Someone else has said, "The instruction received at the mother's knee, together with the pious and sweet souvenirs of the fireside, are never effaced entirely from the soul."

Mother, you have a high and holy calling. By your words and your example, you are to teach your children the fear of the Lord. What a challenge! What a privilege!                                    —HVL

## A Walk in the Park

*Make every effort to keep the unity of the Spirit through the bond of peace.* —EPHESIANS 4:3

After I confronted my friend by email over a matter on which we had differed, she didn't respond. Had I overstepped? I didn't want to worsen the situation, but neither did I want to leave things unresolved before she went on a trip overseas. As she popped into my mind throughout the following days, I prayed for her, unsure of the way forward. Then one morning I went for a walk in our local park and saw her, pain etched on her face as she glimpsed me. "Thank you, Lord, that I can talk to her," I breathed as I approached her with a welcoming smile. We talked openly and were able to resolve matters.

Sometimes when hurt or silence intrudes on our relationships, mending them seems out of our control. But as the apostle Paul says in his letter to the church at Ephesus, we are called to work for peace and unity through God's Spirit, employing gentleness, humility, and patience as we seek God's healing in our relationships. The Lord yearns for us to be united, and through His Spirit He can bring His people together—even unexpectedly when we go walking in the park.                          —ABP

# Women with Empty Arms

*Carry each other's burdens,*
*and in this way you will fulfill the*
*law of Christ.* —GALATIANS 6:2

Children armed with crayons excitedly design cards full of wobbly letters and heartfelt love. Husbands bring home gift-wrapped presents. The family lets Mom have a leisurely day. Each year on Mother's Day, women with children receive the adoration they richly deserve. It's a day of happiness and satisfaction.

But it's not that way in every home. In some, Mother's Day is a date to dread, for it's an inescapable reminder that there are no children to draw funny pictures and fix breakfast. The distress Hannah felt because she was barren is a painful reality to these women.

Perhaps we can help bear the burdens of the childless. First, let's avoid comments that crush the spirit of a woman who longs to hold a baby who will call her "Mom." We shouldn't ask questions like, "When are you going to start a family?" Then, let's also show them our love without treating them as second-class women. Let's befriend couples without children and include them in family activities and church functions.

As we honor mothers, let's not forget the women with empty arms.                    —DB

## Try a Little Kindness!

*Do not be overcome by evil,*
*but overcome evil with good.*
—ROMANS 12:21

This is the true story of a boy who seemed destined for a life of trouble. Coming from a difficult home, he was hostile, undisciplined, and a real menace. One day a young mother was appalled to find this young-ster, hammer in hand, furiously pounding nails into her house. In anger she could have issued a sharp rebuke and a stern warning. But she remained calm, and she quietly reached into her apron pocket, took out a dime, and held it out to the boy.

"Please promise you'll never do that again," she said. "Also, would you watch my house so that none of the other boys pound nails into it?" Overwhelmed by this unexpected response, one that reflects the Bible teaching to overcome evil with good, the youngster readily agreed. This kind deed had defused his rebel-lious heart and had taught him respect for property, for older people, and for himself. And, who knows, that may have been the turning point away from a downward path for this boy!

Kindness does not always meet with such appar-ent success. But we'll never know its power for good until we give it a try.                          —DD

## Join the Cry

*I urge, then, first of all, that petitions,
prayers, intercession and thanksgiving be
made for all people.* —1 TIMOTHY 2:1

A women's prayer group in my country holds regular monthly prayer sessions for Ghana and other African countries. When asked why they pray so incessantly for the nations, their leader, Gifty Dadzie, remarked, "We believe God intervenes in the affairs of nations, so we praise Him for His blessings and cry for His intervention."

The Bible reveals that God indeed intervenes in the affairs of nations (2 Chronicles 7:14). And when God intervenes, He uses ordinary people. We may not be assigned huge tasks, but we can play our part to help bring about peace and the righteousness that exalts a nation (Proverbs 14:34). We can do that through prayer. The apostle Paul wrote, "I urge, then, first of all, that petitions, prayers, intercession and thanksgiving be made for all people—for kings and all those in authority, that we may live peaceful and quiet lives in all godliness and holiness" (1 Timothy 2:1–2).

As the psalmist exhorted the ancient Israelites to "pray for the peace of Jerusalem" (Psalm 122:6), so may we pray for the peace and healing of our nations. When we pray in humility, turn from wickedness, and seek God, He hears us. —LD

## Looking and Learning

*Start children off on the way they should
go, and even when they are old they will
not turn from it.* —PROVERBS 22:6

As an umpire stood behind the plate at a girls' soft-ball game, he heard a player's mother start chanting: "We want a new ump! We want a new ump!" Soon, other parents took up the chant. The ump smiled, then turned toward the crowd and yelled, "I want new parents! I want new parents!" The heckling died away.

It's important for parents to set a good example. Christian parents can encourage good habits and behavior by doing things like:

- Praying for and with their children—so they learn how to talk with God. "Devote yourselves to prayer, being watchful and thankful" (Colossians 4:2).
- Reading and teaching them the Bible—so they learn God's truth. "Talk about [God's commands] when you sit at home and when you walk along the road, when you lie down and when you get up" (Deuteronomy 6:7).
- Telling them about Jesus—and leading them to faith in Him. "No one can see the kingdom of God unless they are born again" (John 3:3).

Let's set a good example for our children. While they're looking—they're learning about what matters most.                                  —CHK

## What Is Family?

*The LORD God said, "It is not good for*
*the man to be alone. I will make a helper*
*suitable for him." —GENESIS 2:18*

I found this description of family: "A place of warmth when the world is cold; a place of safety when the world is hostile; a place of light when the world is dark—this is a family. It is the core around which great nations are built. It is the foundation of any great society. A family is many things: a family is love around the dinner table; devotion going to church together; friendship laughing under the same roof. A family is a light on the front porch on a dark night.

"Rudyard Kipling once wrote about families, 'All of us are we—and everyone else is they.' A family shares things like dreams, hopes, possessions, memories, smiles, frowns, and gladness. A family is a clan held together with the glue of love and the cement of mutual respect. A family is a friendly port when the waves of life become too wild. No person is ever alone who is a member of a family."

Thank God for the warmth and fellowship of a happy family! And when Christ is included, it is truly a foretaste of heaven.                    —RD

## Calming Your Soul

*"Come to me, all you who are
weary and burdened, and I will give
you rest."* —MATTHEW 11:28

While attending a concert, my mind detoured to a troublesome issue that insisted on my attention. Thankfully, the distraction was short-lived as the words of a beautiful hymn began to reach deep into my being. A men's group was singing "Be Still, My Soul." Tears welled up as I contemplated the restful peace that only God can give:

Be still, my soul: the Lord is on thy side! Bear patiently the cross of grief or pain; leave to thy God to order and provide; in every change He faithful will remain.

When Jesus was denouncing the unrepentant towns where He had done most of His miracles (Matthew 11:20–24), He still had words of comfort. He said, "Come to me, all you who are weary and burdened. . . . Learn from me, for I am gentle and humble in heart, and you will find rest for your souls" (vv. 28–29).

Immediately following His strong words for those who were rejecting Him, Jesus extended an invitation to all to draw near to Him to find the peace we all yearn for. Jesus is the only one who can calm our restless, weary souls.                    —JS

## Parental Care

*Charm is deceptive, and beauty is
fleeting; but a woman who fears the LORD
is to be praised.* —PROVERBS 31:30

Parents who honor God will strive to be good examples. Their desire is to be the kind of parent He wants them to be. Instead of bringing up children just to fulfill their own needs, they'll want to raise them for the glory of God.

This approach to parenthood stands in contrast to what sometimes happens today. One sociologist has pointed out that many parents are raising overly dependent, neurotic sons and daughters—especially parents who are caught up in the rat race of middle-class values. They unconsciously use their youngsters to gain honor and influence among their own peers. They strive to bring up model children to gain the reputation of being a model parent. The kids' performance becomes all-important, so the parents give their love or withdraw it, depending on the behavior of the child.

A better method is to fear the Lord and find ultimate fulfillment in Him. Moms and dads who do this won't be perfect, but they are special people, for they love God and want their children to love Him. I know what that means, because I was privileged to have parents who trained me for His sake.    —MD

# Breakthrough

*Once you were alienated from God.... But
now he has reconciled you by Christ's physical
body through death to present you holy in his
sight, without blemish.* —COLOSSIANS 1:21–22

A boy born with cerebral palsy was unable to speak
or communicate. But his mother, Chantal Bryan,
never gave up. When he was ten years old, she figured
out how to communicate with him through his eyes
and a letter board. After this breakthrough, she said,
"He was unlocked, and we could ask him anything."
Now Jonathan reads and writes, including poetry, by
communicating through his eyes. When asked what
it's like to "talk" with his family and friends, he said,
"It is wonderful to tell them I love them."

Jonathan's story leads me to consider how God un-
locks us from the prison of sin. Paul wrote to the Christians at Colossae that once we were "alienated from
God" (Colossians 1:21), our evil behavior making us
His enemy. But through Christ's death on the cross we
are now presented to God as "holy in his sight" (v. 22).
We may now "live a life worthy of the Lord" (v. 10).

We are no longer locked to a life of sin. As we
continue in our faith, we can hold firm to our hope
in Christ.                                    —ABP

## Evening

*After he had dismissed them, he went up on
a mountainside by himself to pray. Later that
night, he was there alone.* —MATTHEW 14:23

The evening is one of my favorite times of day. It's
a time to look back, take stock, and reflect on the
events of the day—whether good or bad. It's a time
for careful thought and evaluation, for thanksgiving,
and for prayer.

Our Lord had a similar practice during His earthly
ministry. At the end of a wearying and demanding
day, He went up on a mountain by himself for a few
moments of reflection and prayer in the presence of
His Father (Matthew 14:23).

The value of the quiet presence of our heavenly
Father and the careful examination of how we have
engaged life on a given day has great significance. Perhaps this was the goal of the apostle Paul's challenge
for us to redeem the time (Ephesians 5:16); that is,
to make sure we are making the best use of the time
God gives us for living and serving.

As the day winds to a close, take some time for
quiet reflection. In the serenity of the evening, we can,
in God's presence, get a more accurate perspective on
life and how we are living it.                          —BC

# Life's Storm-Tossed Sea

*Cast all your anxiety on him because
he cares for you.* —1 PETER 5:7

Emilie, wife of nineteenth-century German pastor Christoph Blumhardt, envied his ability to pray for his parishioners and then effortlessly fall asleep. So one night she pleaded, "Tell me your secret!"

He answered, "Is God so powerless that my worrying would help the well-being of our parish?" Then he added, "There comes a moment each day when we must simply drop what weighs on us and hand it over to God."

One evening Jesus and His disciples were crossing the Sea of Galilee. Weary after a long day of ministry, He fell asleep in the stern of the boat. A fierce squall suddenly arose—so fierce that even the Lord's fishermen-turned-disciples were terrified. But Jesus continued to sleep serenely until His frightened followers woke Him, crying out, "Teacher, don't you care if we drown?" (Mark 4:38). You see, Jesus was in the habit of entrusting himself to His heavenly Father. Having made that commitment, He could sleep through the turbulent squall.

When worries begin to gnaw at our mind, let's surrender them to the Lord and not take them back again (1 Peter 5:7). That's the secret of soul-serenity when we're on life's storm-tossed sea.          —VG

## Denying the Faith

*Anyone who does not provide for their
relatives, and especially for their own
household, has denied the faith and is worse
than an unbeliever.* —1 TIMOTHY 5:8

A friend stopped me in midsentence as I was making a favorable comment about a wealthy man who gives lavishly to Christian causes. "That's all well and good," he said, "but I wish he would remember his elderly parents. They are lonely and poor. He could make them very happy if he would just give them a little of his time and money." I was surprised to discover that this supposedly devout believer was neglecting his needy parents.

Paul had something to say about Christians like this well-to-do acquaintance of mine. He wrote, "Anyone who does not provide for their relatives, and especially for their own household, has denied the faith and is worse than an unbeliever " (1 Timothy 5:8). That's strong language, and we need to take it seriously.

In a day when we tend to be so preoccupied with our own pleasures or problems that we forget aging parents or disabled siblings, we need to be reminded of the apostle's words. Yes, as God's children, we must be willing to care for needy members of our own family. It's not an option; it's our Christian obligation.

—HVL

## Time Off

*And as for you, brothers and sisters,*
*never tire of doing what is good.*
—2 THESSALONIANS 3:13

The teenager's mom, exasperated by the failure of her youngest child to show maturity, sighed and said, "Two more years of junior high." To which he, in typical style, replied with a smile, "Mom, why don't you just take the next two years off!"

That idea sounds tempting. When we have a chronically sick family member, we may be tempted to just "check out" for a while. When children make parenting a struggle, we'd prefer a long vacation from the hassle. And there are times when we face great spiritual battles that we would like to skip altogether.

Paul spoke briefly about such struggles in 2 Thessalonians 3. He mentioned the problem of dealing with people who "are idle and disruptive, . . . busybodies" (v. 11). Facing up to people problems can be frustrating. But Paul gave part of the solution when he said, "never tire of doing what is good" (v. 13). Another part of the equation is to listen to the psalmist, who said, "Cast your cares on the LORD" (Psalm 55:22).

When we can't "take the next two years off," we need to keep doing good and keep casting our care on God.                                —DB

## Scattering Seeds

*"But the seed falling on good soil refers
to someone who hears the word and
understands it. This is the one who
produces a crop."* —MATTHEW 13:23

I received an email from a woman who wrote, "Your mom was my first-grade teacher at Putnam City in 1958. She was a great teacher and very kind, but strict! She made us learn Psalm 23 and say it in front of the class. But it was the only contact I had with the Bible until 1997 when I became a Christian. And the memories of Mrs. McCasland came flooding back as I re-read it."

Jesus told a large crowd a parable about the farmer who sowed his seed on different types of ground—a hard path, rocky ground, clumps of thorns, and good soil (Matthew 13:1–9). While some seeds never grew, "the seed falling on good soil refers to someone who hears the word and understands it" and "produces a crop, yielding a hundred, sixty or thirty times what was sown" (v. 23).

Clearly, my mother scattered seeds of kindness and the message of God's love. Her former student's email concluded, "I have had other influences in my Christian walk. But my heart always returns to [Psalm 23] and [your mom's] gentle nature."

A seed of God's love sown today may produce a remarkable harvest.                    —DM

# Broken Bones

*As a prisoner for the Lord, then, I urge you to live
a life worthy of the calling you have received. Be
completely humble and gentle; be patient, bearing
with one another in love.* —EPHESIANS 4:1–2

Sarah had always been quiet and reserved. Then a new
family began attending her church, and she developed
a close relationship with the wife, Michelle. Sarah was
delighted that she had finally found a friend she could
confide in.

Suddenly, Michelle turned cool. Sarah felt hurt,
and she withdrew. Then Michelle asked if they could
talk. Sarah agreed, but she was afraid. She was sure
she had done something to offend Michelle.

To Sarah's surprise, Michelle apologized. "I'm
sorry we drew apart," she said. "It's always been hard
for me to be trusting because of my family back-
ground. Please forgive me." Sarah forgave her, and
the two women are now better friends than ever.

Whenever we get close to someone, we take risks.
A Christian author wrote, "The love that unites will
bring us suffering by our very contact with one another, because love is the resetting of the body of broken bones."

Are you experiencing a break in your relationship
with a fellow believer in Christ? Do some bones need
resetting? When we bear with one another in love
and forgiveness (Ephesians 4:2, 32), healing can occur.
—DE

# Not One Sparrow

*Precious in the sight of the LORD is the death
of his faithful servants.* —PSALM 116:15

My mother, so dignified and proper her entire life, now lay in a hospice bed, held captive by debilitating age. Struggling for breath, her declining condition contradicted the gorgeous spring day that danced invitingly on the other side of the windowpane.

Nothing can sufficiently brace us for the stark reality of goodbye. Death is such an indignity!

I diverted my gaze to the birdfeeder outside the window. A grosbeak helped itself to some seed. Instantly a familiar phrase popped into my mind: "Not a single sparrow can fall to the ground without your Father knowing it" (Matthew 10:29 NLT). Jesus had said that to His disciples, but the principle applies to all of us. "You are worth more than many sparrows," He told them (v. 31).

My mom stirred and opened her eyes. Reaching back to her childhood, she used a Dutch term of endearment for her own mother and declared, "Muti's dead!"

"Yes," my wife agreed. "She's with Jesus now." Uncertain, Mom continued. "And Joyce and Jim?" she questioned of her sister and brother. "Yes, they're with Jesus too," said my wife. "But we'll be with them soon!"

"It's hard to wait," Mom said quietly.      —TG

## Take Time

*Within your temple, O God, we meditate
on your unfailing love.* —PSALM 48:9

A donut shop posted a picture of a peaceful lake scene. A father and son were visible through the early morning mist, fishing in a rowboat. All was quiet and serene. The boat, the fishermen, and their bobbers were motionless on the placid lake. In the corner of the poster were printed these two words: Take time.

Those two words sound like a foreign language to us. We tend to speed along in life. Our lives are a blur of frantic activity. We're in the "fast lane," traveling as quickly as our bodies and minds will allow. In so doing, we often forget about God.

Yes, even though the busyness of our lives is made up of worthwhile activities, including our work and service in the church, we may have left Him back in the dust somewhere. We need to slow down and do as the writer of Psalm 48 did. He thought about God and His lovingkindness. And that takes time.

If you don't think you have time to pause from the race of life once in a while, think again. Above all, God wants you to take time for Him.          —DE

# When the Bible Comes Alive

*When you received the word of God, which
you heard from us, you accepted it not as
a human word, but as it actually is, the
word of God.* —1 THESSALONIANS 2:13

Someone has said there are three phases of Bible
study. First is the "cod-liver oil" stage, where you
take it like medicine because it's good for you. The
second is the "shredded-wheat biscuit" stage—dry
but nourishing. And third is the "peaches and cream"
stage—really enjoyable.

A young boy who was in the habit of going to
church was unable to attend one Sunday because he
was ill. So he went upstairs to his bedroom to read his
Bible. He was unusually quiet, and his mother began
wondering if he was up to some mischief. Finally, she
called out, "What are you doing, Andy?" He replied,
"I'm watching Jesus raise Lazarus from the dead!"
What a beautiful answer! He was reading John 11,
and his childlike faith made the scene come alive.

Are the Scriptures as real to you as they were to
that boy? When Christ is at the center of your life,
the Word of God becomes a spiritual banquet to feed
your soul. Read it with the Holy Spirit's help and
watch it come alive for you!                    —HB

## The Sympathy of Silence

*Then they sat on the ground with him*
*for seven days and seven nights. No one*
*said a word to him, because they saw*
*how great his suffering was.* —JOB 2:13

A pastor told of visiting a family and being greeted by the mother, who said, "I just knew you'd stop in today! I need your help. I don't know what to do." She then told him about her problems, which brought tears to the pastor's eyes but were beyond his ability to solve. He continued to listen patiently until the woman, smiling through her tears, exclaimed, "Thanks for coming! This is exactly what I needed!" Sympathy, not wisdom, was needed.

Commenting on the scene in Job 2:13, English pastor W. F. Adeney wrote, "Sympathy may be shown in silence. . . . Job's comforters began well. If they had gone home at the end of the week, they would have been known as model comforters." Adeney concluded, "What is wanted in trouble is not advice but sympathy; and this is best shown by the unbidden tear, the silent pressure of the hand, the look of love."

When others share a burden with us, they often just want someone to listen with compassion. That's when our sympathy can best be shown in silence.

—RD

## An Ordinary Life

*You know that the Lord will reward each one
for whatever good they do.* —EPHESIANS 6:8

Barb listened with quiet envy as the speaker at the women's retreat talked in glowing terms of the way the Lord had marvelously provided for her need. Barb wished that would happen to her.

Later in the retreat, she was spellbound as another speaker told of the amazing opportunity the Lord had given her to testify and how several women in deep despair had opened their hearts to Christ. Barb longed for God to use her in a powerful way, but she didn't expect it to happen.

Barb's routine involved getting her husband off to work and her children to school, caring for her home, working three days a week, and helping in their church. She didn't think there was much opportunity to be used mightily by God.

It's easy to lose sight of the fact that God is the God of everyday living. While we look for some great display of God's power, He desires for us to focus on doing His will from our heart each day, delighting in humble service for Him (Ephesians 6:6–7).

Don't miss the wonderful ways God wants to use you in the day-in, day-out activities of ordinary life.

—DE

## Getting a Softer Face

*Praise be to the God and Father of our Lord
Jesus Christ, the Father of compassion and
the God of all comfort, who comforts us in
all our troubles, so that we can comfort those
in any trouble with the comfort we ourselves
receive from God.* —2 CORINTHIANS 1:3–4

The consolation we receive from God in our suffering
can soften our heart and fill us with a compassion
and sensitivity that draws hurting people to us.

An example of this can be found in James Barrie's
book *Margaret Ogilvy*. In the chapter "How Mother
Got Her Soft Face," Barrie described what happened
when news came that his brother, a thirteen-year-old
who was away at school, had died. Barrie's mother
went home and looked long at a tiny outfit her de-
ceased son had worn to church as an infant. Turning
her face to the wall, she felt intense despair. In that
moment, however, God flooded her heart with solace.
Barrie writes, "This is how she got her soft face, . . .
and why other mothers ran to her when they had
lost a child."

People who are hurting can sense when we are
compassionate, and they will long for the same comfort we have received. Then we will be able to comfort
them with the same comfort with which God comforted us (2 Corinthians 1:4).                  —HVL

## The Whole House

*"Believe in the Lord Jesus, and you will be
saved—you and your household."* —ACTS 16:31

Nineteenth-century pastor Thomas De Witt Talmage
told the story of the effect his grandmother's prayer
had on her children long before he was born. One
night she returned home from a gospel meeting and
was determined to pray for the salvation of her teenage children, who were planning to go off for an evening of partying. Just before they left, she called her
children to her room. She said, "Now, I want you to
remember while you are away that I am going to be in
this room praying the whole time for your salvation."

Off they went to the party. But amid the raucous
hilarity of the night, they were unable to forget what
their mother had told them. Talmage said that the
next day his grandmother and her husband heard
someone crying and found their daughter pleading with God to save her. Soon similar conviction
touched them all, and each trusted Jesus.

God wants to save all the members of your family.
How long has it been since you spent time praying
for their conversion? Claim your household for God.
—PVG

## Hammock Musings

*How many are your works, LORD! In*
*wisdom you made them all; the earth is*
*full of your creatures.* —PSALM 104:24

My life often feels frenzied and hectic. Out of sheer exhaustion one Sunday, I collapsed into the hammock in our backyard. At first, I planned to sit for just a moment or two, but in the undistracted stillness, I began to notice things that invited me to linger longer. I could hear the creak of the hammock swinging gently, the buzz of a bee in the nearby lavender, and the flap of a bird's wings overhead. The sky was a brilliant blue, and the clouds moved on the wind.

I found myself moved to tears in response to all God had made. When I slowed long enough to take in the many wonderful things within my eyesight and earshot, I was stirred to worship in gratitude for God's creative power. The writer of Psalm 104 was equally humbled by the work of God's hands, noting "you fill the earth with the fruit of your labor" (v. 13 NLT).

In the midst of a harried life, a quiet moment can remind us of God's creative might! He surrounds us with things that show His power and tenderness; "In wisdom [He] made them all" (v. 24).            —KH

## Peace and Trust

*And the peace of God, which transcends all
understanding, will guard your hearts and
your minds in Christ Jesus.* —PHILIPPIANS 4:7

When I was six years old, I rode a roller coaster for
the first time. As soon as we hit a turn at a high speed,
I started to yell: "Stop this thing! I want to get off!"
The roller coaster didn't stop, and I had to "white
knuckle" it—hanging on tight for the rest of the ride.

Sometimes life can feel like an that, with "down-
hill" drops and hairpin curves we never see coming.
The Bible reminds us that our best recourse in trial
is to place our trust in God. During a tumultuous
time when invasion threatened his country, Isaiah dis-
cerned this powerful promise from God: "You will
keep in perfect peace those whose minds are steadfast, because they trust in you" (26:3).

The peace our Savior gives us as we turn to Him
"transcends all understanding" (Philippians 4:7). I'll
never forget the words of a woman struggling with
breast cancer. After our church prayed for her one
evening, she said, "I don't know what will happen,
but I know I'll be okay, because the Lord was here
with us tonight."

Life has its difficulties, but our Savior, who loves
us more than life itself, is greater than them all. —JB

## The Best Gift

*"So I say to you: Ask and it will be given to
you; seek and you will find; knock and the
door will be opened to you."* —LUKE 11:9

When I was packing up to go home to London, my
mother handed me a gift—one of her rings I had long
admired. Surprised, I asked, "What's this for?" She
replied, "I think you should enjoy it now. Why wait
until I die?" With a smile I received her unexpected
gift—an early inheritance that brings me joy.

My mom gave me a material gift, but Jesus promises that His Father will give so much more—the
Holy Spirit (Luke 11:13). If parents who are marred
with sin can provide necessities (such as fish or eggs)
for their children, how much more will God give
to His children! Through the gift of the Holy Spirit
(John 16:13), we can experience hope, love, joy, and
peace even in times of trouble; and we can share these
gifts with others.

We may have had parents who were unable to love
and care for us fully. Or we may have had mothers
and fathers who were shining examples of sacrificial
love. Whatever our situation, we can hold onto the
promise that our heavenly Father loves us unceas-
ingly. He gave His children the gift of the Holy Spirit.
—ABP

# The Who in Whoever

*He is the atoning sacrifice for our sins,
and not only for ours but also for the
sins of the whole world.* —1 JOHN 2:2

George Cutting, in his book *Light for Anxious Souls*, told of a case of mistaken identity. A mother in England, whose son was in the military, was informed by friends that they had seen his name in a newspaper listing of men who had died.

The grief-stricken mother shared the sad news with her pastor, who contacted authorities to verify the report. Imagine that mother's relief when she learned that her son had not died! The casualty was another soldier with the same name.

Cutting said if God were to record the names of everyone for whom Jesus died, a lifetime wouldn't be long enough to read the list. And even if you found your name, you might wonder if it referred to you or to someone else.

But we don't have to wonder about that! The Holy Spirit inspired John to write "whoever" in John 3:16. "Whoever believes in him shall not perish but have eternal life."

Yes, *whoever* believes in Christ has everlasting life. You and I are included. No one is excluded. So, *whoever* you are, believe and be saved.                —RD

# Not Your Typical Romance

*The women living there said, "Naomi has a son!" And they named him Obed. He was the father of Jesse, the father of David.* —RUTH 4:17

Widows in biblical times often faced a life of poverty. That's the situation for Ruth and her mother-in-law, Naomi, after each woman lost her husband. But God had a plan to provide security for them while involving Ruth in a much bigger plan.

Boaz, a wealthy landowner, knew of and admired Ruth (Ruth 2:5–12), but he was surprised when he awoke one night to see her lying at his feet (3:8). She asked him to "spread the corner" of his garment over her to indicate that as a close relative he was willing to be her "guardian-redeemer" (v. 9). This was more than a request for protection; she was requesting marriage. Boaz agreed to marry her (vv. 11–13; 4:13).

Not exactly your typical romantic tale. But Ruth's choice to follow Naomi's instructions (3:3–6) set up a series of events that placed her in God's plan of redemption! Generations later, Joseph was born into the family, and he became the "legal father" of Mary's child (Matthew 1:16–17; Luke 2:4–5)—our Guardian-Redeemer, Jesus.

As did Ruth and Naomi, we too can count on God to provide for us when life is unsure.          —CHK

## Phony Faith

*I am reminded of your sincere faith.*
—2 TIMOTHY 1:5

True Christians are characterized by a genuine faith. A good synonym for the word *genuine* is the word *sincere* in 2 Timothy 1:5. It comes from two Latin terms—*sine* and *cere*, meaning "without wax."

Years ago, a potter would often put his seal, or stamp, upon a completed vessel with the words *sine cere*. This meant that to his knowledge there was no flaw in that work. If a potter did crack a vessel, he would carefully patch that flawed vase or bowl by filling in the crack with wax. Then he would glaze it over. But it no longer merited the stamp *sine cere*.

Timothy had a genuine, unhypocritical faith, which undoubtedly found its roots in the influence of his godly mother Eunice and his grandmother Lois. He could say with the apostle Paul, "I know whom I have believed" (2 Timothy 1:12).

A phony faith will not stand the test. God knows whether our profession of faith in Christ is real or whether it is merely a way of trying to satisfy a parent, a spouse, or a friend. Don't settle for a phony faith. Make sure it is genuine.                    —PVG

## "For This I Have Jesus"

*"Never will I leave you; never will I
forsake you." —HEBREWS 13:5*

In an evangelistic meeting in Ireland, the speaker was explaining what it means to abide in Christ and to trust Him completely in every trial. He repeated several times, "It means that in every circumstance you can keep on saying, 'For this I have Jesus.'"

The meeting was then opened for testimonies. One young woman said, "A few minutes ago I was handed this telegram. It reads, 'Mother is very ill; take train home immediately.' When I saw those words, I knew tonight's message was meant just for me. I said, 'For this I have Jesus.' Instantly a peace and strength flooded my soul."

Three or four weeks later the evangelist received a letter from this woman. It read, "Thank you again for your message. Life has become an uninterrupted psalm of victory, for I realize that no matter what life brings, for this I have Jesus."

That woman found in her Savior the One who would be with her "through fire and water," and who would bring her "to a place of abundance" (Psalm 66:12).

Are you enduring a great trial of affliction? For this you have Jesus!                              —HB

## Noisy Lids

*And this is my prayer: . . . that you*
*may be able to discern what is best*
*and may be pure and blameless for the*
*day of Christ.* —PHILIPPIANS 1:9–10

A little boy told a salesclerk he was shopping for a birthday gift for his mother and asked to see some cookie jars. At a counter displaying a large selection, the youngster carefully lifted and replaced each lid. His face fell as he came to the last one." Aren't there any covers that don't make any noise?" he asked.

This delightful story presents an accurate commentary on human nature. It also reminds us that right motives should accompany right actions. Sin has so affected our entire being that it's possible to do what's right for the wrong reason.

We must regularly examine under the searchlight of God's Word our reason for doing what we do. For example, Paul asked God that the Philippian believers would be pure and blameless (1:10), so their inner motives would correspond with their conduct.

Let's ask God to show us wrong motivations so with Paul we'll be able to say that "we have conducted ourselves in the world . . . with integrity and godly sincerity" (2 Corinthians 1:12). Then we won't have to worry about "noisy lids."          —DD

## Word Watch

*I tell you that everyone will have to give
account on the day of judgment for every empty
word they have spoken.* —MATTHEW 12:36

We sin when we say more than we know for certain
and when we say something that needlessly hurts
someone.

When I was a teenager, I said of a man I knew
only casually, "Too much wine, women, and song." A
mother of one of my friends looked at me reproach-
ingly and said, "Herbert, do you know that to be
true? And if it is, was it necessary for you to say it?"
Wow! Saying what I did was unkind and unnecessary.

The Bible warns us about being quick to testify
against someone (Proverbs 25:8). It also admonishes
us not to disclose some things (v. 9). From this we can
conclude that speaking out too quickly or divulging
a secret can get us into trouble.

Jesus added another reason for being careful of
what we say, one that is awesome. He declared that
our words, even those we think are insignificant, reveal what's in our heart and will be brought to our
attention at the final judgment (Matthew 12:36–37).

We should say nothing about a person until it passes
the triple test: Is it true? Is it kind? Is it necessary?

—HVL

## Living under Authority

*Children, obey your parents in the Lord, for this is right. . . . Fathers, do not exasperate your children; instead, bring them up in the training and instruction of the Lord.* —EPHESIANS 6:1, 4

I am reminded of the mother who wanted to have the last word but couldn't handle the hassle that resulted whenever she said no to her young son. After an especially trying day, she finally flung up her hands and shouted, "All right, Billy, do whatever you want! Now let me see you disobey *that*!"

Early in life, children must be taught that God has given parents the right to make certain decisions for the children's physical and spiritual well-being. Youngsters should also know that Dad and Mom themselves are expected to live under the lordship of Jesus Christ, and that although they sometimes fail, they are striving to obey Him.

While parents must be strong enough to say no and stick to it, they should also look for every opportunity to say yes. While it is difficult to know what is right in every situation, the more you live under God's authority, the more clearly we see the right path to follow. We all live under authority—which makes life work best if we all understand our roles.

—DD

## His Demands, Not Ours

*I say to God: Do not declare me
guilty, but tell me what charges
you have against me.* —JOB 10:2

Job experienced a series of tragedies, and the Lord
never told him why. He cried out to the Lord, but in
so doing he made demands on God that he had no
right to make (see 10:1, 2). We too are inclined to give
God orders and expect Him to respond immediately.

I was idly watching a mother and daughter shopping in the mall. The girl, about three years old,
wanted a chocolate chip cookie. Her mother denied
her request. So the girl replied, "Get me a cookie."
"Not now," Mom replied, "you'll spoil your lunch." "I
don't care," the child responded. "Buy me a cookie."
"No," the mother said firmly. Stamping her feet, the
daughter shouted, "I want a cookie! Get me one
now!" Firmly, and in control, that mother gave her
daughter what was best for her—some needed discipline.

Sometimes we make demands of God. Oh, how
foolish! It's God who has the right to make demands
on us—demands of obedience and loyalty and faith.
And they are always for our good.              —DE

## Ice Cream Man

*Flee the evil desires of youth and pursue
righteousness, faith, love and peace,
along with those who call on the Lord
out of a pure heart.* —2 TIMOTHY 2:22

Little Jeff was trying his best to save money to buy his mother a present. It was a terrible struggle because a brightly colored ice-cream van came through the neighborhood regularly.

One night after his mother had tucked him in bed, she overheard him pray, "Please, God, help me run away when the ice cream man comes tomorrow." He was starting to learn the key to overcoming temptation.

All believers are tempted to sin. Yet they need not give in. The Lord provides the way to be victorious over evil enticements (1 Corinthians 10:13). But we must do our part. Sometimes that involves avoiding situations that would contribute to our spiritual defeat.

The apostle Paul admonished Timothy to run away from the evil desires of youth (2 Timothy 2:22). He was to keep his distance from the temptations that might cause him to yield because of their strong appeal. That's good advice.

If possible, we should never let ourselves be in the wrong places or with people who will tempt us to do the things we should be avoiding. When necessary, run away!                                        —RD

## To Love and to Be Loved

*I have calmed and quieted myself, I am
like a weaned child with its mother; like a
weaned child I am content.* —PSALM 131:2

Toward the end of lunch with my sister and her children one afternoon, my sister told my three-year-old niece, Annica, it was time to get ready for her nap. Her face filled with alarm. "But Aunt Monica did not hold me yet today!" she objected, tears filling her eyes. My sister smiled. "Okay, she may hold you first—how long do you need?" "Five minutes," she replied.

As I held my niece, I was grateful for how, without even trying, she constantly reminds me what it looks like to love and be loved. We sometimes forget that our faith journey is one of learning to experience love—God's love—more fully than we can imagine (Ephesian 3:18). When we lose that focus, we can find ourselves, like the older brother in Jesus's prodigal son parable, trying desperately to win God's approval while missing out on all He has already given us (Luke 15:25–32).

Through time with Him we can return to a place of peace (Psalm 131:2), finding the hope we need (v. 3) in His love—as calm and quiet as if we were children again in our mothers' arms (v. 2).       —MB

## Feathers and a Refuge

*He will cover you with his feathers, and under his wings you will find refuge; his faithfulness will be your shield and rampart.* —PSALM 91:4

When I think of protection, I don't automatically think of a bird's feathers. Though a bird's feathers might seem like a flimsy form of protection, there is more to them than meets the eye.

Bird feathers are an amazing example of God's design. Feathers have a smooth part and a fluffy part. The smooth part of the feather has stiff barbs with tiny hooks that lock together like the prongs of a zipper. The fluffy part keeps a bird warm. Together both parts of the feather protect the bird from wind and rain. But many baby birds are covered in a fluffy down, and their feathers haven't fully developed. So a mother bird has to cover them in the nest with her own feathers to protect them from wind and rain.

The image of God "[covering us] with his feathers" in Psalm 91:4 and in other Bible passages (see Psalm 17:8) is one of comfort and protection. The image that comes to mind is a mother bird covering her little ones with her feathers.

We can face trouble and trial without fear as long as our faces are turned toward God. He is our "refuge" (91:2, 4, 9).                              —LW

## Give Your Children to God

*So now I give him to the LORD. For his whole
life he will be given over to the LORD." And he
worshiped the LORD there.* —1 SAMUEL 1:28

Godly parents should give their children away. That's
what Hannah did. Even before her son was born, she
promised to "give him to the LORD for all the days of
his life" (1 Samuel 1:11). She vowed to return him to
the Lord as an expression of her love and worship.

An elderly mother in Scotland went to a missionary society meeting where only contributing members
were admitted. The doorkeeper asked, "Are you a
contributor?" "I am afraid not," she answered. She
left disappointed. But then she thought of her son,
who years before had gone as a missionary to Sierra
Leone, West Africa. His body now lay buried in that
distant land. She retraced her steps and explained to
the man, "You asked me if I was a contributor. I gave
my only boy, and he is buried out in Sierra Leone."
The doorkeeper removed his cap, bowed graciously,
and said, "Come in." He then led her to a front seat.

It may seem like a huge sacrifice, but what more
secure future could we want for our children than to
give them to God! Only He can guide and keep them.

—PVG

## Of Spiders and God's Presence

*I pray that out of his glorious riches he may
strengthen you with power through his Spirit
in your inner being.* —EPHESIANS 3:16

*Spiders.* I don't know any kid who likes them.

As she was getting ready for bed, my daughter spied one dangerously close to her bed. "Spiiiderrr!!!!!" she hollered. Despite my determination, I couldn't find the eight-legged interloper. "He's not going to hurt you," I reassured her. She wasn't convinced. It wasn't until I told her I'd stay next to her top bunk and stand guard that she agreed to get in bed.

As my daughter settled in, I held her hand. I told her, "I love you so much. I'm right here. But you know what? God loves you even more than Daddy and Mommy. And He's very close. You can always pray to Him when you're scared." That seemed to comfort her, and peaceful sleep came quickly.

Scripture repeatedly reassures us God is always near (Psalm 145:18; Romans 8:38–39; James 4:7–8), but sometimes we struggle to believe it. We can lose track of God's proximity. But just as I lovingly held my daughter as she went to sleep that night, so our loving heavenly Father is always as close to us as a prayer.                                         —AH

## God's Kind Will

*"Whoever does God's will is my brother
and sister and mother."* —MARK 3:35

A lady who had just one child said to her pastor's wife, "I don't dare pray, 'Your will be done,' because I am afraid God will take away my little boy." To this the other woman replied, "Suppose your child should come to you and say, 'I want to do just what you desire today, Mommy.' Would you say to yourself, 'Now is my opportunity to make my son do all the disagreeable duties I want done; I will take advantage of his willingness to please me by making things hard for him and telling him he can't go out and play today?'" "Oh no," said the mother, "I would give him the best day I could possibly plan."

"And do you think that God is less loving than you?"

The lady recognized that her fear was unfounded. She committed herself to doing God's will, leaning on the Holy Spirit, and experiencing intimate communion with the Savior.

How pleasing it is to the Lord when we do what we know is right. That's when we find that even though the way is difficult His will is always kind!

—HB

## Weeping . . . for Now

*Jesus wept.* —JOHN 11:35

I called a longtime friend when his mother died. She had been a close friend of my mother, and now both had passed on. As we spoke, our conversation slipped easily into a cycle of emotion—tears of sorrow now that Beth was gone and tears of laughter as we recalled the caring and fun person she had been.

Many of us have experienced that strange crossover from crying one moment and laughing the next. It's an amazing gift that emotions of both sorrow and joy can provide a physical release in this way.

While I can imagine that Jesus must have had a wonderful sense of humor, we also know that He knew the pain of grief. When his friend Lazarus died, Jesus saw Mary weeping, and "he was deeply moved in spirit and troubled" (John 11:33). A short time later, He too began to weep (John 11:33–35).

Our ability to express our emotions with tears is a gift, and God keeps track of each tear we cry (Psalm 56:8). But one day—we are promised (Revelation 7:17)—God "will wipe away every tear."      —CHK

## Learning from Leandra

*"I am the vine; you are the branches.*
*If you remain in me and I in you, you*
*will bear much fruit; apart from me*
*you can do nothing."* —JOHN 15:5

One day I was babysitting my three-year-old grand-daughter Leandra and her brother Max as Max played computer games. Suddenly she announced that she was going to get a snack. "I do it myself!" she said emphatically.

"I'll help you," I said and began to follow her. She repeated firmly, "I do it myself!" She turned, saw me, and said, "You stay upstairs, Grandpa. Keep an eye on Max." I tried not to laugh. At the bottom of the stairs she turned, put one hand on her hip, and said, "I mean it, Grandpa!" I backed out of sight, laughing. Later I checked on her. She had opened the refrigerator, found some packaged pudding, and gotten "her" spoon, but she needed help opening the container.

There's a lot of that spirit of independence in us. We too want to "do it ourselves" when it comes to growing and serving as Christians—and in trying to produce good fruit in our children. Although we may think we don't need God's help, we really do. Without it, we are unable to produce the kind of life Jesus talked about in John 15:5: "Apart from me you can do nothing."                              —DE

## Another Reason to Praise

*Blessed are those whose help is the
God of Jacob, whose hope is in the
LORD their God.* —PSALM 146:5

Shoes. Nobody had thought about shoes. The hectic
pace of summer kept speeding along, and it was time
for Julie's basketball camp. Just a few minutes before
she was to leave, it suddenly dawned on us that Julie
didn't have adequate basketball shoes.

We weren't prepared for a $40 surprise like that.
Plus, it was too late to buy them. So, Julie would have
to show up at the gym wearing an old pair of ill-fitting
shoes. But when we opened the door to go to the car,
there stood Connie, our next-door neighbor. And what
was in her hands? Shoes. Basketball shoes. Too small
for her Erin, but just right for Julie. Although we had
not thought about shoes, Someone had.

Did you ever read through the list of reasons to
praise the Lord in Psalm 146? It mentions many ways
in which God has demonstrated His providential care
for those who live by faith in Him. The almighty
Creator of the world lovingly cares for the needs of
His people.

The Lord provides what we need today too. Things
like shoes. Things that give us one more reason to
praise Him.                                      —DB

## "Peel It!"

*Always giving thanks to God the Father
for everything, in the name of our Lord
Jesus Christ.* —EPHESIANS 5:20

The story is told of a mother and her four-year-old daughter who were strolling through an open-air market. As the little girl stared at a large pile of oranges, a generous vendor took one from the table and gave it to her.

"What do you say to the nice man?" the mother asked her daughter. The little girl looked at the orange, then thrust it toward the man and said, "Peel it!"

Thankfulness is something we learn and grow into. What might be excusable in a four-year-old would be rude and ungrateful from an older child or adult.

Yet, how easy it is to fall into the trap of responding to God's gracious gifts by thinking, "This is nice, but I'd like a little more."

An attitude of gratitude toward God is a mark of a developing spiritual maturity. In Paul's letter to the growing Christians in Ephesus, his challenge to follow Christ included "always giving thanks to God" (Ephesians 5:20).

Let's practice thankfulness to God—instead of complaining about what we don't have.

Instead of saying "Peel it!" let's say "Thanks."

—DM

# A Mother's Influence

*I am reminded of your sincere faith, which*
*first lived in your grandmother Lois and in*
*your mother Eunice and, I am persuaded,*
*now lives in you also.* —2 TIMOTHY 1:5

As a lawyer, as a congressman, as governor of
Ohio, and as president of the United States, William
McKinley had a close relationship with his mother. He
either visited her or sent a message to her every day.

When she became seriously ill, he arranged to have
a special train standing by, ready to take him to her
bedside. Mrs. McKinley died December 12, 1897, in
the arms of her fifty-four-year-old son. Her gentle,
Christian virtues helped mold the president's character, for when he was gunned down in Buffalo, New
York, about four years later, he showed no bitterness
toward his assassin. With Christian courage he said,
"God's will be done." Before he died, he asked to hear
once again the hymn "Nearer, My God, to Thee,"
which his mother had taught him.

If you've been blessed with a Christian heritage,
let the precious memories of your parents, who have
been pointed you to God, awaken in your heart a
new desire to live for Him. Praise God for the influence of a godly mom or dad.                    —DD

## A Clean Slate

*"I have swept away your offenses like a cloud, your sins like the morning mist. Return to me, for I have redeemed you."* —ISAIAH 44:22

When I was a youngster, we didn't use paper and pencils at school. Instead, we each had a slate and some chalk. And we each had a moist sponge for erasing. How thankful I was for that eraser! It saved me from embarrassment more than once when the teacher walked over as my friends began to giggle at what I had drawn. But enough of that! The memory of those days brings to mind a story.

A little boy who had been reading his Bible came to his mother and said, "Mom, I don't understand this verse, 'I have blotted out, as a thick cloud, thy transgressions' (Isaiah 44:22 KJV). How can He do that?" His mother said, "Bring me your slate." Then she said, "I know you had some words on it earlier. Where are they?" He replied, "They're gone. I rubbed them out." "So too, God erases our past sins through Jesus's precious blood. I don't know where they went, but they're gone!" That mother taught her son the wondrous meaning of God's redeeming grace.

What a joy it is to know that our sins have been "blotted out!" We have a clean slate!          —MRD

## Compassion, Yes; Pity, No

*When Jesus landed and saw a large crowd, he*
*had compassion on them, because they were*
*like sheep without a shepherd. So he began*
*teaching them many things.* —MARK 6:34

In his book *Out of My Mind*, Joseph Bayly told of an elderly mother and her son who lived in a row house of Philadelphia. The mother was paralyzed, and the son just sat around the house and ate. As a result, he gained so much weight that he couldn't care for his feet. Hearing about the need, a young pastor began stopping by to wash the son's feet and cut his toenails. The son would always heap on him abusive language, but the pastor kept coming back, proving that compassion persists in finding a way to help.

Nowhere in the New Testament do we read that Jesus took pity on the needy, the outcast, and the demon-oppressed. We do read often, however, that He was "moved with compassion" (Matthew 9:36; 14:14 NKJV). This caused Him to touch and cleanse a leper (Mark 1:41), to give sight to the blind (Matthew 20:34), and to raise a man from the dead (Luke 7:13–15).

We live in a suffering world. People in famine-stricken areas need food. Despairing people need encouragement. People on the outer edges need a loving touch. Let's show compassion. That's what Jesus would do!                              —DD

## "Not Know"

*Surely God is my salvation; I will trust*
*and not be afraid.* —ISAIAH 12:2

Two-year-old Max was securely buckled in his seat in Grandpa's pickup truck. He was waiting for Dad and Grandpa to stop talking so he could go for a ride. His mother poked her head in the truck and said, "Where are you going, Max?" "Not know," he replied, raising his little arms.

"What are you going to do?" she asked. "Not know," came the answer again.

"Well," she asked, "do you want to come back in the house with me?"

"No!" came the quick reply as he settled himself more firmly, waiting to begin his adventure.

"That little boy taught me a lesson I needed right then," his mother Sheryl told me later. "He didn't know where he was going or what he was going to do, but he trusted Grandpa completely. Max's confidence in Grandpa is the kind of trust I need in my heavenly Father."

When we are faced with periods of uncertainty, it might help to think about it that way. God wants us to have the confidence in Him to say, like the prophet Isaiah, "I will trust [in God] and not be afraid" (12:2).
—DE

## Grace's "Secret"

*Now may the Lord of peace himself give you*
*peace at all times and in every way. The Lord*
*be with all of you.* —2 THESSALONIANS 3:16

Grace is a very special lady. One word comes to mind when I think of her: *peace*. The quiet and restful expression on her face has seldom changed in the six months I have known her, even though her husband was diagnosed with a rare disease and then hospitalized.

When I asked Grace the secret of her peace, she said, "It's not a secret, it's a person. It's Jesus in me. There is no other way I can explain the quietness I feel in the midst of this storm."

The secret of peace is our relationship to Jesus Christ. He is our peace. When Jesus is our Savior and Lord, and as we become more like Him, peace becomes real. Peace reassures us that God holds our lives in His hands (Daniel 5:23), and we can trust that things will work together for good.

Have we experienced this peace that goes beyond logic and understanding? Do we have the inner confidence that God is in control? My wish today echoes the words of the apostle Paul: "May the Lord of peace himself give you peace." And may we feel this peace "at all times and in every way" (2 Thessalonians 3:16).
                                                        —KO

## A Little Bit of Love

*In all their distress he too was
distressed.* —ISAIAH 63:9

A little girl accidentally caught her finger in the swinging door of her father's study. He was a busy man, preoccupied with his work, so he paid little attention to her crying. He interrupted what he was doing just long enough to call downstairs to his wife and say, "You'd better come up here and look after your child." The mother came quickly, hugged the sobbing girl, and planted a tender kiss on her forehead. While she massaged the aching finger, she asked, "Does it hurt, dear?" "Yes, Mommy," said the child, "but the worst is Daddy didn't even say, 'Oh!'"

The sorrows of life are unbearable if no one helps bear the pain. That's why we should be quick to give a warm handclasp or to empathize when someone we know faces a bitter trial. We should be like our Lord, whose heart was filled with compassion whenever He saw human need! Of Him the Bible declares, "In all their distress he too was distressed" (Isaiah 63:9).

The love of Christ should make us "devoted to one another!" (Romans 12:10). Let's not forget that the world is dying for a little bit of love.          —HB

## A Sermon from Nature

*A rod and a reprimand impart wisdom,*
*but a child left undisciplined disgraces*
*its mother.* —PROVERBS 29:15

Have you ever seen a mother wren angrily dive-bomb someone? I'll never forget seeing my father come under such an attack when I was young. He had placed a number of wren houses around the yard and was always happy when his tenants returned each year to raise their families. One of his birdhouses was made with a hinged cover so Dad could lift the top and look into the nest.

One day, wanting to see a new family that had just hatched, my father approached the birdhouse—but not without a severe scolding from the mother wren. Disregarding her warning, my father was just about to lift the lid when this furious little mother flew full speed right down on top of his head. She gave him such a vicious peck that it drew blood!

This can remind us of the concern we should have for our children. We must diligently protect them from the evil that could bring them spiritual injury— and tell them about the threats of the world, the flesh, and the devil.

Our children need our attention and care. May God help us to guard them from spiritual harm.

—RD

## Grandma's Ice Cream

*Then we your people, the sheep of your pasture, will*
*praise you forever; from generation to generation*
*we will proclaim your praise.* —PSALM 79:13

My phone beeped, indicating an incoming text. My
daughter wanted my grandmother's recipe for Peppermint Ice Cream Pie. As I thumbed through the
yellowed cards in my aged recipe box, my eyes spotted the unique handwriting of my grandmother—and
several jotted notes in the small cursive of my mother.
It occurred to me that with my daughter's request
Peppermint Ice Cream Pie would make its entrance
into a fourth generation within my family.

I wondered, What other family heirlooms might
be handed down generation to generation? What
choices regarding faith would play out in the lives of
my daughter and her offspring?

In Psalm 79, the psalmist bemoans a wayward Israel, which had lost its faith moorings. He begs God
to rescue His people from the ungodly and to restore
Jerusalem to safety. This done, he promises a restored
commitment to God's ways. "Then we your people
. . . will praise you forever (v. 13).

I eagerly shared the recipe, knowing my grandmother's dessert legacy would enjoy a new layer in
our family. And I prayed sincerely for the most lasting
hand-me-down of all: the influence of our family's
faith on one generation to the next.          —EM

## Profitable Praying

*For I know my transgressions, and my
sin is always before me.* —PSALM 51:3

A little guy had been sent to his room because he had been bad. A short time later he came out and said to his mother, "I've been thinking about what I did, and I said a prayer." "That's fine," she said, "if you ask God to make you good, He will help you." "Oh, I didn't ask Him to help me be good," replied the boy. "I asked Him to help you put up with me."

Do we sometimes pray that way? We focus on secondary problems by asking the Lord to adjust our circumstances to our liking. Praying about our spiritual growth becomes effective only when we first come clean with the Lord about our own sin. Look at David's prayer in Psalm 51. He acknowledged his sin (v. 3). He asked for mercy (v. 1), for a clean heart (v. 10), and for a restoration of the joy of his salvation (v. 12). David made no excuse for his sin.

Let's be willing to do the hard word of having total honesty when we talk with the Lord. That kind of praying is not always comfortable—but oh, how profitable!                                              —DD

## Where Is Peace?

*"In me you may have peace."*
—JOHN 16:33

"Do you still hope for peace?" a journalist asked Bob Dylan in 1984.

"There is not going to be any peace," Dylan replied. His response drew criticism, yet peace remains ever elusive.

About 600 years before Christ, most prophets were predicting peace. God's prophet wasn't one of them. Jeremiah reminded the people that God had said, "Obey me, and I will be your God and you will be my people" (Jeremiah 7:23). Yet they repeatedly ignored the Lord. Their false prophets said, "Peace, peace" (8:11), but Jeremiah predicted disaster. Jerusalem fell in 586 BC.

Peace is rare. But amid Jeremiah's book of dire prophecies we discover a God who loves relentlessly. "I have loved you with an everlasting love," the Lord told His rebellious people. "I will build you up again" (31:3–4).

God is a God of love and peace. Sin destroys the world's peace and robs each of us of inner peace. Jesus came to this planet to reconcile us to God and give us that inner peace (John 16:33; Romans 5:1).

Whether we live in a combat zone or dwell in a serene neighborhood with nary a whisper of war, Christ invites us into His peace.                    —TG

## Seasons of Motherhood

*There is a time for everything, and
a season for every activity under the
heavens.* —ECCLESIASTES 3:1

As a pastor, I shared with many women the seasons
of motherhood. I have called on mothers in the hospital and rejoiced with them for their precious newborn baby. I have counseled with anxious mothers
and tried to assure them that their teenage daughter's
marriage would work out. I have stood with mothers
at the bedside of an injured or ill child and felt their
pain. And I have cried with them in their grief when
their son or daughter died.

Mary, the mother of Jesus, also experienced these
times of joy and sorrow. What joy when the Christ
child was born! What excitement when the shepherds
came to worship Him! What uneasiness when Simeon
prophesied that a sword would pierce her soul! And
what heart-wrenching grief as she watched her Son
dying on the cross! But her seasons of motherhood
didn't end there. She saw Jesus alive after He rose
from the grave. And because she trusted Him as her
Savior, she is now in heaven with Him.

A mother experiences great joys and intense sorrows. But if she submits her life to God, as Mary did,
every season of her motherhood serves His eternal
purposes.                                       —HVL

## The Better Position

*"So do not be afraid of them, for there is nothing concealed that will not be disclosed, or hidden that will not be made known."* —MATTHEW 10:26

When I was in my early teens, someone stole my bicycle. I was distressed and angry, and I expressed my bitter feelings to my mother. Like many times before, her wisdom helped me.

"Dave," she said, "you are really the winner. It's far better to be the one who lost the bicycle than the one who stole it. Think of what he's got to live with. And what can he say to God in the judgment?" I saw her point immediately and was consoled.

It wasn't until later that I began to understand all that was involved in Mom's statement. She had faith in God and His justice. She knew that even though this person might get away with stealing in this world, one day he would answer to God for this sin.

Are you experiencing deep hurt because you've been wronged? Perhaps someone you love and trust has betrayed you. Maybe you've suffered a terrible loss and the person who inflicted it has gotten away with it. Because God is just and makes all things right, you are in the better position!          —DE

## An Age-Old Question

*He replied, "You are talking like a foolish*
*woman. Shall we accept good from God,*
*and not trouble?" In all this, Job did*
*not sin in what he said.* —JOB 2:10

Seventeen-year-old Jeremy was struggling with a question theologians have wrestled with for centuries. He was trying to understand why his mother had to have brain surgery. He asked, "Why do good people suffer, Mom?"

She told him, "Suffering is part of living in a sin-cursed world, and good people suffer like anybody else. That's why I'm glad we have Jesus. If I die, I'll go to a better place, and someday I'll see you again." She said she could understand his frustration, but she told him not to put the blame on God.

We can put the question about suffering squarely before God, argue with Him if we must, and struggle with our doubts. But let's not blame Him.

God didn't explain to Job what He was doing but said that He could be trusted to do what is right (Job 38–42). And He has assured us in His Word that Jesus suffered on our behalf, rose from the dead, and is preparing a suffering-free place for us.

These may not be the answers we want, but they are the answers we need to help us live with the often unanswerable question of suffering.          —DD

## Thunderstorm Thoughts

*Whatever you have learned or received
or heard from me, or seen in me—put
it into practice. And the God of peace
will be with you.* —PHILIPPIANS 4:9

I laugh every time I hear the radio commercial that has a woman shouting to her friend in conversation. She's trying to talk above the sounds of the thunderstorm in her own head. Ever since a storm damaged part of her home, that's all she hears because her insurance company isn't taking care of her claims.

I've heard thunderstorms in my head, and maybe you have too. It happens when a tragedy occurs—to us, to someone close to us, or to someone we hear about in the news. Our minds become a tempest of "what if" questions. We focus on all the possible bad outcomes.

It's natural for us to be fearful in a storm (literal or figurative). The disciples had Jesus right there in the boat with them, yet they were afraid (Matthew 8:23–27). He used the calming of the storm as a lesson to show them who He was—a powerful God who also cares for them.

We can find moments of peace when we're anchored to the truth that Jesus is in the boat with us and He cares.                                                       —AC

## How God Makes Comforters

*The God of all comfort, who comforts us in*
*all our troubles, so that we can comfort those*
*in any trouble with the comfort we ourselves*
*receive from God.* —2 CORINTHIANS 1:3–4

A mother whose son died asked an elderly Chinese philosopher how to overcome her deep grief. "I can help you, but you must first bring me some mustard seed," he said. "But you must get it at a home where there has never been any loss or sorrow."

The woman started her search, but in every home she visited was someone who had lost a loved one or had known loss. Returning without any mustard seed, she exclaimed, "Sorrow is common to all." "Ah," said the philosopher, "you have learned a valuable lesson. Because you know sorrow, you can sympathize with others and comfort them. When you do, your own sorrow will be lessened."

Someone has written, "Sorrow can lead us into one of four lands: the barren land in which we try to escape; the broken land in which we sink under it; the bitter land in which we resent it; or the better land in which we bear it and become a blessing to others." In that better land, we accept God's comfort and reach out to others.

The best comforters are those God has comforted who are willing to comfort others.            —HB

## No Pain, No Gain

*Start children off on the way they should
go, and even when they are old they will
not turn from it.* —PROVERBS 22:6

Christian educator and author Howard Hendricks cautioned parents not to bribe or threaten their children to get them to obey. What they need is firm, loving discipline.

Hendricks recalled being in a home where a bright-eyed grade-schooler sat across the table from him.

"Sally, eat your potatoes," said her mother. "If you don't, you won't get any dessert!"

Sally winked at Hendricks. Sure enough, mother removed the potatoes and brought Sally some ice cream. He saw this as a case of parents obeying their children rather than "Children, obey your parents" (Ephesians 6:1).

Many parents are afraid to do what they know is best for their youngsters. They're afraid their children will turn against them. Hendricks says, "Your primary concern is not what they think of you now, but what they'll think twenty years from now."

Even our loving heavenly Father's correction is difficult, yet afterward "it produces a harvest of righteousness and peace for those who have been trained by it" (Hebrews 12:11). As loving parents, dare we have less long-term vision than our heavenly Father has?                                        —JY

## We Need to Go!

*Not giving up meeting together, as some
are in the habit of doing, but encouraging
one another—and all the more as you see
the Day approaching.* —HEBREWS 10:25

Josef Gabor grew up in Czechoslovakia when it was
dominated by communism, and religion was despised
as weakness. His father taught communist doctrine
classes. But Josef's mother, who believed in Jesus
Christ, took Josef and his brother with her to church.

They got up early each Sunday morning and took
a three-hour train ride to Prague. Then they walked
to the church and sat through a two-and-a-half-hour
service. After eating lunch in a nearby park, they returned to church for another two-and-a-half-hour
meeting. Then they took the three-hour ride home.

Josef Gabor became a missionary to his own people in Czechoslovakia. When he would tell about going to church as a child, his eyes would fill with tears
of gratitude for a mother who cared enough about
his spiritual welfare to help him come to know and
serve Christ.

Some Christians would do anything to be in
church, but for health or other reasons they can't.
They know how important it is to worship and fellowship with believers. They don't want to give up
meeting together (Hebrews 10:25).

They know "we need to go."                    —DE

## We've Been Adopted

*He predestined us for adoption to sonship
through Jesus Christ, in accordance with
his pleasure and will.* —EPHESIANS 1:5

Penelope Duckworth, a college chaplain, talked with a Christian woman who had adopted a Jewish daughter. She explained that after Hitler had annexed Poland, the Nazis came to her village to round up Jews. She had been shopping near the train station where German soldiers were loading Jews into rail cars—destined to die in a concentration camp.

That woman saw a soldier pushing a Jewish woman toward the station, and she had a little girl toddling behind. He stopped her and demanded, "Is she your daughter?" The terrified mother looked into the Christian woman's eyes, who then was standing nearby and said, "No, the child is hers." From that moment the Christian woman took that Jewish girl as her own daughter.

By grace God has claimed us for His own. We were condemned, not as innocent victims, but as sinners. We were powerless to save ourselves. We were headed for the second death, which is eternal exile from heaven's life and light and love. But God redeemed us through Jesus's death on the cross.

Praise God—once alienated; now by faith adopted!

—VG

# "Mother, I Heard That!"

*He said, "Young man, I say to you, get up!" The*
*dead man sat up and began to talk, and Jesus*
*gave him back to his mother.* —LUKE 7:14–15

Luke 7 pictures for us the touching scene of a grief-stricken widow taking her only son to be buried. Her sorrow is almost unbearable.

W. P. Siebert gives this description: "The long walk to the cemetery has begun. Finally, the procession reaches the city gates. Soon her loved one will be removed from her sight forever. Then the mourners meet a Man whose words ring with such a note of authority that her sobbing is replaced by a tranquil peace. This compassionate One addresses the corpse, 'Young man, I say to you, get up!' (v. 14). To the amazement of all, he did."

Someone once imagined the boy asking his mom later about the scene. "How did it all happen, Mother?" She explained the situation and the arrival of Jesus: "Then He looked at you and said, 'Young man, arise.'" "Mother, I heard that!" exclaimed the happy youth. "You don't have to say any more, I know the rest!"

This same Jesus still sympathizes with His sorrowing children and tells us not to weep, for someday our loved ones too "will hear his voice and come out" (John 5:28–29).                                    —HB

## Unexplained Peace

*You will not abandon me to the realm*
*of the dead. . . . You make known to me*
*the path of life; you will fill me with joy*
*in your presence.* —PSALM 16:10–11

It always amazes me the way peace—powerful, un-explainable peace (Philippians 4:7)—can somehow fill our hearts even in our deepest grief. I experienced this at my father's memorial service. As a long line of sympathetic acquaintances passed by offering their condolences, I was relieved to see a good high school friend. Without a word, he simply wrapped me in a long bear hug. His quiet understanding flooded me with the first feelings of peace within grief that diffi-cult day, a powerful reminder that I wasn't as alone as I felt.

The kind of peace and joy God brings into our lives isn't caused by a choice to stoically stomp down the pain during hard times. David implies that it's more like a gift we can't help but experience when we take refuge in our good God (Psalm 16:1–2).

The life God has given us—even in its pain—is still beautiful and good (vv. 6–8). And we can surrender to His loving arms that tenderly carry us through our pain into a peace and joy that even death can never quench (v. 11).                                    —MB

## That Extra Mile

*"Whoever compels you to go one mile, go with him two."* —MATTHEW 5:41 NKJV

A young boy was sent by his mother to pick a quart of raspberries. He didn't want to pick raspberries; he hated to pick raspberries. But his mom had spoken, so he made his way slowly, reluctantly toward the raspberry patch. Then a happy thought came to his mind. Why not pick two quarts and surprise his mother! Suddenly a new motivation of love dissolved his strong dislike. Everything changed. He could hardly wait to see the approving smile on his mother's face when he showed her the extra quart.

As Christians, we encounter similar situations. When we are called upon to love the unlovely, everything within us cries out in loud protest. An inner battle begins. We say, "No, Lord, not that—anything but that! It's not fair!" The protest continues, but the thought is overpowering: "The extra mile. Why, that's what Jesus did for me when He went to the cross. And that's what He expects of me—to go the extra mile. Certainly He would not ask me to do what He wouldn't enable me to do. Help me, Lord! I'll do it!"

Let's go that extra mile.                          —DD

## Pass on the Praise

*One generation commends your
works to another; they tell of your
mighty acts.* —PSALM 145:4

A baby had just been born. Grandmother was at the hospital to visit her daughter and new granddaughter. The three were alone in the patient's room. "Did I ever tell you about your birth?" the new grandmother asked her daughter. "As far as we were concerned, God worked a miracle."

"Please tell me about it," said the new mother.

"You decided to come early, during a blizzard. We lived in the country, and your dad put me in our old car and we headed for town. On a remote part of the road the car suddenly quit, and Dad couldn't get it started. Then a car came by and stopped. A man we had never seen before got out, started our car, and followed us to the hospital. If we hadn't arrived when we did, you would have died, because there were complications. To this day we don't know who that man was. God wanted you born, and He's been taking care of you ever since."

That new mother was overwhelmed. Years later she told the story to her daughter, giving God the praise. That daughter is my aunt.

Let's be sure to tell our loved ones how God has worked in our lives.                                        —DE

## Acceptable Service

*"His master replied, 'Well done, good and*
*faithful servant! You have been faithful*
*with a few things; I will put you in charge*
*of many things. Come and share your*
*master's happiness!'"* —MATTHEW 25:23

A four-year-old boy sensed his mother's enthusiasm as she prepared to entertain guests. He wanted to help get things ready. After the visitors had come and gone, she wrote this to a friend about her son's willingness: "Desiring to be of service to his mama, the dear little fellow got out the brass polish and began polishing and singing. Of course, he left white polish streaks all over the place! But I'm more than willing to put up with the extra work just to see his little heart so willing."

I think this is how our heavenly Father observes our service for Him. Even when we have done what He has commanded us to do, we must admit, "We are unworthy servants" (Luke 17:10). Yet, one day our Lord will say, "Well done, good and faithful servant" (Matthew 25:23).

Paul said, "If the willingness is there, the gift is acceptable according to what one has, not according to what one does not have" (2 Corinthians 8:12). Are you afraid what you're doing for God is not adequate? Serve Him out of love and willingly. Someday you'll hear Him say, "Well done."                    —PVG

## Within Reach

*For in Christ all the fullness of the Deity*
*lives in bodily form.* —COLOSSIANS 2:9

A little girl once said to her mother, "Mamma, I like you better than God."

"Oh, you must not say that!" replied the mother.

"Yes, but really, Mamma, I do like you better than God."

Shocked, her mother inquired, "Dear, what makes you say that?"

The child answered simply, "Because I can hug you!"

That little girl expressed the universal desire of humans to desire contact with God in a personal, tangible way. A spirit without a body is difficult for us to conceive, but a real "flesh and bones" man is a concrete reality we can understand. In the incarnation, therefore, Jesus brought God within embracing distance.

Someone has said, "The kindest thing God ever did was to become a Man!" It is indeed a thrilling truth. Because of the incarnation, we can now have a much clearer understanding of God, and we can experience a warm, personal contact with Him through the person of His Son. No wonder the apostle John declared, "We have seen his glory, the glory of the one and only Son, who came from the Father, full of grace and truth" (John 1:14).

Have you embraced Christ as your Savior?  —HB

## Burned-Out Jugglers

*But those who hope in the LORD will renew*
*their strength. They will soar on wings like*
*eagles; they will run and not grow weary, they*
*will walk and not be faint.* —ISAIAH 40:31

Today's wife and mother is a professional juggler. She balances home, work, church, and community responsibilities, and often runs a family taxi service.

My daughter Tina is a juggler who admits that she sometimes feels like resigning, but she's learned where to go with her struggle. Here's how it began.

One morning Tina woke up with the I-can't-juggle-it-all feeling and started to panic. Reaching for pen and paper, she began recording some spiritual "first aid," such as: "God is not stressed-out. God is not frustrated. God is not exhausted. God is not confused. God is not panicking."

After listing what God is not, she began listing what He is: "God is relaxed. God's timing is perfect. God is in control. God knows everything." Then she wrote, "This God is living in me. He is working through me." Tina's panic feelings subsided. Before she had a chance to say, "God, I want to resign," she realized that He wanted to renew her strength.

Are you a juggler needing God's first aid for your soul? Guided by today's Bible reading of Isaiah 40, ponder the Lord's limitless attributes. Then let Him renew you.                                    —JY

## Quiet Times

*"Be still, and know that I am
God."* —PSALM 46:10

My friend Mary told me that she had always valued
the time she spent fishing with her dad. Not being a
fishing aficionado myself, I was curious about what
she found so enjoyable. "I just like being with my
dad," she said. "So you just fish and talk?" I asked
her. "Oh, no, we don't really talk," she said. "We just
fish."

It wasn't the conversation—it was the company.

Did you ever think about how much time we spend
talking? In what we like to call our "quiet time" with
God, we usually fill in any silence with our prayers.
But do we ever practice just being "still"?

God said, "Be still, and know that I am God"
(Psalm 46:10). When Jesus noticed that the disciples
were so busy that they didn't even have time to eat,
He told them, "Come with me by yourselves to a
quiet place and get some rest" (Mark 6:31).

Are you allowing quiet moments alone with God
to be a part of your life? Let Him teach you how to
"be still." And listen when Jesus invites you: "Come
with me and get some rest."                    —CHK

# Looking Our Best

*Rather, it should be that of your inner
self, the unfading beauty of a gentle
and quiet spirit, which is of great
worth in God's sight.* —1 PETER 3:4

Charles William Eliot (1834–1926), longtime president of Harvard University, had an inoperable birthmark on his face. It has been said that the moment he was told it couldn't be removed was "the dark hour of his soul."

Charles's mother told him: "My son, it is not possible for you to get rid of that hardship. . . . But it is possible for you, with God's help, to grow a mind and soul so big that people will forget to look at your face."

I'm encouraged by those words. I have Parkinson's disease, and one of its symptoms is a "facial mask" in which the face takes on a stiff, plastic appearance with little expression. It's embarrassing to look like an "old sourpuss." But I know it is possible, with God's help, to develop character qualities that will overshadow any physical imperfections.

Peter wrote about the "unfading beauty of a gentle and quiet spirit" (1 Peter 3:4). Christlike character is more desirable than the finest external physical features.

May our lives reflect the love of Christ, the peace of God, and the joy of the Lord—qualities that make us look our best!         —RD

## Leave the Light On

*"You are the light of the world. A town built
on a hill cannot be hidden. . . . In the same
way, let your light shine before others, that
they may see your good deeds and glorify
your Father in heaven."* —MATTHEW 5:14, 16

At the end of a radio commercial for a motel chain, a voice reassuringly says, "We'll leave the light on for you." My mother used to say the same thing. No matter what time I got home, the porch light was burning. Its warm beams seemed to say, "This is where you belong. Someone loves you here. You are home."

One night the porch light wasn't on. I remember my feelings. Were my parents angry with me? Had I done something wrong? Was I no longer welcome? The explanation was simple: the bulb had burned out. Everything was okay.

Jesus is the true light, but as His followers we reflect His light. Our faithful walk of obedience is a beacon of God's love and truth. We are like a porch light, drawing unbelievers to Jesus, assuring them that Someone loves them and waits to welcome them home.

Perhaps your brother or sister is still in the darkness. Or a friend or coworker. Or a son or daughter. Don't stop praying for them. Keep finding ways to draw their attention to the Lord. Leave the light on for them. —DE

## Seeking Peace

*Let the peace of Christ rule in your hearts,*
*since as members of one body you were called*
*to peace. And be thankful.* —COLOSSIANS 3:15

"What do you think about peace?" my friend asked as we ate lunch together. "Peace?" I said, puzzled. "I'm not sure—why do you ask?" He answered, "Well, as you jiggled your foot during the church service, I wondered if you're agitated about something. Have you considered the peace God gives to those who love Him?"

That day some years ago, I was a bit hurt by my friend's question, but it started me on a journey. I began exploring the Bible to see how God's people embraced this gift of well-being, of peace, even in the midst of hardship. As I read Paul's letter to the Colossians, I chewed over the apostle's command to let the peace of Christ rule in their hearts (Colossians 3:15).

We all will encounter times when we can choose to embrace or refuse the rule of Christ's peace in our hearts. As we turn to Him, asking Jesus to dwell in us, He will gently release us from the anxiety and cares that weigh down us. As we seek His peace, we trust that He will meet us with His love.          —ABP

## Held in Their Hands

*I give them eternal life, and they shall never perish; no one will snatch them out of my hand.* —JOHN 10:28

When Pastor Thomas Collins called on a family from his church, he found the mother to be despondent—feeling that God had forsaken her. Looking at the baby in the woman's arms, Pastor Collins said to her, "Drop that baby on the floor." Startled, she looked at him in disbelief. "Well," he said, "for what price would you do it?" Indignantly she replied, "Not for as many dollars as there are stars!" He then said kindly, "Tell me, do you really think you love your child more than the Lord does His?"

In times of deep trial, we are sometimes tempted to feel abandoned by God. It's then we must remind ourselves that we have the double protection of being held firmly in Christ's hand and in the Father's hand (John 10:28–29). There is no more secure place than that!

Take comfort, doubting Christian. If it's absurd to think that a loving mother would deliberately drop her helpless infant, it's unthinkable that our heavenly Father and His Son would ever loosen the grip of their all-powerful hands on us.                    —PVG

# Why, God, Why?

*The LORD blessed the latter part of Job's life
more than the former part.* —JOB 42:12

When death snatches a loved one from us through disease, an accident, or some other tragedy, grief can overwhelm us and we may question, "Why, God, why?" Although He does not reveal all His reasons for what happens, sometimes He gives us a partial answer.

A young mother in nineteenth-century England, Mrs. Josephine Butler, returned home one day and witnessed the tragic death of her child. Her little daughter Evangeline, seeing her coming, had rushed to the porch railing to greet her. As she leaned over, she lost her balance and fell to her death. Mrs. Butler's world was shattered. In her search for comfort, she turned to a godly neighbor, an old Quaker woman, who said to her, "God hath taken to himself her whom thou dost love; but there are many forlorn young hearts who need that mother-love of thine." Those words led Mrs. Butler into a life of social reform and Christian service that brought hope to thousands.

Have you suffered a loss? God won't give a full explanation, but He will give strength to go on. —DD

# The Call of the Present

*"I am the Lord's servant," Mary answered.*
*"May your word to me be fulfilled."*
*Then the angel left her.* —LUKE 1:38

The life of Jesus's mother was simple and plain. She did the tasks others did at her age, learning how to be a good homemaker for her future husband. There was nothing out of the ordinary about her external life—at least not revealed in Scripture.

Yet what treasures of grace lie concealed in Mary's attitude! When the angel announced that her child would be called "the Son of God," (Luke 1:35) she responded, "Let it be to me according to your word" (v. 38 NKJV).

Her answer contained all that our Lord requires—submission of the soul to His will. This was the secret of Mary's deep spirituality: She abandoned herself to God's will and received His grace to do it.

What is God asking you to do? It may be to respond actively to a command of Scripture or to submit patiently to present suffering. Eighteenth-century writer Jean-Pierre de Caussade called our submission to God "the holiest thing that could happen to us."

Are you able to accept each moment with grace and submission? Can you respond to the Lord as Mary said to the angel, "May your word to me be fulfilled"?                                        —DR

## Mothers Who Pray

*She kept on praying to the LORD.*
—1 SAMUEL 1:12

In the Old Testament we read how Hannah's prayer was granted in the birth of her son Samuel, whom she dedicated to the Lord as she had promised. And in Paul's letter to Timothy, reference is made to the faith of Timothy's mother, which I'm sure was often expressed in earnest prayer on his behalf. Mothers who pray will often see their prayers rewarded.

I know a pastor's wife who is a woman of prayer. When her husband would leave for an important meeting or call, she would pray, asking the Lord's guidance and protection. When he would leave for services away from home, she would ask God to give him wisdom and strength. She prayed aloud, and the children heard her. Imagine her delight with what her daughter said when she was preparing to leave for college. She said that going would be easier because she knew that as soon as she left, her mother would pray for her—and keep on praying!

Ever feel frustrated because of limitations on what you can do for your children? You can always pray—and prayers are among the most cherished gifts of all.

—DE

## It's for Keeps!

*Therefore what God has joined together,*
*let no one separate.* —MARK 10:9

On the day after their wedding, the honeymooners were visiting Niagara Falls. In the evening they watched the thundering cascades of water plunge over the rocky cliffs, and then they walked hand in hand in the romantic glow of a full moon. The starry-eyed bride stopped, looked lovingly into her dream-man's eyes, and exclaimed, "Just think, fifty years from yesterday, we'll be celebrating our Golden Anniversary!"

Her comment may bring a smile to our faces, but that bride had the right idea. To her, marriage was a permanent relationship. It was not some trial arrangement. Its continuing existence was not conditioned on the whims of the partners involved. No, she had entered into a lifelong covenant.

Marriage is the most blessed of all human relationships. The union of husband and wife is unique. Jesus declared, "For this reason a man will leave his father and mother and be united to his wife, and the two will become one flesh" (Mark 10:7–8). Our Lord concluded, "Therefore what God has joined together, let no one separate" (v. 9).

God expects you to honor your wedding vows. Marriage is for keeps!                        —RD

## Childhood Beginnings

*"For even the Son of Man did not come to*
*be served, but to serve, and to give his life*
*as a ransom for many."* —MARK 10:45

One summer our church invited a young man to join
the staff. As Caleb shared how he grew up in Costa
Rica while his family was serving Christ there, he
reflected on the words of 2 Timothy 3:14–17. From
his childhood, he reminisced, he had known the Bible.
His mother and father had taught him the truths of
the Scriptures that were "able to make [him] wise for
salvation through faith in Christ Jesus" (v. 15). He
acknowledged that his preparation to be a pastor had
begun when he was still a child.

Our congregation had the opportunity to "meet"
his family in Costa Rica via a video-conferencing call.
Caleb's dad challenged his son using the words of
Jesus about himself in Mark 10:45. He said, "Caleb,
remember our family motto, 'We are here to serve,
not to be served.'" It was easy to understand how
this young man had developed his maturity of faith.

The children God has entrusted to us are precious
gifts. With God's help we can pass on the baton of
faith to future generations. What a great privilege to
be servants like Jesus!                        —CHK

## Mom's Translation

*For Ezra had devoted himself to the
study and observance of the Law of
the LORD, and to teaching its decrees
and laws in Israel.* —EZRA 7:10

Four pastors were discussing the merits of the various translations of the Bible. One liked a particular version best because of its simple, beautiful English. Another preferred a more scholarly edition because it was closer to the original Hebrew and Greek. Still another liked a contemporary version because of its up-to-date vocabulary.

The fourth minister was silent for a moment, then said, "I like my mother's translation best." Surprised, the other three men said they didn't know his mother had translated the Bible. "Yes," he replied. "She translated it into life, and it was the most convincing translation I ever saw."

This pastor reminded them that the most important focus should be learning God's Word and doing it. That was the top priority of Ezra's life. As a scribe, he studied the Law, obeyed it, and taught it to the Israelites (Ezra 7:10). For example, God commanded His people not to intermarry with neighboring nations who served pagan gods (9:1–2). Ezra confessed the nation's sin to God (9:10–12) and corrected the people, who then repented (10:10–12).

Let's follow Ezra's example by seeking the Word of God and translating it into life.          —AC

## Kindness a Mark of Grace

*Be completely humble and gentle; be patient,*
*bearing with one another in love.* —EPHESIANS 4:2

During the Civil War, Abraham Lincoln often visited the hospitals to cheer the wounded. On one occasion, according a story verified by the *Epoch Times*, he saw a young fellow who was near death. "Is there anything I can do for you?" asked the compassionate president. "Please write a letter to my mother," came the reply.

Unrecognized by the soldier, Lincoln sat down and wrote as the youth told him what to say. The letter read, "My Dearest Mother, I was badly hurt while doing my duty, and I won't recover. Don't sorrow too much for me. May God bless you and Father. Kiss Mary and John for me." Lincoln signed the letter for him and added this postscript: "Written for your son by Abraham Lincoln." Seeing the note, the soldier was astonished. "Are you really our president?" he asked. "Yes," was the quiet answer.

Kindness is a powerful tool. We cannot always do exceptional deeds, but there are thousands of small, generous acts we can perform that will help others and bring glory to God. May we stand out as servants of Christ because of our kindness and our sincere love.                                                    —HB

## A Giving Heart

*All day long he craves for more, but the righteous
give without sparing.* —PROVERBS 21:26

Followers of Christ should generously give to help
others materially or through acts of encouragement.
We should follow the example of our heavenly Father,
who did not spare His only Son but gave Him up for
our sins.

A Christian mother has the following words taped
to her refrigerator door:

Happy are those who . . .

- Give love rather than demand it.
- Reach out to others rather than expect to be
  reached out to.
- Desire to be a friend more than to have friends.
- Express appreciation rather than expect it.
- Relieve suffering rather than think only of their
  own suffering.
- Pray "God bless others" more than "God bless
  me."
- Think of others' good points, not their failings.
- Forget themselves in doing deeds that will be
  remembered.

Do you see what is behind each of these sayings?
It's a way of thinking that focuses on other people
rather than on ourselves.

*Lord, help me to put the concerns of others above
my selfish desires. Grant me a giving heart.*     —DE

## Pushed to the Limit

*I discipline my body and bring it into
subjection, lest, when I have preached
to others, I myself should become
disqualified.* —1 CORINTHIANS 9:27 NKJV

I met a woman who has pushed her body and mind to the limit. She climbed mountains, faced death, and even broke a Guinness world record. Now she's engaged in a different challenge—raising her special-needs child. The courage and faith she employed while ascending the mountains she now pours into motherhood.

In 1 Corinthians, the apostle Paul speaks of a runner competing in a race. After urging the church people, who were in love with their own rights, to begin showing consideration for each other (chapter 8), he explains that he saw the challenges of love and self-sacrifice to be like a marathon of endurance (chapter 9). As followers of Jesus, they were to relinquish their rights in obedience to Him.

Just as athletes train their bodies to win, we can train our bodies and minds so our souls can flourish. As we ask the Holy Spirit to transform us, we leave our old selves behind. Empowered by God, we stop ourselves from actions that are not godly.

As we train to run in the Spirit of Christ, how might God want to mold us today?          —ABP

## Tips on Marriage

*However, each one of you also must love his wife as he loves himself, and the wife must respect her husband.* —EPHESIANS 5:33

A good marriage requires much love and giving by both parties. Too often when the first rosy glow of romance has faded to the deeper purple of reality, some of the sweetness that accompanies courtship is lost in the bitter experiences of life. Faults become as obvious as virtues. It takes work to make a marriage endure.

Perhaps these suggestions can help: (1) Build on the same spiritual base and work toward the same spiritual goals. Your greatest bond is salvation in Christ and a desire to grow in His grace. (2) Never go to bed angry at each other. Make up before going to sleep. (3) Don't let a "lively discussion" involving disagreement blow up into an ugly name-calling argument. (4) Identify frustrations and talk about issues, but never attack the person. (5) Share feelings and enjoy talking about mutual interests.

No marriage is perfect, but with effort, a loving marriage can be your greatest earthly treasure.

—HB

## Four Ways to Look

*I will consider all your works and meditate
on all your mighty deeds.* —PSALM 77:12

Joan was struggling with some difficult issues with
her children when she heard a speaker share encouragement for those who feel like quitting. These four
thoughts Joan heard helped her to keep going:

*Look up and pray.* Asaph prayed all night long
and even expressed feelings that God had forgotten
and rejected him (Psalm 77:9–10). We can tell God
everything! We can ask Him anything. He won't criticize us for asking.

*Look back and remember* what God has done in
the past for you and others. Asaph didn't talk to God
only about the pain; he also recalled God's power and
mighty works for him and God's people. He wrote, "I
will remember the deeds of the LORD" (v. 11).

*Look forward.* Think about the good that might
come out of the situation. What might you learn?
What do you know God will do because His ways
are perfect? (v. 13).

*Look again.* This time look at your circumstances
with eyes of faith. Remind yourself that He is the
God of great wonders and can be trusted (v. 14).

May these ideas help us gain perspective and keep
moving in our faith journey with Jesus.　　　　—AC

## No Grudges after Sunset

*"In your anger do not sin": Do not let the sun go
down while you are still angry.* —EPHESIANS 4:26

A little boy got into a fight with his brother and the
whole experience left him feeling bitter. When his
brother wanted to make things right, he refused to
listen. In fact, he would not speak to his brother all
day.

Bedtime came, and their mother said to the boy,
"Don't you think you should forgive your brother
before you go to sleep? Remember, the Bible says,
'Do not let the sun go down while you are still angry'" (Ephesians 4:26). The boy thought for a few
moments and then blurted out, "But how can I keep
the sun from going down?"

Don't we do this? We're angry at certain people
and hold grudges. When we are urged to make things
right, we sidestep the issue and refuse to heed the
clear instruction of Scripture. True, we cannot change
another person's heart, but we are responsible for our
own attitude. The Bible says, "Be kind to one another,
tenderhearted, forgiving each other, just as God in
Christ forgave you" (Ephesians 4:32 NKJV).

No, we can't keep the sun from going down. But
we can keep it from setting—on our anger. And that
means we must forgive.                          —RD

## Perfect Freedom

*I will walk about in freedom, for I have
sought out your precepts.* —PSALM 119:45

Aaron wanted to go swimming in a nearby gravel
pit, but his mother said he couldn't because it was
too dangerous. He raised a ruckus, so she punished
him by making him sit on a chair in the kitchen.
After a time of silence he asked, "Mommy, can God
do anything He wants to do?" The mother replied,
"Yes, Aaron, He can." Again he was quiet. Then he
said, "God doesn't have parents, does He?"

Aaron thought he'd be perfectly free if it weren't
for his mother. He didn't realize that what he wanted
to do was foolish. Nor did he understand that when
he became an adult he still wouldn't be able to do
everything he desired.

As Aaron grows older, he'll learn that he'll always need people and laws to keep him from doing
something wrong or dangerous. He'll discover that
Christians alone can look forward to true freedom—
perfect freedom—in heaven. Only then will we do
what is always right and good.                    —HVL

## Love's Transformation

*At once he began to preach in the synagogues
that Jesus is the Son of God.* —ACTS 9:20

Before I met Jesus, I'd been wounded so deeply that I avoided close relationships in fear of being hurt more. My mom remained my closest friend, until I married Alan. Seven years later and on the verge of divorce, I toted our kindergartener, Xavier, into church. I sat near the exit door—afraid to trust but desperate for help.

Thankfully, believers reached out, prayed for our family, and taught me how to nurture a relationship with God. Over time, the love of Christ and His followers changed me.

Two years later, Alan, Xavier, and I were baptized. Sometime later, my mom said, "You're different. Tell me more about Jesus." Soon she too trusted Christ as her Savior.

Jesus transforms lives . . . lives like Saul's, one of the most feared persecutors of the church (Acts 9:1–5). Others helped Saul learn more about Jesus (vv. 17–19). His transformation added to the credibility of his Spirit-empowered teaching (vv. 20–22).

As people notice how Christ's love changes us, we'll have opportunities to tell others what He did for us.                                        —XD

## The Best Question

*LORD, who may dwell in your sacred tent? Who may live on your holy mountain?* —PSALM 15:1

Nobel Prize-winning physicist Martin Perl was asked what he attributed his success to. "My mother," he answered. "Every day when I came home from school she asked me, 'So, Marty, did you ask any good questions today?'"

David asked the best question of all: "Lord, who may dwell in your sacred tent?" (Psalm 15:1). In effect, he was asking, "What kind of person dwells close to God?"

The answer came in a series of character traits: "The one whose walk is blameless, who does what is righteous, who speaks the truth from their heart" (v. 2).

It's one thing to know the truth; it's another to obey it. God delights to live on His holy hill with those who are holy—who reflect the reality of the truth they believe. He loves men and women who "ring true."

This psalm, however, is not about any holiness of our own that we think will qualify us to gain entrance to His presence. It is rather about the beauty of holiness that God forms in us as we dwell in fellowship with Him.

The closer we get to God, the more like Him we will become.                                              —DR

## A Guaranteed Pension

*God is not unjust; he will not forget
your work and the love you have shown
him as you have helped his people and
continue to help them.* —HEBREWS 6:10

Joanna Ambrosius was the wife of a poor farmer in the German Empire of the late nineteenth century. She and her husband spent many long hours in the fields, so she knew little of the outside world. But hers was the soul of the poet. With her hope in God, she wrote down the thoughts that filled her heart. She had great sympathy for the struggling people around her, and her mother-heart expressed its joys and sorrows in poetry.

Somehow, a bit of her verse found its way into print and later into the hands of the Empress of Germany. The royal lady was so impressed by the beauty of what Joanna wrote that she supplied her immediate needs and gave her a pension for life.

Perhaps you're serving God today in a place of obscurity. No one seems to notice what you are doing. Don't be discouraged. God will reward you for your labors. He sees your struggles; He knows the load you bear; He notes your faithfulness. He is caring for you now, and when He comes again He'll make it all worthwhile.

Take courage. Your eternal pension is guaranteed. God "will not forget your work."          —PVG

## True Sacrifice

*Because he almost died for the work of Christ.
He risked his life to make up for the help you
yourselves could not give me.* —PHILIPPIANS 2:30

Teenagers amaze me. So many of them love life with grand passion and face it with unrelenting optimism. Sometimes they demonstrate the Christian life in ways adults can only hope to emulate.

Such is the case with Carissa, a teen I worked with a few years ago on mission trips. When she was twelve, her mother was diagnosed with cancer, and that was when Carissa began helping to care for her mom.

During the next few years, Carissa often fed her mom, dressed her, and helped her do anything she couldn't do for herself. "It was so hard to learn," she said. "Can you imagine, a mother and daughter literally changing roles? I truly learned to be a humble servant."

Carissa helped her dad take care of her mom until she was fourteen when Carissa and the family said goodbye to Mom for the last time. As Carissa puts it, "God took her home and made her perfect."

Carissa reminds me of Epaphroditus, who sacrificially cared for Paul's needs (Philippians 2:25–30). What examples of caring, love, and compassion! Their sacrifice can teach us all about the value of servanthood.                                            —DB

## Hard of Hearing

*So Eli told Samuel, "Go and lie down, and*
*if he calls you, say, 'Speak, LORD, for your*
*servant is listening.'" So Samuel went and*
*lay down in his place.* —1 SAMUEL 3:9

Joshua, a precocious two-year-old, watched his mother baking cookies. "Please, may I have one?" he asked hopefully. "Not before supper," his mother replied. Joshua ran tearfully to his room, then reappeared with this message: "Jesus just told me it's okay to have a cookie now." "Jesus didn't tell me!" his mother retorted, to which Joshua replied, "You must not have been listening!"

Joshua's motivation was wrong, but he was absolutely right about two things: God longs to speak to us, and we need to listen.

In 1 Samuel 3, another young boy learned those same ageless principles. When Samuel followed Eli's counsel and prayed, "Speak, LORD, for your servant is listening," he was open to receiving God's powerful message (v. 9). Like Samuel, we long to hear God speaking to us but often fail to discern His voice.

As a result of neglect and nonstop activity, some of us have become "hard of hearing." We need a "spiritual hearing aid." There is one in Samuel's prayer: "Speak, for your servant is listening" (v. 10). This humble attitude is a real help for the spiritually hard of hearing.                                    —JY

## A Mother's Strength

*She speaks with wisdom, and faithful
instruction is on her tongue.* —PROVERBS 31:26

My wife Carolyn and I were walking in a park one morning when we spotted a mother squirrel scurrying along a power line with her baby in her mouth. She delivered the little squirrel to a new nest she had built in a tree. Back and forth she scampered until she had deposited all six of her babies in their new home. "Being a mother is hard work!" Carolyn mused.

Indeed it is. How essential it is that a human mother takes care of her children—spiritually and otherwise! Of all concerns, the care for her soul is the greatest—to grow in wisdom and in the knowledge of God.

Susanna Wesley was a busy mother with nineteen children, yet she set aside time each day to meet with God. Some days she spent that time in a chair with her apron over her head, praying.

The woman described in Proverbs 31 placed a high value on wisdom, kindness, and a respect for the Lord (vv. 26, 30). How amazing are women who share their wisdom, show kindness, and who seek above all to honor the Lord!                     —DR

## "Standing Up on the Inside!"

*I urge you, brothers and sisters, in view of*
*God's mercy, to offer your bodies as a living*
*sacrifice, holy and pleasing to God—this is*
*your true and proper worship.* —ROMANS 12:1

I heard about a mother who was frustrated by the behavior of her young boy. She told him again and again to do something, but he refused to obey. Finally, in exasperation she plopped him into a chair and insisted that he stay put or else. He didn't budge an inch, but with a determined look on his face he piped up, "I may be sitting down on the outside, but I'm standing up on the inside!"

That attitude could describe the way some people serve Christ. They submit to God's will outwardly and comply with some of the commands of Scripture. They go through the motions of religious activity, but their hearts aren't in it. They've never come to the place where they realize that there is real joy and satisfaction in serving Jesus.

Knowing that the Lord has saved us by His grace, keeps us by His power, and overshadows us with His love, we should have a genuine desire to do God's "good, pleasing, and perfect will" (Romans 12:2).

Don't be a Christian who is sitting down on the outside but standing up on the inside.          —RD

## From Difficulties to Praise

*When anxiety was great within me, your*
*consolation brought me joy.* —PSALM 94:19

As I awaited the train for my weekly commute, negative thoughts crowded my mind—worry over debt, unkind remarks, helplessness in the face of a recent injustice done to a family member. By the time the train arrived, I was in a terrible mood.

On the train, another thought came to mind: write a note to God, giving Him my lament. After I finished pouring out my complaints, I pulled out my phone and listened to the praise songs on my playlist. Soon my bad mood had completely changed.

Without knowing it, I was following a pattern set by the writer of Psalm 94. The psalmist first poured out his complaints: "Rise up, Judge of the earth; pay back to the proud what they deserve. . . . Who will rise up for me against the wicked?" (Psalm 94:2, 16.) He spoke passionately to God about injustice done to widows and orphans. Following the lament, the psalmist transitioned into praise: "But the LORD has become my fortress" (v. 22).

God invites us to take our laments to Him. He can turn our difficulties into praise.                     —LW

## The Power of Faithfulness

*"Do not fear any of those things which you are about to suffer. . . . Be faithful until death, and I will give you the crown of life."* —REVELATION 2:10 NKJV

Before leaving home to work on a sailing ship, J. H. Crowell promised his mother he would stay true to Jesus. He was the only Christian among a crew of twelve, and the other sailors began to taunt him. They poured buckets of water on his head, but they couldn't put out the fire in his soul. Their persecution increased until finally they tied a rope around his waist and threw him overboard. Thinking he would drown, he asked God to forgive his tormentors, and he pleaded with them to send his body home to his mother. "Tell her I was faithful and died for Jesus!" he said.

As they pulled him back on deck, many of the sailors realized he had something they didn't have. Holy Spirit conviction came upon several of them—including the captain—and they turned to God for salvation.

Christ's admonition to be "faithful until death" (Revelation 2:10 NKJV) came when early believers faced intense persecution—costing some their lives. Through their faithfulness, however, the entire Western world was soon touched by their witness and the preaching of the gospel.

That's the kind of faithfulness that can reach our world for Jesus.        —HB

## Created for Relationship

*The LORD God said, "It is not good for*
*the man to be alone. I will make a helper*
*suitable for him." —GENESIS 2:18*

There's a growing "rent-a-family" industry in many
countries to meet the needs of lonely people. Some
use the service to maintain appearances, so that at a
social event they can appear to have a happy family.
Some hire actors to impersonate estranged relatives,
so that they can feel, if briefly, a familial connection.

This trend reflects a basic truth: humans are created for relationship. In the creation story found in
Genesis, God looks at each thing He has made and
sees that it is "very good" (1:31). But when God con-
siders Adam, He says, "It is not good for the man to
be alone" (2:18). The human needed another human.

The Bible doesn't just tell us about our need for
connection. It also tells us where to find relationships:
among Jesus's followers. Jesus, at His death, told His
friend John to consider Christ's mother as his own.
They would be family to each other even after Jesus
was gone (John 19:26–27). And Paul instructed believers to treat others like parents and siblings (1 Timothy 5:1–2). The psalmist tells us that part of God's
redemptive work in the world is to put "the lonely in
families" (Psalm 68:6), and God designed the church
as one of the best places to do this.

Thanks be to God, who has made us for relationship and given us His people to be our family! —AP

## Acts of Kindness

*In Joppa there was a disciple named Tabitha
(in Greek her name is Dorcas); she was always
doing good and helping the poor.* —ACTS 9:36

"Estera, you got a present from our friend Helen!"
my mom told me when she got home from work. We
didn't have much, so receiving a present in the mail
was like a second Christmas. I felt loved, remembered, and valued by God through Helen.

The poor widows Tabitha made clothes for must
have felt the same way. A disciple of Jesus living in
Joppa, she was well known for her acts of kindness.
She was "always doing good and helping the poor"
(Acts 9:36). Then she got sick and died. Peter was
visiting a nearby city, so two believers went after him
and begged him to come to Joppa.

When Peter arrived, the widows Tabitha had helped
showed him the evidence of her kindness—"the robes
and other clothing that [she] had made" (v. 39). Led
by the Holy Spirit, Peter prayed and God brought her
back to life! The result of God's kindness was that
"this became known all over Joppa, and many people
believed in the Lord" (v. 42).

As we're kind to those around us, may they turn
their thoughts to God and feel valued by Him.

—EPE

## Learning to Lament

*Yet this I call to mind and therefore I*
*have hope.* —LAMENTATIONS 3:21

On February 14, 1884, Theodore Roosevelt's wife, Alice, died giving birth to their daughter, also named Alice. Roosevelt was so distraught that he never spoke of his wife again. But reminders of her absence haunted the family. Because the newborn had the same name as her mother, she was called "Sister"—never Alice. On Valentine's Day, the holiday for sweethearts, few in the Roosevelt household felt inclined to celebrate it or Sister's birthday. Broken hearts made moods strained and stoic.

Burying our feelings doesn't help, but prayerful grieving can. Jeremiah's heart was broken by Israel's disobedience and the Babylonian captivity that followed. Memories of Jerusalem's destruction haunted him (Lamentations 1–2). Yet he had learned to lament. He identified what caused his grief, began to pray, and let his tears flow. Soon his focus shifted from his loss to the steadfast grace of God's provision. "Because of the LORD's great love we are not consumed, for his compassions never fail. They are new every morning; great is your faithfulness" (3:22–23). Grief can give way to thankfulness.

Learning to lament can give us a fresh vision of hope and begin the process of healing and restoration.                                    —DF

## His Good Purpose

*We know that in all things God works for the good of those who love him, who have been called according to his purpose.* —ROMANS 8:28

Romans 8:28—how easily and how often this Bible reference rolls off our tongues! But perhaps we need to grasp more fully what this verse is really saying.

Randy Alcorn, in a book he coauthored with his wife, Nanci, offers some insights on Romans 8:28: "God causes all things to work together for good" (NASB). Randy points out that it doesn't say each individual thing is good but that God works them together for good.

Recalling his boyhood days, Randy tells how he often watched his mother bake cakes. One day when she had all the ingredients set out, he sneaked a taste of each one. Except for the sugar, they all tasted horrible. Then his mother stirred them together and put the batter in the oven. "It didn't make sense to me," he recalls, "that the combination of individually distasteful things produced such a tasty product."

Randy concludes that God likewise "takes all the undesirable stresses in our lives, mixes them together, puts them under the heat of crisis, and produces a perfect result."

Let's look beyond our immediate circumstances and remember that God has an ultimate good purpose.                                                —JY

## Wipe Away Tears

*"'He will wipe every tear from their eyes.*
*There will be no more death' or mourning*
*or crying or pain, for the old order of things*
*has passed away."* —REVELATION 21:4

I had just finished preaching on the heartaches of life when a couple approached me. The woman told me about the burden they bore as a family. Their young son had severe physical problems, and the strain of the constant care of this needy little guy, coupled with the heartache of knowing they couldn't improve his situation, sometimes felt unbearable.

As the couple shared with tears in their eyes, their little daughter stood with them. Seeing their obvious hurt, the girl reached up and gently wiped the tears from her mother's cheek. It was a simple gesture of love and compassion, and a profound display of concern from one so young.

Our tears often blur our sight and prevent us from seeing clearly. In those moments, it can be an encouragement to someone who cares enough to love us in our pain and struggles.

Even though friends can be a help, only Christ can reach beyond our tears and touch the deep hurts of our hearts. His comfort can carry us through the struggles of our lives until that day when God himself wipes away every tear from our eyes (Revelation 21:4). —BC

# A Mother's Sacrifice

*"So now I give him to the LORD. For his whole life he will be given over to the LORD."* —1 SAMUEL 1:28

It's often difficult for parents to "let go" of their children, allowing them to be independent. This is especially true of mothers. They like to keep their children close as long as possible.

My wife and I first experienced this when our two older girls moved on to life on their own (college and marriage). It was extremely tough for Sue and me to see our "little girls" leave home.

But imagine letting go when your child is very young, as Hannah did with Samuel. Today, that kind of sacrifice is inconceivable. Yet that's what Hannah and her husband Elkanah did.

Hannah's sacrifice was a remarkable example of complete trust in God. That's why she could say: "My heart rejoices in the LORD" (1 Samuel 2:1). No bitterness or anger—just total release of her only child to God's work.

Releasing our children to the Lord demands great faith. As they grow up, we need to prayerfully entrust them to God's care. After all, He loves them even more than we do.                    —DB

## Not Good Enough

*"Come now, let us settle the matter," says the
LORD. "Though your sins are like scarlet, they
shall be as white as snow."* —ISAIAH 1:18

A friend told me recently of a young mother who was
trying to explain her father's death to her four-year-
old. The girl wondered where Grandpa was. "I'm
sure he's in heaven," the mother answered, "because
he was very good." The girl replied sadly, "I guess I
won't be in heaven." "Why not?" her mother asked
in surprise. "'Cause I'm not very good."

The story saddened me, as I'm saddened when I
hear of others who believe they must be very good
to get into heaven, especially since we all know deep
down in our hearts that we're not very good at all.

Perhaps like this little girl you're thinking about
your sins and asking, "What must I do to get to
heaven?" The answer has already been given: Jesus,
by His death, has paid in full the price of your sins,
no matter how sordid, tawdry, or shameful they may
be. Your salvation is free.

God promises, "Though your sins are like scarlet,
they shall be as white as snow" (Isaiah 1:18).

No one is good enough to get into heaven. Eternal
life is a gift. Receive Jesus by faith.          —DR

## Finding Purpose

*If anyone speaks, they should do so as one
who speaks the very words of God. If anyone
serves, they should do so with the strength
God provides, so that in all things God may be
praised through Jesus Christ.* —1 PETER 4:11

On a hot day in western Texas, my niece Vania saw a
woman standing by a stoplight and holding up a sign.
As she drove closer, she tried to read what the sign
said, assuming it was a request for food or money.
Instead, she was surprised to see these three words:

"You Have Purpose"

God has created each of us for a specific purpose.
Primarily that purpose is to bring honor to Him, and
one way we do that is by meeting the needs of others
(1 Peter 4:10–11).

A mother of young children may find purpose in
wiping runny noses and telling her kids about Jesus.
A woman who has lost her sight still finds purpose
in praying for her children and grandchildren and
influencing them to trust God.

Psalm 139 says that before we were born "all the
days ordained for [us] were written in [His] book"
(v. 16). We are "fearfully and wonderfully made" to
bring glory to our Creator (v. 14).

Never forget: You have purpose!           —CHK

## Arms of Love

*Dear children, let us not love with
words or speech but with actions
and in truth.* —1 JOHN 3:18

Many college students go on summer mission trips.
But rarely does one do what Mallery Thurlow did.
Mallery, a student at Cornerstone University in
Grand Rapids, went to Haiti to help distribute food.
One day a mother showed up at the distribution center with a sick infant in her arms. The woman was
out of options. The baby needed surgery, but no one
would perform it. Without intervention, the baby
would die. Mallery took the baby into her arms—
and into her heart.

After returning to the United States, Mallery searched
for someone to operate on the child. Most doctors held
out little hope. Finally, the baby was granted a visa
to leave Haiti, and Mallery went back to get her.
Detroit Children's Hospital donated the $100,000
surgery, and it was successful. A life was saved.

It's unlikely that we will have such a dramatic impact on others. Yet challenged by this student's willingness, we can find ways to provide help. She didn't
let circumstances, youth, or inconvenience stop her
from saving a life.

Like Mallery, we are called to love "with actions
and in truth" (1 John 3:18). Who needs you to be
God's arms of love today?                    —DB

# Hating the "Wolves"

*Let those who love the LORD hate evil, for he guards the lives of his faithful ones and delivers them from the hand of the wicked.* —PSALM 97:10

Nineteenth-century pastor Henry Ward Beecher told of a mother in American frontier country who was washing clothes beside a stream. Her only child was playing nearby, but not near enough. A wolf snatched the child and killed it. Heartbroken, she picked up the lifeless body, drew it close to her heart, and tenderly carried it home. Beecher concluded, "Oh, how that mother hated wolves!" Understandably, she detested them because of what they had done to her beloved child.

Every Christian parent should feel that way about evil. Like a wild wolf, it can destroy children. Even mothers and fathers who are careful to guard their youngsters from physical harm don't notice the sinful forces that threaten the spiritual welfare of their boys and girls. They leave them unprotected. Our children's friends, their internet habits, the programs they view can all be problematic if parents are not diligent. If any of these influences are evil, they become a deadly threat. Like the psalmist, we must determine—and help our children say, "I will have nothing to do with what is evil" (Psalm 101:4).

Just as the mother in Beecher's story hated wolves, we as parents need to hate evil with that same passion.

—RD

# A Child's Wonder

*They may arise and declare [God's laws]
to their children, that they may set their
hope in God.* —PSALM 78:6–7 NKJV

In nineteenth-century Scotland, a young mother observed her three-year-old son's inquisitive nature. It seemed he was curious about everything that moved or made a noise. James Clerk Maxwell would carry his boyhood wonder with him into a remarkable career in science. He went on to do groundbreaking work in electricity and magnetism. Years later, Albert Einstein would say of Maxwell's work that it was "the most fruitful that physics has experienced since the time of Newton."

From early childhood, religion touched all aspects of Maxwell's life. As a committed Christian, he prayed: "Teach us to study the works of Thy hands . . . and strengthen our reason for Thy service." The boyhood cultivation of Maxwell's spiritual life and curiosity resulted in a lifetime of using science in service to the Creator.

The community of faith has always had the responsibility to nurture the talent of the younger generation and to orient their lives to the Lord.

Finding ways to encourage children's love for learning while establishing them in the faith is an important investment in the future.          —DF

## God Remembers

*God remembered Noah and all the wild
animals and the livestock that were with
him in the ark, and he sent a wind over the
earth, and the waters receded.* —GENESIS 8:1

A Chinese festival called Qing Ming is a time to express grief for lost relatives. Customs include grooming gravesites and taking walks with loved ones in the countryside. Legend has it that it began when a youth's rude and foolish behavior resulted in the death of his mother. So he decided that henceforth he would visit her grave every year to remember what she had done for him. Sadly, it was only after her death that he remembered her.

How differently God deals with us! In Genesis, we read how the flood destroyed the world. Only those who were with Noah in the ark remained alive. But God remembered them (8:1) and sent a wind to dry the waters so they could leave the ark.

God also remembered Hannah when she prayed for a son (1 Samuel 1:19). He gave her a child, Samuel.

God remembers us wherever we are. Our concerns are His concerns. Our pain is His pain. Commit your challenges and difficulties to Him. He is the all-seeing God who remembers us as a mother remembers her children, and He waits to meet our needs.        CPH

## Reach Out

*Jesus answered him, "Truly, I tell you, today*
*you will be with me in paradise." —*LUKE 23:43

Throughout His earthly ministry, Jesus reached out to the sick, sorrowing, and distressed. Even as He was dying on the cross, He spoke words of hope to a man who repented after bitterly mocking Him just moments before (Matthew 27:44). What joy that rebel must have felt when the Savior assured him that on that very day he would be with Him in paradise!

I know a mother who even on her deathbed continued to express her love for her rebellious son, praying for his salvation. Years later, he became terminally ill. He was afraid, because he knew he deserved God's wrath. He thought he was too bad to be forgiven. But a relative reminded him of his mother's deathbed prayers. This gave him hope. He concluded that if his mother forgave him, God surely would. He placed his trust in Christ and died peacefully.

As we near death, we may not have opportunity to express words of forgiveness and hope. But right now we can reach out in love to others by praying for them, showing them kindness, and encouraging them to put their trust in Christ.          —HVL

## Respect for Life

*I praise you because I am fearfully and
wonderfully made; your works are wonderful,
I know that full well.* —PSALM 139:14

In Psalm 139, David describes God as fashioning his tiny body together in the darkness of his mother's womb. God loved David before he ever existed.

God designed the person David was to be, and He brought that person into being according to His predetermined plan. In this psalm, David used the intriguing metaphor of a journal in which God first wrote His plan and then brought that plan into fruition through His handiwork in the womb: "Your eyes saw my unformed body; all the days ordained for me were written in your book before one of them came to be" (v. 16).

What was true of David is true of you. You are special—along with everyone else in the world.

This being true, we must be pro-life in the purest sense of the word. We are to respect and cherish all human life: the born and those still in the womb; winsome children and weary seniors; the wealthy executive and the financially destitute. All persons are unique productions of our Creator's genius. With David, let's exclaim: "I praise you because I am fearfully and wonderfully made" (v. 14).          —DR

# Not Forgotten

*"Can a mother forget the baby at her breast and have no compassion on the child she has borne? Though she may forget, I will not forget you!"* —ISAIAH 49:15

At her mother's fiftieth birthday celebration, firstborn daughter Kukua recounted what her mother had done for her. The times were hard, Kukua remembered, and funds were scarce. But her single mother deprived herself of personal comfort, selling her precious jewelry and other possessions to put Kukua through high school. With tears in her eyes, Kukua said that no matter how difficult things were, her mother never abandoned her or her siblings.

God compared His love for His people with a mother's love for her child. When the people of Israel felt abandoned by God during their exile, they complained: "The LORD has forsaken me, the Lord has forgotten me" (Isaiah 49:14). But God said, "Can a mother forget the baby at her breast and have no compassion on the child she has borne? Though she may forget, I will not forget you!" (v. 15).

When we feel abandoned by society, family, and friends, God does not abandon us. The Lord says, "I have engraved you on the palms of my hands" (v. 16) to indicate how much He knows and protects us. Even if people forsake us, God will never forsake His own. —LD

# Under New Orders

*Jesus replied: "'Love the Lord your God with*
*all your heart and with all your soul and*
*with all your mind.'"* —MATTHEW 22:37

Herman Wouk's World War II novel *The Caine Mutiny*
contains an excellent illustration of what happens
when someone becomes a follower of God.

In the novel, a young man from an influential
family has enlisted in the Navy. On the day of his
induction, his mother drops him off in her fancy car
and kisses him goodbye. He shakes hands with the
guard as he enters the building, and the door closes
behind him.

His mother, suddenly worried that he might not
have enough money, rushes up to the door. But the
guard politely stops her. When she demands entrance,
he refuses to let her in. She can see her son standing inside the door. "He's my son!" she cries. The
guard gently removes her hand from the knob and
says softly, "I know, ma'am, but he belongs to Uncle
Sam now."

When we believe in Jesus Christ and become His
followers, we are under new authority. Now we belong to Him. What was once important to us loses its
significance. Our new desire is to love and serve the
Lord with all our heart (Deuteronomy 6:5–6). Have
you joined His ranks?                              —DE

## Marriage God's Way

*That is why a man leaves his father and*
*mother and is united to his wife, and*
*they become one flesh.* —GENESIS 2:24

The movie *The Princess Bride* has a wedding scene in which the marrying minister says, "Marriage . . . is what brings us together today."

While that line was meant to be humorous, he spoke a great truth. Marriage is indeed a great unifier. It is a solemn, respectable institution created by God himself, and it joins together a man and a woman in amazing oneness.

Marriage creates one new family out of two: Adam said, "This is now bone of my bones and flesh of my flesh. . . . That is why a man leaves his father and mother and is united to his wife" (Genesis 2:23–24).

It provides a pure outlet for a divinely designed desire: "Since sexual immorality is occurring, each man should have sexual relations with his own wife, and each woman with her own husband " (1 Corinthians 7:2).

It forms a mutually helpful team: "Her husband has full confidence in her and lacks nothing of value. She brings him good, not harm, all the days of her life" (Proverbs 31:11–12).

Celebrate marriage for the ways it brings us together in God's name.                                    —DB

# The Mom Box

*From infancy you have known the Holy
Scriptures, which are able to make
you wise for salvation through faith
in Christ Jesus.* —2 TIMOTHY 3:15

Each Christmas I give both of my daughters a "Mom box." Each box contains items to encourage them to be the best mothers they can be. It might have craft books or special projects, devotional books, first-aid kits, recipes—and often something personal like bubble bath for a little pampering after a tough day of mothering! It's become a tradition that Rosemary and Tanya have looked forward to every year for the last decade.

Encouraging our children to be good parents can begin even earlier. The best way is to start equipping them with the Word of God while they are still young.

The apostle Paul wrote that "from infancy" Timothy had known "the Holy Scriptures" (2 Timothy 3:15). And 2 Timothy 1:5 mentions the "sincere faith" of Timothy's mother and grandmother. That faithful teaching and spiritual influence helped to enable Timothy to be a godly man.

The Bible is our richest resource to help us raise children who will know and love Jesus. Nothing is more essential than "the Holy Scriptures" to equip them for all of life's challenges.

What are you doing to make the next generation "wise for salvation through faith" (3:15)?     —CHK

## Tangible Love

*When Jesus saw his mother there, and the*
*disciple whom he loved standing nearby, he said*
*to her, "Woman, here is your son."* —JOHN 19:26

The Chester Beatty Library in Dublin, Ireland, houses a wonderful collection of ancient Bible fragments. One very small fragment is a portion of John 19. This piece of John's gospel describes the moment, as Jesus was being crucified, when He spoke to His mother in a display of love and concern for her. The words are from verse 26, where we read, "When Jesus saw his mother there, and the disciple whom he loved standing nearby, he said to her, 'Woman, here is your son!'"

As I stared at that ancient fragment, it struck me afresh how tangible Jesus's love was for His mother and friend. He let the world know of His love and affection by showing His concern that Mary be cared for by His friend John when He was gone. Hanging on the cross, Jesus said to John, "'Behold your mother!' And from that hour that disciple took her to his own home" (v. 27 NKJV).

Let's make this our note to Mom—one tangible way to say thank you for her love and her importance in our lives.                                        —BC

# Give Them Love!

*Children are a heritage from the LORD,
offspring a reward from him.*
—PSALM 127:3

A wealthy woman was so caught up in her love for worldly pleasures that she had little time for her daughter. Even when her child became seriously ill, the mother's attitude remained the same. She felt she could shower her with gifts to compensate for her lack of attention.

Once, she left the girl in the care of a nurse and went to Europe. While there, she remembered her daughter's birthday and sent her a rare and beautiful vase. When it arrived, the nurse brought it to the girl. Refusing even to look at the present, the girl cried, "Take it away!" And then, as if her mother were in the room, she tearfully exclaimed, "Oh, Mother! Don't send me any more things. I have enough things. I want YOU!"

Shallow, outward pretenses of affection are not enough for our children. They can't be bought. Even though they may express great interest in gifts, they need our love and tender concern above all else. What will meet their deepest need is sharing, teaching, and caring.

Should we give gifts to our children? Of course. But most important, let's give our children the gift of love.                                    —HB

## How to Begin the Day

*He will respond to the prayer of the destitute;*
*he will not despise their plea.* —PSALM 102:17

I read about a five-minute rule a mother had for her children. They had to be ready for school and gather together five minutes before it was time to leave each day.

They would gather around Mom, and she would pray for each one by name, asking for the Lord's blessing on their day. Even neighborhood kids would be included in the prayer circle if they happened to stop by. One of the children later said that she learned from this experience how crucial prayer is to her day.

The writer of Psalm 102 knew the importance of prayer. This psalm is labeled, "A prayer of an afflicted person who has grown weak. . . ." He cried out, "Hear my prayer, LORD . . . ; when I call, answer me quickly" (vv. 1–2). God looks down "from his sanctuary on high, from heaven he viewed the earth" (v. 19).

God wants to hear from you. No matter what your method, talk to the Lord each day. Your example may have a big impact on your family or someone close to you.                                              —AC

## Ike's Anger Problem

*Better a patient person than a warrior,*
*one with self-control than one who*
*takes a city.* —PROVERBS 16:32

On June 6, 1944, Dwight D. Eisenhower, Supreme
Allied Commander, was the most powerful man
on earth. Under his authority, the largest amphib-
ious army ever assembled prepared to liberate the
Nazi-dominated continent of Europe. How was
Eisenhower able to lead such a vast army? Part of
the answer can be linked to his remarkable skill in
working with different kinds of people.

What many do not know, however, is that Ike
hadn't always gotten along with others. As a boy,
he often got into fistfights at school. But fortunately,
he had a caring mother who instructed him in God's
Word. One time, when she was bandaging his hands
after an angry outburst, she quoted Proverbs 16:32,
"Better a patient person than a warrior, one with
self-control than one who takes a city." Years later,
Eisenhower wrote, "I have always looked back on
that conversation as one of the most valuable moments of my life."

Inevitably, each of us will at times be tempted to
lash out in anger. Yet through God's work in our lives
we can learn to control our anger. What better way to
influence people than through a gentle spirit. —DF

# The Card Sender

*Therefore encourage one another and
build each other up, just as in fact you
are doing.* —1 THESSALONIANS 5:11

There are several ways to encourage others. Some do it verbally—offering a word of comfort or encouragement. Others find that saying the right words is tough, so they send their words of cheer by way of cards.

We can have a wonderful ministry as card-senders. On the surface, a person may seem fine—especially at church. But beneath that "doing great" exterior may be a spirit so bowed down that it's ready to give up hope. A card can help.

Let me illustrate. Susan's personal problems were enormous. Tough issues from the past and current problems with money and relationships troubled her greatly. Somehow, she kept up a good front at work.

At Christmastime, she received a card from her boss with these handwritten words: "I don't know what we'd do without you. Thank you for being so competent and helpful." Later she commented, "I framed that card! It's like a sign that says, 'You're okay!'"

So send that card. Write that note. Offer that word of encouragement in the name of Christ. You may be giving someone just the lift he or she needs.     —DE

# The Real Prize

*Husbands, love your wives, just as
Christ loved the church and gave
himself up for her.* —EPHESIANS 5:25

I've been amazed at the impact that my wife, Martie, has had on the lives of our kids. Likewise, I know for certain that my character and faith have been shaped and molded by my mom, Corabelle. Let's face it, where would we be without our wives and mothers?

It reminds me of one of my favorite memories in sports history. Phil Mickelson walked up the eighteenth fairway at the Masters Golf Tournament in 2010 after his final putt to clinch one of golf's most coveted prizes for the third time. Right away, he made a beeline through the crowd to his wife, who was battling life-threatening cancer. They embraced, and the camera caught a tear running down Phil's cheek as he held his wife close for a long time.

Our wives need to experience the kind of sacrificial, selfless love that has been shown to us by the Lover of our souls. As Paul put it, "Husbands, love your wives, just as Christ loved the church and gave himself up for her" (Ephesians 5:25). Prizes come and go, but it's the people you love—and who love you—that matter most.                              —JS

## "I'll See You over There"

*God will bring with Jesus those who have
fallen asleep in him.* —1 THESSALONIANS 4:14

Every loved one who has died in the Lord will be with
Jesus when He returns to gather His own to himself.
In 1 Thessalonians 4:17, Paul declared that "we who
are still alive and are left will be caught up together
with them." There will be a joyous coming together
of all believers.

This hope burned brightly in my mother's heart
as her life drew to a close. On the day before she
died, my brother and I were called to her bedside.
She quoted some favorite Bible verses and spoke of
"going Home." After we had been with her for several hours, she urged us not to stay but to go home
and get some rest. As I was about to leave, she said,
"If I don't see you tomorrow, I'll see you over There!"
Those were her last words to me, and they were precious.

Christians don't say a final goodbye! While death
breaks our earthly ties, we know that those who die
as believers are living in the presence of Jesus.

Has death taken a believing loved one from you?
Think of the glorious reunion that awaits you—over
There!                                          —DD

## The Goodness of the Lord

*Oh, how I love your law! I meditate
on it all day long.* —PSALM 119:97

Some years ago, I came across a short essay written by Sir James Barrie, an English baron. In it he gives an intimate picture of his mother, who deeply loved God and His Word and who literally read her Bible to pieces. "It is mine now," Sir James wrote, "and to me the black threads with which she stitched it are a part of the contents."

My mother also loved God's Word. She read and pondered it for sixty years or more. I keep her Bible on my bookshelf in a prominent place. It too is tattered and torn, each stained page marked with her comments and reflections. As a child, I often walked into her room in the morning and found her cradling her Bible in her lap, poring over its words. She did so until the day she could no longer see the words on the page. Her Bible was the most precious book in her possession.

The psalmist wrote, "How sweet are your words to my taste, sweeter than honey to my mouth!" (119:103). Have you tasted the goodness of the Lord?
—DR

## The Courage of Esther

*"Who knows but that you have
come to your royal position for such
a time as this?"* —ESTHER 4:14

At Yad Vashem, Israel's Holocaust museum, my husband and I went to the Righteous Among the Nations garden, which honors those who risked their lives to save Jewish people during the Holocaust. While there, we met a group from the Netherlands. One woman was visiting to see her grandparents' names listed on the large plaques. Intrigued, we asked about her family's story.

Members of a resistance network, the woman's grandparents Rev. Pieter and Adriana Müller took in a two-year-old Jewish boy and passed him off as the youngest of their eight children from 1943–1945.

Moved by the story, we asked, "Did the little boy survive?" An older gentleman in the group stepped forward and proclaimed, "I am that boy!"

The bravery of many to act on behalf of the Jewish people reminds me of Queen Esther. Perhaps she could have avoided the threat of death under King Xerxes's decree to annihilate the Jews around 475 BC by continuing to conceal her ethnicity. But she risked everything to confront her husband and rescue her people.

If we're ever required to speak out against an injustice, may God grant us the courage He gave the Müllers and Queen Esther.                    —LS

## Only a Sketch

*For now we see only a reflection as in a mirror; then we shall see face to face. Now I know in part; then I shall know fully, even as I am fully known.* —1 CORINTHIANS 13:12

In *The Weight of Glory*, C. S. Lewis tells of a woman who gave birth to a son while confined as a prisoner. Since the boy had never seen the outside world, his mother tried to describe it by making pencil drawings. Later when he and his mother were released from prison, the simple pencil sketches were replaced by the actual images of our beautiful world.

Similarly, the inspired picture the Bible gives us of heaven will someday be replaced by joyful, direct experience. Paul understood that our perception of heaven is limited until the future day when we will be in Christ's presence. "Now we see only a reflection as in a mirror; then we shall see face to face. Now I know in part; then I shall know fully" (1 Corinthians 13:12). Paul's confidence in future glory gave him strength: "I consider that our present sufferings are not worth comparing with the glory that will be revealed in us" (Romans 8:18).

Our current idea of the glories of heaven is only a simple sketch. But Jesus has gone to prepare a place for us (John 14:1–3). The best is yet to come!  —DF

## "Now She Knows Everybody"

*"'He will wipe every tear from their eyes.
There will be no more death' or mourning
or crying or pain, for the old order of things
has passed away."* —REVELATION 21:4

Heaven is a wonderful place. In that glorious land God will forever banish all suffering, pain, disappointment, and tears—including the distresses of Alzheimer's disease. The victims of that disorder become so forgetful that they fail to recognize friends and family, even their own husband or wife. Once-familiar people seem like strangers.

My friend Wilbur C. Rooke shared with me what his eight-year-old grandson said when he heard that Wilbur's wife Myrtle had died after suffering for fifteen years from Alzheimer's. Without hesitation, David exclaimed, "Well, praise the Lord! Grandma's in heaven, and now she knows everybody!"

Wilbur commented, "Little did David know how important his words were, and what they would mean to so many. If you have ever observed loved ones losing their memory, you can relate to how David felt when he exclaimed, 'Now Grandma knows everybody!' His words were a great comfort to those of us who cared the most."

Yes, on that day when we shall all be changed, the mist of forgetfulness will be banished by the sunlight of remembrance.                    —RD

## Correct Them

*"Why do you honor your sons more*
*than me by fattening yourselves on the*
*choice parts of every offering made by*
*my people Israel?"* —1 SAMUEL 2:29

Therapist and mother Lori Gottlieb says that parents who are obsessed with their children's happiness may actually contribute to their becoming unhappy adults. These parents coddle their children, don't equip them to deal with the real world, and neglect disciplining them.

In 1 Samuel, we read that the high priest Eli sometimes looked the other way. We don't know what he was like as a father when his boys were young, but he failed to deal with their behavior as grown men serving in God's temple. They were selfish, lustful, and rebellious—putting their own needs first. When Eli rebuked them, they wouldn't listen. Instead of removing them from service, he let them continue in their sin. Because of his sons' sins and because Eli honored his sons above the Lord (1 Samuel 2:29), the Lord warned Eli that his family would suffer judgment (v. 34; 4:17–18).

As Christian parents, we have the awesome responsibility to lovingly discipline our children (Proverbs 13:24; 29:17; Hebrews 12:9–11). As we impart God's wisdom to them, we have the blessing of helping them develop into responsible, God-fearing adults.                                        —MW

## Keep On Praying

*Far be it from me that I should sin against
the Lord by failing to pray for you.*
—1 SAMUEL 12:23

A godly mother told about her two middle-aged sons who had turned their backs on the Lord. Neither could hold a job. In and out of jail. Tears fell as she told of their terrible language and disregard for the laws of God and man. "I still pray for them every day," she said. "I plead with the Lord not to give up on them—to bring them back to himself. I'm not giving up."

In 1 Samuel 12, we read a story that's both terrible and marvelous. Israel had been rebellious. The people had sinned against the Lord throughout the period of the judges, and now they were demanding a king. To show them their wickedness, Samuel asked the Lord to send thunder and hail on the wheat harvest (vv. 16–18). When the Lord answered, the people were terrified. But Samuel assured them that he would keep on praying for them as they began living under Saul, their new king.

How many times have we wanted to give up praying for someone? Samuel didn't give in to his frustration and disappointment. Let's follow his example. Keep on praying!    —DE

## Questioning God's Love

*"How have you loved us?"*
—MALACHI 1:2

As a teenager, I went through the typical season of rebellion against my mother's authority. My father died before I entered adolescence, so my mom had to navigate these turbulent parenting waters without his help.

I recall thinking that Mom didn't want me to have any fun—and maybe didn't even love me—because she frequently said no. I see now that she said no to activities that weren't good for me precisely because she does love me.

The Israelites questioned how much God loved them because of their captivity in Babylon. But that captivity was God's correction for their continued rebellion. When God sent the prophet Malachi to them, his opening words from the Lord were, "I have loved you" (Malachi 1:2). Israel replied skeptically, as if to say, "Really? How?" But God, through Malachi, reminded them of the way He had demonstrated that love: He had chosen them over the Edomites.

When we are tempted to question God's love during difficult times, let's recall the many ways He's shown us His unfailing love. When we stop to consider His goodness, we find that He is indeed a loving Father.                                  —KH

## Just Kids

*Don't let anyone look down on you because you are young, but set an example for the believers in speech, in conduct, in love, in faith and in purity.* —1 TIMOTHY 4:12

After high school, Darrell Blizzard left the orphanage where he grew up to join the US Army Air Corps. World War II was in full swing, and soon he faced responsibilities usually given to older and more experienced men. He told a reporter years later that a four-mule plow team was the biggest thing he'd driven before he became the pilot of a four-engine B-17. Now in his late eighties, he said, "We were all just kids flying those things."

In the Bible, we find accounts of many people who followed God courageously when they were young. For instance, in a situation of corrupt spiritual leadership, "Samuel ministered before the LORD, even as a child" (1 Samuel 2:18 NKJV). David faced the giant Goliath in spite being just "a youth" (17:33 NKJV). Jesus's mother Mary was most likely very young when she was told she would bear the Son of God. She responded by saying, "May your word to me be fulfilled" (Luke 1:38).

God values each one in His family. In His strength, the young can be bold in their faith, while those who are older can encourage those who are "just kids."

—DM

# The Pure and Gentle Way

*The wisdom that is from above is first pure,*
*then peaceable, gentle, willing to yield, full of*
*mercy and good fruits.* —JAMES 3:17 NKJV

The parents were heartbroken when their young daughter died in an unusual accident. She suffocated when the drawstring of the hood on her jacket became caught in a playground slide. Design flaws in both the clothing and the slide made this an accident waiting to happen.

Some people might have seen in this tragedy an opportunity for a lucrative lawsuit. But the parents refused to sue. In a television interview, the mother said they would have seen any remuneration as "blood money." She and her husband knew that the leaders of the companies involved never intended their products to harm anyone. So the parents appealed to the clothing and slide manufacturers to correct the problems that led to the death of their daughter. Both firms took immediate action. The mother then led a crusade to promote child safety.

Although there may be cases that call for legal action, I was moved by the choice of those parents to follow the pure, peaceable, and gentle way (James 3:17). What an impact we make in our society when we who profess to believe on Jesus follow their example!                                          —HVL

# Open Arms

*"While he was still a long way off, his father
saw him and was filled with compassion
for him; he ran to his son, threw his arms
around him and kissed him."* —LUKE 15:20

At the funeral of former US First Lady Betty Ford,
her son Steven said, "Nineteen years ago when I went
through my alcoholism, my mother . . . gave me one
of the greatest gifts, and that was how to surrender to
God, and to accept the grace of God in my life. And
truly in her arms I felt like the prodigal son coming
home, and I felt God's love through her."

Jesus's parable about a young man who squan-
dered his inheritance and then in humiliation returned
home leaves us amazed at his father's response: "His
father saw him and was filled with compassion for
him; he ran to his son, threw his arms around him
and kissed him" (Luke 15:20). Then he threw him a
party. Why? Because "this son of mine was dead and
is alive again; he was lost and is found" (v. 24).

Steven Ford concluded his tribute with the words,
"Thank you, Mom, for loving us, loving your husband, loving us kids, and loving the nation with the
heart of God."

May God enable us to open our arms to others.

—DM

## The Power of a Compliment

*"I tell you, her many sins have been forgiven—
as her great love has shown. But whoever has
been forgiven little loves little."* —LUKE 7:47

In the incident recorded in Luke 7, Jesus paid a high compliment to a woman who had been hearing nothing but insults. He commended her sorrow over sin and her love for Him. Jesus's words must have given her new hope that her life was valuable.

A woman in our church also experienced the power of a compliment. She's a busy mother, working hard to meet the needs of her family, and she carries several key responsibilities in the church. During a time when her schedule was particularly heavy, she began to feel depressed. It seemed that she was being taken for granted by everyone. Then a bouquet of flowers was delivered to her door. The note said simply, "We just wanted you to know how much we appreciate you. You're a wonderful wife and mother." It was signed, "Your husband and children." She sat down on the floor and wept. And with her tears went her depression.

Have you been taking someone for granted? Not showing appreciation? Thinking mostly about yourself? Today, tell that person he or she is special to you, and give a sincere compliment.                    —DE

## His Arm around Us

*Take my yoke upon you and learn from me,*
*for I am gentle and humble in heart, and you*
*will find rest for your souls.* —MATTHEW 11:29

A Sunday school teacher read Matthew 11:30 to the children in her class, and then asked: "Jesus said, 'My yoke is easy.' Who can tell me what a yoke is?" A boy raised his hand and replied, "A yoke is something they put on the necks of animals so they can help each other."

Then the teacher asked, "What is the yoke Jesus puts on us?" A quiet little girl raised her hand and said, "It is God putting His arm around us."

When Jesus came, He offered an "easy" and "lighter" yoke compared to the yoke of the religious leaders (Matthew 11:30). They had placed "heavy burdens" of laws on the people (Matthew 23:4; Acts 15:10), which no one could possibly keep.

As we humble ourselves and recognize our need for forgiveness, Jesus comes alongside us. He places His yoke on us, freeing us from guilt and giving us His power to live a life that's pleasing to God.

Do you need Jesus's help? He says, "Come to me. . . . Take my yoke upon you and learn from me" (Matthew 11:28–29). He longs to put His arm around you.                    —AC

## The Good Old Days

*I remember the days of long ago; I meditate
on all your works and consider what
your hands have done.* —PSALM 143:5

Sometimes our minds run back through the years and yearn for that better time and place—the "good old days."

But for some, the past harbors only bitter memories. Deep in the night, they ponder their own failures, disillusionments, and fantasies, and they think of the cruel hand life has dealt them.

It's better to remember the past as David did— by contemplating the good that God has done, to "meditate on all [His] works and consider what [His] hands have done" (Psalm 143:5). As we call to mind the lovingkindness of the Lord, we can see His blessings through the years. These are the memories that evoke a deep longing for more of God and more of His tender care. They transform the past into a place of fellowship with our Lord.

I heard a story about an elderly woman who would sit in silence for hours in her rocking chair, eyes gazing off into the far distance. One day her daughter asked, "Mother, what are you thinking about?" Her mother replied softly, "That's just between Jesus and me."

I pray that our memories and meditations would draw us into His presence.                     —DR

## "You've Still Got Me"

*If we have food and clothing, we will be
content with that.* —1 TIMOTHY 6:8

"What's the matter, Mom?" asked the three-year-old boy. Kimberly had just received some disappointing news. She was discouraged, and her son sensed it. After a moment of hesitation, her little boy said, "That's okay, Mom. You've still got me!"

Later she commented, "His confident assurance brought tears as I thought about how fortunate I am. I have a healthy, loving family, caring and supportive friends, a Christ-centered church, food, clothing, and a warm house. I am not just fortunate. Compared with many, I am prosperous!"

Why do we keep thinking about what we don't have rather than what we have? What causes us to let a canceled trip or a lost sale affect us so deeply? When a woman and her husband missed the chance to buy a certain house, I heard her complain, "It ruined my whole life!" Is anything on this earth really that important? When we're tempted to feel that way, we need to remember 1 Timothy 6:8.

Instead of letting life sour over missed acquisitions and lost opportunities, let's examine our hearts and ask the Lord to teach us thankfulness. Then we can truly rejoice in all that He has provided and be content.                                    —DE

## The Parable of the Watch

*Those parts of the body that seem to be weaker
are indispensable.* —1 CORINTHIANS 12:22

In 1 Corinthians 12:12–23 is a principle that encourages believers to serve faithfully wherever God places them in the body of Christ. Even the smallest task is important to the proper functioning of the whole church.

Here's how one woman learned this lesson from her mom. As a child, she came home from school crying because she had been given just a small part in the school play while her friend got the leading role. Her mother took off her watch and put it in the girl's hand. "What do you see?" she asked. "A gold case, a face, and two hands," the youngster replied. Then she opened the watch and asked the same question. "Tiny wheels," she replied. "This watch would be useless," the mom said, "without every part—even the ones you can hardly see." The girl remembered that important lesson throughout her life.

Whether we teach a small Sunday school class, serve as an usher, or work behind the scenes in some other role, every task in the church is essential. And faithfulness in fulfilling it is what God requires.

—HB

## Mom's Finish Line

*I have fought the good fight, I have finished
the race, I have kept the faith.*
—2 TIMOTHY 4:7

When Jeff learned that his mother's health was rapidly declining, he immediately caught a plane to be with her. He sat at her bedside holding her hand, singing hymns, comforting her, and expressing his love for her. She passed away, and at her funeral many told Jeff what a blessing his mother had been. She had finished strong for Christ.

To honor his mother's life, Jeff ran in a marathon. During the race he thanked God for her life and grieved her loss. When he crossed the finish line, Jeff pointed his index finger toward heaven—"Where Mom is," he said. She had honored Christ to the end, which reminded him of the words of the apostle Paul: "I have fought the good fight, I have finished the race, I have kept the faith" (2 Timothy 4:7).

We are involved in a "long-distance race." Let's run in such a way that we may obtain the prize of "an imperishable crown" (1 Corinthians 9:25 NKJV). Nothing could be more desirable than to finish strong for Christ and to be with Him forever.          —DF

## Turn It Off

*Because so many people were coming and going
that they did not even have a chance to eat, he
said to them, "Come with me by yourselves to
a quiet place and get some rest."* —MARK 6:31

When our kids were young, we took a trip to northern Wisconsin to visit my grandparents. They didn't get very good reception on their television. After I had seen our son Scott fiddling with the TV set for a while, he asked with frustration, "What do you do if you can get only one channel and you don't like what's on that one?"

"Try turning it off," I said with a smile. Not exactly the advice he was hoping for.

It's even more difficult to do now, especially when there are so many devices that entertain, inform, and distract us.

Sometimes we do need to just turn it all off and rest our minds for a little while. Jesus often drew aside for a time—especially when He wanted to take time to pray (Matthew 14:13). He encouraged the disciples to step away as well (Mark 6:31). That kind of solitude and time for reflection is beneficial for each of us. In those moments we are able to draw near to God.

Follow the example and wisdom of Christ. Get away by yourself and "get some rest." It will be good for your body, mind, and spirit.                    —CHK

## Self-Made Captains

*Since they did not know the righteousness of God*
*and sought to establish their own, they did not*
*submit to God's righteousness.* —ROMANS 10:3

Donald Grey Barnhouse told the story of a young immigrant who became successful as an author. He made a fortune by writing several volumes, including a Broadway play. With his newfound wealth he bought a yacht. One day he took his aged mother for a cruise on his yacht, which was managed by a crew.

Once on board, he excused himself and went below deck. Shortly he returned, attired in an officer's uniform—hat, coat, and all the trimmings. He said, "See, Mama, I'm a captain!" She looked up at him and said, "Izzie, by me, you is a captain; and by you, you is a captain. But by captains, you is no captain!"

Likewise, a person may dress himself up with good works and say, "I'm good." But by God's standard, he is not good. Paul explained, "There is no one righteous, not even one" (Romans 3:10).

All of us fall short of God's requirement. We must put our faith in the spotless Son of God, who died in our place. Only His sacrifice can make us accepted by the Father and save our soul. There are no self-made Christians.                                        —PVG

## Clean the Closet

*Search me, God, and know my heart; test me
and know my anxious thoughts.* —PSALM 139:23

To this day I can still hear my mother telling me to go
and clean up my room. Dutifully, I would go to my
room to start the process, only to get distracted by
reading the comic book that I was supposed to put
neatly in the stack. But soon the distraction was interrupted by my mother warning that she would be
up in five minutes to inspect the room. Unable to
effectively clean the room in that time, I would pro-
ceed to hide stuff in the closet and then wait for her
to come in—hoping she wouldn't look in the closet.

This reminds me of what many of us do with our
lives. We clean up the outside of our lives hoping that
no one will look into the "closet" where we have
hidden our sins.

The psalmist encourages us to submit to the cleansing inspection of God: "Search me, God, and know
my heart; test me and know my anxious thoughts.
See if there is any offensive way in me, and lead me in
the way everlasting" (Psalm 139:23–24). Let's invite
Him to inspect and cleanse every corner of our lives.
—JS

## We Have Fruit!

*"I gave you a land on which you did not toil
and cities you did not build; and you live in
them and eat from vineyards and olive groves
that you did not plant."* —JOSHUA 24:13

The young mother sighed as she scraped together lunch for her three-year-old daughter. Spying the empty fruit basket on the table in their tiny kitchen, she sighed and said aloud, "If we just had a basket of fruit, I would feel rich!" Her little girl overheard her.

Weeks passed. God sustained the small family. Still, the struggling mom worried. Then one day her little girl bounded into the kitchen. "Look, Mommy, we're rich!" she exclaimed, pointing at the full fruit basket on the table. Nothing had changed except that the family had purchased a bag of apples.

When Joshua, the leader of the Israelites, was about to die, he shared a message from the Lord that recounted all God had done for them. He said, "[God] gave you a land on which you did not toil and cities you did not build; and you live in them and eat from vineyards and olive groves that you did not plant" (Joshua 24:13).

Today if you visit the family above, you'll find a bowl of fruit in their kitchen. It reminds them of God's goodness and how a three-year-old infused her family with faith, joy, and perspective.          —TG

## Playing with Fire

*"Whoever has my commands and keeps them is the one who loves me. The one who loves me will be loved by my Father, and I too will love them and show myself to them."* —JOHN 14:21

When I was a young boy, my mom warned me never to play with fire. Yet one day I decided to see what would happen if I did. Taking a book of matches and some paper, I went into the backyard to experiment. I knelt on the ground, struck the match, and set the paper aflame.

Suddenly I saw my mother approaching. Not wanting to get caught, I put my legs over the flames to hide what I was doing. But Mom shouted, "Denny, move your legs! There's a fire!" Fortunately, I moved my legs quickly enough and was not burned. I realized then that my mother's rule was not to spoil my fun but because of her concern to keep me safe.

Sometimes we don't understand the reasons behind God's commands—thinking He's setting up rules and regulations to keep us from enjoying ourselves. But God asks us to obey Him because He has our best interests at heart. As we obey, we "remain in his love" and are filled with joy (John 15:10–11).

So when God warns us not to sin, let's listen. He wants to protect us from "playing with fire" and getting burned.                                         —DF

## It's No Sin to Say No

*At daybreak, Jesus went out to a solitary place. The people were looking for him and when they came to where he was, they tried to keep him from leaving them.* —LUKE 4:42

While Jesus was here on earth, He sometimes found it necessary to say no. In Luke 4, for example, He denied a request to stay in Capernaum. On other occasions He refused to accept His brothers' plan (John 7:1–9), He turned down a request to give a miraculous sign to doubters (Mark 8:11–13), and He rejected Satan's ideas (Matthew 4:1–10). Jesus never fell into sin, and He never became too busy, because He knew how to say no.

A young mother I know became overwhelmed because she couldn't say no. With two preschoolers and another child on the way, she let herself become so busy in church that she endangered her health. One morning she collapsed. Her doctor told her in no uncertain terms to slow down! She did, and she was soon fine.

Do you think you have to say yes to every worthy request? But you're neglecting your family. You're tired and irritable. You no longer look forward to Sundays. Remember, it's no sin to say no!      —DE

# Not What I Planned

*Be still before the LORD and wait patiently
for him; do not fret when people succeed
in their ways, when they carry out their
wicked schemes.* —PSALM 37:7

This isn't the way I expected my life to be. I wanted to marry at nineteen, have a half dozen children, and settle into life as a wife and mother. But instead I went to work, married in my forties, and never had children. For a number of years, I was hopeful that Psalm 37:4 might be for me a God-guaranteed promise: "He will give you the desires of your heart."

But God doesn't always "bring it to pass" (v. 5 NKJV), and unmet desires stir up occasional sadness. Like mine, your life may have turned out differently than you planned. A few thoughts from Psalm 37 may be helpful.

We learn from verses four and five that the keys are to take "delight in the LORD" and "commit [our] way to the LORD" (NKJV). Bible teacher Herbert Lockyer Sr. explains that we are to roll our burdens on the Lord "as one who lays upon the shoulders of one stronger than himself a burden he is not able to bear."

When we confidently entrust everything to God, we can "rest in the LORD" (v. 7 NKJV), for He is bringing about His best for our lives.                    —AC

## The Supreme Motive

*So that you may live a life worthy of the*
*Lord and please him in every way: bearing*
*fruit in every good work, growing in the*
*knowledge of God.* —COLOSSIANS 1:10

A little first-grader beamed with satisfaction as he handed me a spelling test on which his teacher had written a large "100—Good work!" The boy said, "I showed this to Dad and Mother because I knew it would please them." His desire to make Dad and Mom happy was obviously an important motivating factor in his life.

When Paul used the simile of a soldier who serves with single-minded devotion in order to please his commanding officer (2 Timothy 2:3), he wanted Timothy to know the supreme reason for serving God, even when the going gets tough. Wholehearted devotion, marked by hard work and careful attention to God's standards, brings great glory to the Lord when it comes from a yielded, loving heart.

Our Savior, who in His humanity shrank from the prospect of being made the sin-offering for mankind, nevertheless prayed, "Not my will, but yours be done" (Luke 22:42). His supreme motive was His desire to please His Father. That should be our incentive too. —HVL

## On Having Peace with God

*Therefore, since we have been justified through
faith, we have peace with God through
our Lord Jesus Christ.* —ROMANS 5:1

Dr. F. B. Meyer tells of an experience he had with a
woman in England. He had been speaking to her of
receiving God's grace by faith. She could not understand his message, and told him so. At tea with her a
day later, he suddenly turned and said, "Madam, may
I please have a cup of tea?" She looked at his table
and said, "Why, Dr. Meyer, you have a cup of tea."
After he did this three times, she said, "Oh, Dr. Meyer,
I see it all now. You are telling me that the Lord's
blessing, power, and forgiveness is right here before
me, yet I keep asking for it, instead of taking it and
finding peace through our Lord Jesus Christ."

Some people say, "I prayed and prayed that God
would receive me when I came earnestly seeking salvation, but I still do not know if I have it!" The very
first time you came, He received you! For He has
promised, "Whoever comes to me I will never drive
away" (John 6:37). You can't make peace, He has
made it—all you have to do is accept it!          —HB

## Calm in a Crisis

*This is what the Sovereign LORD, the Holy*
*One of Israel, says: "In repentance and*
*rest is your salvation."* —ISAIAH 30:15

Some people panic when they encounter a crisis. If they have an automobile accident, a financial reversal, or a problem with the children, they lose all perspective. They run from person to person, pouring out their story and asking what to do. They seem to be unable to cope with adversity when it strikes.

This doesn't have to be the case for Christians. They can maintain composure in the most critical moments because they believe in God and know that He is in control of this world. They can derive assurance from the many promises of Scripture. Furthermore, the indwelling Holy Spirit reminds them of the truths of God's Word to give them strength. Yes, though outward circumstances may be turbulent, the believer's heart can remain calm.

If we trust God and claim His promises, we can become like the depths of a storm-tossed lake. Although the winds of crisis may surge violently about us, our hearts can remain at peace, secure in the wise purposes of an all-loving God. When testing comes or trouble arises, we must keep trusting in Him. That's how to be calm in the midst of a crisis.          —DE

# The Appeal of the Forbidden

*When the woman saw that the fruit of the tree
was good for food and pleasing to the eye, and
also desirable for gaining wisdom, she took some
and ate it. She also gave some to her husband,
who was with her, and he ate it.* —GENESIS 3:6

The story is told about a young boy who spied a beautiful vase in a china cabinet and asked his nanny for it. When she refused, he began crying. His mother came to see what the problem was. "What do you want, darling?" she asked. He pointed to the vase, so she gave it to him. Soon he was crying again. "Now what does my little darling want?" the mother asked. "I want—I want," blubbered the boy between sobs, "I want anything I'm not supposed to have!"

The desire for what is off-limits is a human tendency that goes back to the beginning of human history—back to the forbidden fruit of the "tree of the knowledge of good and evil" (Genesis 2:17).

When we try to live according to biblical principles, we recognize that many practices and attitudes common in today's society must be rejected. So we must know God's will, identify evil allurements, and resist temptation. "Put on the full armor of God, so that you can take your stand against the devil's schemes" (Ephesians 6:11).

Beware of the appeal of the forbidden!        —RD

## What's in a Smile?

*A happy heart makes the face cheerful, but heartache crushes the spirit.* —PROVERBS 15:13

Changes of the heart can show up on the face. But can changing our expression also help to change our heart? Writer Daniel Goleman says there is a relationship between facial expression and resulting mood. He cites experiments in which researchers found that pronouncing the word *cheese* prompted a smile and pleasant feelings, while pronouncing the word *few* tended to create another expression, resulting in negative emotions.

Smiling isn't the only thing we can do to change the way we feel. In Psalm 4, we find many actions that troubled people can take. When distress grips our soul, we can ask the Lord for relief and mercy (v. 1). We can take comfort in knowing we are among those who are favored by Him, remembering that He hears us when we call (v. 3). We can acknowledge our feelings and be quiet before Him (v. 4). We can do what is right (v. 5) and trust in Him to give us overflowing gladness (v. 7). And we can rest in the assurance of His peace and safety (v. 8).          —MD

# Pumpkins, Pots, and God's Power

*But we have this treasure in jars of clay to show that this all-surpassing power is from God and not from us.* —2 CORINTHIANS 4:7

In one of my favorite pictures of my daughter as an infant, she is gleefully sitting in the belly of a hollowed-out pumpkin. There she sat, the delight of my heart, contained in an overgrown squash. The pumpkin withered in the ensuing weeks, but my daughter continued to grow and thrive.

The way Paul describes knowing the truth of who Jesus is reminds me of that photo. He likens the knowledge of Jesus in our heart to a treasure stored in a clay pot. Remembering what Jesus did for us gives us the courage and strength to persevere through struggles in spite of being "hard pressed on every side" (2 Corinthians 4:8). Because of God's power in our lives, when we are "struck down, [we're] not destroyed" (v. 9).

We may feel the wear and tear of our trials. But the joy of Jesus in us continues to grow in spite of those challenges. Our knowledge of Him—His power at work in our lives—is the treasure stored in our frail clay bodies. We can flourish in the face of hardship because of His power at work within us.     —KH

## Assembly Required

*Do not be anxious about anything,*
*but in every situation, by prayer and*
*petition, with thanksgiving, present your*
*requests to God.* —PHILIPPIANS 4:6

When our daughter and her fiancé began receiving wedding presents, it was a happy time. One gift they received was a bench cabinet that had to be assembled—and I volunteered for the task. Although it took a couple of hours, it was much easier than expected. All of the wooden pieces were precut and predrilled, and all the hardware for assembly was included. The instructions were virtually foolproof.

Unfortunately, most of life isn't that way. Life doesn't carry with it simple instructions, nor do we find all of the necessary parts in hand. We face situations with no clear idea of what we're getting into or what it will take to pull it off. We can easily find ourselves overwhelmed with these difficult moments.

But we need not face our burdens alone. God wants us to bring them to Him: "Don't be anxious about anything, but in every situation, by prayer and petition, with thanksgiving, present your requests to God (Philippians 4:6).

We have a Savior who understands and offers His peace in the midst of our struggles.          —BC

## He Quiets the Storm

*There is a river whose streams make glad
the city of God, the holy place where
the Most High dwells.* —PSALM 46:4

One autumn day, a thunderous storm blew across Lake Michigan for thirty-six hours straight. Sustained winds of sixty miles per hour, with gusts much stronger, whipped up the highest waves in fifteen years. One frothing roller after another, some up to eighteen feet high, crashed over the breakwaters and pounded the shore with great fury.

The writer of Psalm 46 must have experienced a sustained spiritual and emotional crisis like the incessant pounding of a giant storm, for he wrote of troubled waters and roaring seas. He also mentioned the quaking of the mountains (vv. 2–3).

That may describe how life in this world feels to you right now. If so, continue on to verse 4, which tells of a quiet river that delights and refreshes the people of God. Its cool, peaceful waters flow continually as a never-ending source of joy and blessing.

Let the Lord quiet the storms in your heart. For He says, "Be still, and know that I am God; I will be exalted among the nations, I will be exalted in the earth" (v. 10).                              —DE

## Sleeping in Safety

*In peace I will lie down and sleep, for you alone,*
*Lord, make me dwell in safety.* —PSALM 4:8

Someone has said, "The rest of your life depends on the rest of your nights." Many people, though, feel like the little boy who was having trouble falling asleep. He told his mother, "My body is lying down, but my mind keeps sitting up!"

If anxious thoughts keep you awake, ask the Lord to quiet your heart and give you the faith to be able to relax and let Him solve the problems that disturb you. That's what David did when he was in trouble, for he wrote, "I will both lie down in peace, and sleep; for you alone, O Lord, make me dwell in safety" (Psalm 4:8 NKJV).

During World War II, an elderly woman in England had endured the nerve-shattering bombings with amazing serenity. When asked to give the secret of her calmness amid the terror and danger, she replied, "Well, every night I say my prayers. Then I remember that God is always watching, so I go peacefully to sleep. After all, there is no need for both of us to stay awake!"

Having trouble sleeping? Remember that your heavenly Father is tenderly watching over you.

—HB

## Reflecting the Son

*The light shines in the darkness, and the darkness has not overcome it.* —JOHN 1:5

Due to its location among sheer mountains, Rjukan, Norway, does not see natural sunlight from October to March. To lighten up the town, the citizens installed large, moveable mirrors on the mountainside to reflect the sunrays and beam sunlight into the town square.

I like to think of the Christian life as a similar scenario. Jesus said His followers are "the light of the world" (Matthew 5:14). John the disciple wrote that Christ the true light "shines in the darkness" (John 1:5). So too, Jesus invites us to reflect our light into the darkness around us: "Let your light shine before others, that they may see your good deeds and glorify your Father in heaven" (Matthew 5:16). That is a call for us to show love in the face of hatred and peace in moments of conflict. As the apostle Paul reminds us, "For you were once darkness, but now you are light in the Lord. Live as children of light" (Ephesians 5:8).

Jesus also said, "I am the light of the world. Whoever follows me will never walk in darkness, but will have the light of life" (John 8:12). Our light is a reflection of Jesus the Son.                    —LD

# When Life Is Hard

*He knows the way that I take; when he has*
*tested me, I will come forth as gold.* —JOB 23:10

During an interview, singer and songwriter Meredith Andrews spoke about being overwhelmed as she tried to balance outreach, creative work, marital issues, and motherhood. Reflecting on her distress, she said, "I felt like God was taking me through a refining season—almost through a crushing process."

The Old Testament character Job was overwhelmed after losing so much. And although Job had been a daily worshiper of God, he felt that the Lord was ignoring his pleas for help. Job claimed he could not see God whether he looked to the north, south, east, or west (Job 23:2–9).

In the middle of his despair, Job had a moment of clarity. He said, "[God] knows the way that I take; when he has tested me, I will come forth as gold" (v. 10). Sometimes God uses difficulty to burn away our self-reliance, pride, and earthly wisdom.

Pain and problems can produce the shining, rock-solid character that comes from trusting God when life is hard.                                    —JBS

# Trust Him First

*Praise be to the Lord, to God our Savior,*
*who daily bears our burdens.* —PSALM 68:19

"Don't let go, Dad!"

"I won't. I've got you. I promise."

I was little, and terrified of the water, but my dad wanted me to learn to swim. He would purposefully take me away from the side of the pool into a depth that was over my head, where he was my only support. Then he would teach me to relax and float.

This was a lesson in trust. I knew my father loved me and would never let me be harmed intentionally, but I was also afraid—thus I would cling tightly to his neck. Eventually his patience and kindness won out, and I began to swim. But I had to trust him first.

When I feel "over my head" in a difficulty, I sometimes think back on those moments. They help me call to mind the Lord's reassurance to His people: "I have made you and I will carry you" (Isaiah 46:4).

The Lord has promised that He will never leave us (Hebrews 13:5). As we rest in His care and promises, He helps us learn to trust in His faithfulness and find peace in Him. —JB

## Rest Easy

*Even the darkness will not be dark to
you; the night will shine like the day, for
darkness is as light to you.* —PSALM 139:12

For eighteen years the routine is the same. Each night
you make sure each child is asleep before turning out
the lights and locking the door. You can rest easy only
when you know the family is safe.

Then that day comes when your oldest child leaves
home. Perhaps to college as our oldest daughter did.
Maybe to a hitch in the military. Or just across town
to an apartment.

As much as you prepared for that day, those first
nights are difficult. Now when you lock the doors
and turn out the lights, you no longer have the security of knowing where each child is. You no longer
can rest quite as well—unless you trust God.

In Psalm 139, David provided some comforting
words that can help all of us who have to say goodbye to our children as they go out on their own. We
cannot escape God's presence. He is with us, and with
our children, wherever we go.

Psalm 33:13 says, "From heaven the LORD looks
down and sees all mankind." That helps me rest easy—
even when one of the children is out of the house.

—DB

## "Rejoice!"

*Rejoice in the LORD and be glad,*
*you righteous; sing, all you who are*
*upright in heart!* —PSALM 32:11

I heard about a man who for years had cheated himself out of the joy of forgiveness. He felt guilty about the part he had played in a college prank that took the life of a classmate. Although he had confessed his wrong to God, he continued to be so torn up on the inside that he couldn't keep a job or maintain a good relationship with his wife.

One day the mother of the student who had died stopped in to see him. She was astounded that he had been carrying this load of guilt. She assured him that she had forgiven him long ago and no one held any ill feeling toward him. She also reminded him that God had erased this unfortunate escapade from the record. When he finally came to accept forgiveness, he felt a new sense of freedom. He was able to renew his relationship with his wife and seek out a good job.

When we allow a sin that we have confessed to plague our conscience, we displease the Lord and cheat ourselves out of joy. Let's accept the God's forgiveness and "rejoice in the Lord."          —DD

## A Look Back

*There is a time for everything, and*
*a season for every activity under the*
*heavens.* —ECCLESIASTES 3:1

While flying recently, I watched a mother and her children a few rows ahead of me. While the toddler played contentedly, the mother gazed into the eyes of her newborn, smiling at him and stroking his cheek. He stared back with a wide-eyed wonderment. I enjoyed the moment with a touch of wistfulness, thinking of my own children at that age.

I reflected, however, about King Solomon's words in the book of Ecclesiastes about "every activity under the heavens" (v. 1). He describes "a time to be born and a time to die, a time to plant and a time to uproot" (v. 2). Perhaps King Solomon in these verses despairs at what he sees as a meaningless cycle of life. But he also acknowledges the role of God in each season, that our work is a "gift of God" (v. 13) and that "everything God does will endure forever" (v. 14).

While we may remember times in our lives wistfully, we know that the Lord promises to be with us in every season of our life (Isaiah 41:10). We can count on His presence and find that our purpose is in walking with Him.       —ABP

## Hope beyond Hope

*May the God of hope fill you with all joy
and peace as you trust in him, so that you
may overflow with hope by the power
of the Holy Spirit.* —ROMANS 15:13

Grant Murphy of Seattle was the active type, a man who ran at full throttle. Idling and coasting were not in his nature.

Then multiple sclerosis hit, and the activity slowed little by little. Near the end, he was totally helpless and hardly strong enough to talk. A friend recalls, however, that "he expressed only joy and thankfulness with a constant anticipation of being in the Lord's presence."

On the friend's last visit, Grant quoted Romans 15:13 in a voice no more than a whisper, then added, "I can't do anything now."

It's when we can't do anything that God does everything. And herein lies a profound paradox of the Christian's experience. Faith is simultaneously an exercise of our will and the impartation of divine strength. And from that marvelous mixture spring joy and peace and an abundance of hope.

Are you in a helpless situation? Strength gone? All options exhausted? If you have trusted Jesus as your Savior, God will strengthen you to keep on believing. As you trust Him, He'll give you not only joy and peace but also hope when all hope is gone.     —DD

# Holy Awe

*The LORD is in his holy temple; let all the earth be silent before him.* —HABAKKUK 2:20

Times of silence are opportunities to think about God and our relationship to Him. Time to contemplate the peace and hope that come from knowing the living God.

After pronouncing God's judgment on the cruel, immoral, and drunken people of his day, Habakkuk pointed out the foolishness of worshiping idols. Then he said, "The LORD is in his holy temple; let all the earth keep silent before him" (2:20). It's as if he was saying, be quiet so God can get through to you.

Although we can benefit from times of silence, we tend to shy away from being alone with our thoughts. For example, in my car I sometimes listen absent-mindedly to the radio when I could be reflecting on the greatness of God. Some of my most enriching spiritual experiences have come in times of silence. I recall sensing God's presence and power when I stepped outside on a cold, still morning. I stood in silence. During the night God had with unseen fingers deftly covered the landscape with silvery frost. I couldn't help but marvel at His handiwork.

Yes, the Lord is in His holy temple. We stand silent before Him in holy awe. —HVL

# Your Walking Does the Talking

*And so you became a model to all the believers in Macedonia and Achaia.* —1 THESSALONIANS 1:7

When we do what is right without saying anything, we can have a far greater impact for good than when we tell others what they should do without doing it ourselves.

That's why Christian mothers and fathers want to make sure their walk supports their talk. Their exemplary living in itself provides clear and consistent guidelines. Of course, we must never discount the importance of verbal instruction—along with a worthy example. Although we usually think that the only preachers are those who speak from the pulpit, the truth is that we are all "preaching" every day. Our conduct at home, our handling of business matters, our response to difficulties, our reaction to temptation—everything our youngsters, friends, and associates observe about us is "preaching." Someone has wisely said, "What you're doing speaks so loudly I can't hear what you're saying."

How important it is that all of our actions are in harmony with God's revealed will! Remember, whether we realize it or not, our walking is doing our talking.                    —RD

# Make Parenting a Priority

*Children are a heritage from the LORD,*
*offspring a reward from him.* —PSALM 127:3

An old cartoon in a Christian magazine portrays how moms sometimes feel. It showed a mother sprawled out in an overstuffed chair, her hair disheveled and a frazzled look on her face. Toys and crayons cluttered the floor. As her husband came into the room, he gave her a quizzical look. Exhausted, she commented, "I'll be glad when the kids are grown so I'll have time to be a good parent."

Moses told Jewish parents to seize every opportunity to convey God's laws and precepts to their youngsters—when they sat down together, when they walked together, before they went to bed, and when they got up in the morning.

If a perfect house is more important than time for the spontaneous interruption of children, perhaps we need to back off a bit from perfection. A fast pace, pressure to succeed, and the lure of materialism can all sap us of the emotional energy needed to build relationships with our children.

We glorify our heavenly father when we make parenting a priority.                    —DD

## Message from the Sky

*The heavens declare the glory of God; the skies proclaim the work of his hands.* —PSALM 19:1

Depending on where we live on this planet, finding moments of solitude where we can gaze at the silent night sky is increasingly difficult. Yet, according to Psalm 19, if we were able to steal away to a spot where the only sound was our heartbeat and the only sight the canopy of the stars, we could hear a message from those heavens.

In such a moment, we could hear with the ears of our innermost being the noiseless testimony of God's breathtaking creation.

We could hear from the heavens as they "declare the glory of God" (v. 1). And we could watch in amazement as the skies "proclaim the work of his hands" (v. 1).

We could listen as "day after day they pour forth speech" (v. 2) that fills our minds with the unmistakable awareness of God's splendid creation.

We could marvel through the night as the firmament shows in unmistakable splendor the knowledge of God's handiwork.

Our Creator tells us to "be still, and know that I am God" (Psalm 46:10). A great way to do this is to spend time in His creation admiring His handiwork. Then we will certainly know that He is God!  —DB

## Love in Return

*This is love: not that we loved God, but that
he loved us and sent his Son as an atoning
sacrifice for our sins.* —1 JOHN 4:10

A mother was writing letters at her desk as her little
girl played with her doll in another room. After some
time, she called for her daughter to come and see
her. The little girl said, "Mommy, I'm glad you called
for me. I love you so much." "Do you, darling?" she
asked as she tenderly hugged her beaming five-year-
old. "I am glad you love me. You weren't lonely while
I was writing, were you? You and your dolly seemed
to be having such a good time together." "We were
having fun, but I got tired of loving her. She never
loves me back." "Is that why you love me?" "That's
one reason, Mommy; but not the best." "And what is
the best?" Her bright eyes were earnest as she replied,
"Mommy, can't you guess? I love you because you
loved me and took care of me when I was too little
to love you back."

When we consider that God loved us "while we
were still sinners," and even when "we were God's
enemies" (Romans 5:8, 10), there is but one response
that should flow from our hearts—a return of love
because He first loved us.                        —PVG

# What Prayer Is Not

*Being in anguish, he prayed more earnestly,*
*and his sweat was like drops of blood*
*falling to the ground.* —LUKE 22:44

Praying is not always easy. If it is painless, we may not be communicating what is really in our hearts. Christ's great struggle in Gethsemane was His cry to God out of the most urgent matter of the moment. It was His battle with the enemy over His impending death on the cross for the sins of the world.

*Prayer is not one-way communication.* Jesus not only spoke but He also listened. Sometimes prayer is our answer to what God has said to us through His Word by His Spirit. But we cannot know His voice—His leading—unless we quiet our hearts and listen in reflection and meditation.

*Prayer is not wishful thinking.* A young woman was telling a counselor about the mess she had made of her life. He stopped her and said, "Debbie, do you ever pray?" "No," she replied, "never." Then she added with a quick smile, "But sometimes I send a wish upward." Instead, effective prayer directs our attention to the living God.

*Prayer is not always easy.* It involves talking and listening, and is God-centered. Those are the secrets to real prayer.                                    —DE

## Morning Prayer

*Pray in the Spirit on all occasions with all kinds of prayers and requests. With this in mind, be alert and always keep on praying for all the Lord's people.* —EPHESIANS 6:18

Singer-songwriter Robert Hamlet wrote "Lady Who Prays for Me" as a tribute to his mother who made a point of praying for her boys each morning before they went to the bus stop. After a young mom heard Hamlet sing his song, she committed to praying with her own little boy before he left the house. The result was heartwarming! Five minutes later he returned— bringing kids from the bus stop with him! The boy explained to his mom, "Their moms didn't pray with them."

In the book of Ephesians, Paul urges us to pray "on all occasions with all kinds of prayers" (6:18). Demonstrating our daily dependence on God is essential in a family. Many children first learn to trust God as they observe genuine faith in the people closest to them (2 Timothy 1:5). There is no better way to teach the utmost importance of prayer than by praying for and with our children.

When we "start children off" by modeling a "sincere faith" in God (Proverbs 22:6; 2 Timothy 1:5), we give them a special gift, an assurance that God is an ever-present part of our lives.            —CHK

# A Day Off

*By the seventh day God had finished the work*
*he had been doing; so on the seventh day*
*he rested from all his work.* —GENESIS 2:2

I saw a magazine ad that stopped me short and made me really think. It said, "Even God Took a Day Off!" The writers were referring to the seventh day of creation, when God rested from all His labors.

I've never thought of the seventh day as a "day off" for the Lord. But it does underscore the work-rest principle that began in Genesis and runs throughout the entire Bible.

In the Old Testament, Israel was commanded to honor the seventh day by not doing any work. The Sabbath was to be a day of recovery as well as a day of sacrifice and worship. Even the land was to be left idle every seventh year. And in the New Testament, we read that the Lord Jesus led His disciples to a quiet place after a prolonged preaching tour so they could rest (Mark 6:31).

How's your schedule? Is your calendar always crammed full? Are Sundays the most hectic of all? Perhaps you can slow down and give yourself time for rest. The Bible calls for it and your body and emotions desperately need it.

Remember, even God took a day off.          —DE

## Looking Like Jesus

*"The King will reply, 'Truly I tell you,*
*whatever you did for one of the least*
*of these brothers and sisters of mine,*
*you did for me.'"* —MATTHEW 25:40

When a friend cared for her housebound mother-in-law, she asked her what she longed for the most. "For my feet to be washed," she replied. My friend told me, "How I hated that job! Each time she asked me to do it I was resentful and would ask God to hide my feelings from her."

But one day her grumbling attitude changed in a flash. As she got out the bowl and towel and knelt at her mother-in-law's feet, she said, "I looked up, and for a moment I felt like I was washing the feet of Jesus himself. She was Jesus in disguise!" After that, she felt honored to do it.

When I heard this moving account, I thought of Jesus's story about the end of time, which He taught on the Mount of Olives. The King welcomes into His kingdom His sons and daughters, saying that when they visited the sick or fed the hungry, they did it for Him (Matthew 25:40). We too serve Jesus himself when we visit those in prison or give clothes to the needy.

Today, might you echo my friend, who now wonders when she meets someone new, "Are you Jesus in disguise?"            —ABP

## When to Speak Up

*Love is patient, love is kind. It does
not envy, it does not boast, it is not
proud.* —1 CORINTHIANS 13:4

Good communication is essential for a happy marriage. Poet Ogden Nash seems to have hit on a formula to help us remember how to communicate effectively. Nash, in his witty style, wrote:

If you want your marriage to sizzle
With love in the loving cup,
Whenever you're wrong, admit it;
Whenever you're right, shut up!

There's some immensely helpful truth in that four-liner—truth that is supported by Scripture.

First, if we are wrong we need to admit it. Not only marriage, but all relationships benefit from this kind of honesty (Proverbs 12:22). Protecting ourselves when we're wrong makes resolution impossible.

On the other hand, we can be equally hard to live with if we insist that we're always right—and afraid to let our spouse know that we are fallible. According to 1 Corinthians 13:4, love "does not boast, it is not proud." No one likes to be around someone who always seems to be patting herself on the back.

Two simple guidelines for a marriage that pleases God: Admit wrong and keep quiet about being right. It's a good way to keep the relationship strong.

—DB

## Pushed beyond Your Limits

*When He had sent the multitudes away,*
*He went up on the mountain by Himself*
*to pray.* —MATTHEW 14:23 NKJV

The cartoon said it all. Beneath a picture of a frustrated young man was this caption: "God put me on this earth to accomplish a certain number of things. Right now I'm so far behind I will never die."

We usually don't associate that kind of pace with Jesus's life. Yet consider His mission and ministry. He came into the world to provide salvation for sinners. Multitudes of sick and needy people thronged Him. The religious establishment violently opposed Him. He came to do His Father's will and had to train a small band of loyal followers to spread the gospel after He left them. And all within three years. What an agenda for pressure!

How did He accomplish His mission? He made doing His Father's will His top priority. He took time to get away to rest, and He used that solitude to pray (Matthew 14:23).

When the world closes in on you, remember Jesus's example. Slip away and find a quiet place to pray. It's the best response when you're pushed beyond your limits.                                                    —DD

## Pray On! God Is Listening!

*Hear my prayer, LORD; let my cry for help*
*come to you. . . . Turn your ear to me; when*
*I call, answer me quickly.* —PSALM 102:1–2

When the psalmist was in distress, he cried out for deliverance, but at times it seemed that the Lord had hidden His face from him and would not answer his prayers (Psalm 88:14). All of us feel that way now and then. Yet when we suffer periods of darkness, we must not conclude that God has turned His back on us. He lets us go through these periods of loneliness to prepare us for service here on earth.

A mother told this story: "When it became necessary to break my little daughter's habit of sleeping in my room, I tucked her in her crib, gave her a good-night kiss and turned out the light. She sobbed, thinking I didn't hear or that I no longer loved her. Yet I wasn't far away—though hidden in the darkness—and my heart was actually aching for her. I longed to do what she wanted, but I refrained so that she might grow up emotionally." So too, God may appear to withdraw himself from us that we might grow up spiritually.

God will respond to our plea in His own way and time. Don't despair. Pray on! God is listening! —HB

## Alone with God

*When you pray, go into your room,
close the door and pray to your Father,
who is unseen.* —MATTHEW 6:6

A committee was assigned to tour a factory to judge its efficiency. They were shown the various departments where there were many large, noisy machines. Then they were led to a much smaller and quieter room containing nothing but control panels.

One of them said, "This isn't very important; nothing's happening here."

The guide smiled, "Oh, but this is the most important room of all. This is where the power is distributed to the entire factory."

Maybe we could equate that power room with prayer. We need a quiet place where we can be alone with God—where we can speak to Him and reverently allow Him to speak to us as we meditate on His Word.

In Matthew 6:6, Jesus taught the value of intimate fellowship with heaven, which can be attained only in the sacred solitude of our prayer closet. He did not discourage public prayer, but He did warn against the evil of seeking attention by parading our piety before others.

How long has it been since you've shut the door on the distractions of life and poured out your heart before the Father's throne?                        —HB

## The Troubled Sea

*The wicked are like the tossing sea, . . .*
*whose waves cast up mire.* —ISAIAH 57:20

I fight a losing battle with black silt on the lake bottom near our cabin. In the morning before my grandchildren awaken, I rake the lake bottom close to the dock so they can wade on clean sand.

It works well—until noon. That's when the powerboaters begin to run, making waves that carry fresh silt to the shore. Even when no high-speed craft appear, the wind usually rises about then, creating neat little whitecaps. They too stir up the silt and deposit it, covering the cleared lake bottom with black gunk.

Imagine a sea that is always churning with turbulence. The foaming restlessness never quiets, sending up plumes of dirt and mire. Isaiah described the wicked that way (57:20). Their lives are like a frothy, wave-tossed, unsettled, restless sea—never calm, never at peace (v. 21).

Peace is available to all who believe in Christ, which puts us at peace with God (John 14:27).

If you don't have peace, if you are worn out by the turbulence of unrest, turn in faith to Jesus. He has the power to calm the restless sea of your life.      —DE

## Trying to Impress

*For out of the heart come evil thoughts—*
*murder, adultery, sexual immorality, theft,*
*false testimony, slander. These are what defile*
*a person; but eating with unwashed hands*
*does not defile them."* —MATTHEW 15:19–20

When a college class went on a field trip, the instructor almost didn't recognize one of his pupils. In the classroom she had concealed six-inch heels beneath her pant legs. But in her walking boots she was less than five feet tall. "My heels are how I want to be," she laughed. "But my boots are how I really am."

Our physical appearance doesn't define who we are; it's our heart that matters. Jesus had strong words for those masters of appearances—the super-religious "Pharisees and teachers of the law." They asked Jesus why His disciples didn't wash their hands before eating, as their religious traditions dictated (Matthew 15:1–2). Jesus asked, "Why do you break the command of God for the sake of your tradition?" (v. 3). Then He pointed out how they had invented a legal loophole to keep their wealth instead of caring for their parents (vv. 4–6), thus dishonoring them and violating the fifth commandment (Exodus 20:12).

Jesus said, "Out of the heart come evil thoughts—murder, adultery, sexual immorality," and the like (Matthew 15:19). Only God, through the righteousness of His Son Jesus, can give us a clean heart.

—TG

## A Better Gift

*"He is the one who will build a house
for me, and I will establish his throne
forever."* —1 CHRONICLES 17:12

My birthday is the day after my mother's. As an adolescent, I would strive to think of a gift I could afford that would delight my mom. She always received my purchases with appreciation, and on the following day, my birthday, she would present her gift to me. Because her resources far outshone mine, her gift likewise outshone mine.

My gift-giving reminds me of David's wish to build a home for God. Struck by the contrast between his palace and the tent-tabernacle, David longed to build God a temple. Instead of granting David's wish, however, God responded by giving David a much better gift. God promised that not only would his son Solomon build the temple (1 Chronicles 17:11) but that He would also build David a house, a dynasty. That promise began with Solomon but found its fulfillment in Jesus, whose throne was indeed established forever (v. 12). David wanted to give from his finite resources, but God promised something infinite.

May we always be moved to give to God out of gratitude and love—always noticing how much more abundantly He has given to us in Jesus.          —KH

## Quiet Rest

*In peace I will lie down and sleep,
for you alone, LORD, make me
dwell in safety.* —PSALM 4:8

My son Brian and I agreed to haul some equipment into an isolated Idaho backcountry ranch for a friend. There are no roads into the area, at least none my truck could negotiate. So Ralph, the young ranch manager, arranged to meet us at road's end with a mule-drawn wagon.

Ralph lived on the property year-round. "What do you do in the winter?" I asked, knowing that winters in the high country were long and bitter, and that the ranch had no electricity or telephone service, only a satellite radio. "How do you endure it?"

"Actually," he drawled, "I find it right peaceable."

In the midst of our pressure-filled days, we sometimes crave peace and quiet. There is too much noise in the air; there are too many people around. We want to "come . . . to a quiet place and get some rest" (Mark 6:31). Can we find a place to do this?

Yes, there is such a place. When we take a few moments to reflect on God's love and mercy, we will find in that quiet God-filled space the peace that the world has taken away. —DR

## Include the Unaccepted

*Accept one another, then, just as*
*Christ accepted you, in order to bring*
*praise to God.* —ROMANS 15:7

Christ's followers are called to live an inclusive lifestyle. We are instructed in God's Word to reach out to those who might not be accepted by others. But we get so comfortable with our church friends that we may feel it's too much to ask.

In *The Covenant Home Altar*, Erika Carney wrote, "When I was growing up, my mom was deeply involved with the various activities I participated in. She would often tell me, 'Make sure Heather feels included,' or 'Ask Julie to be your partner,' or 'Invite Kristen to sit with you and your friends.' I sometimes dreaded hearing those words. What if I just wanted to be with my friends? Why should I have to make sure other people were having fun?"

Erika's mother was teaching her daughter to obey the principle taught in Romans 15:7. We are to welcome and accept Christians who may not feel comfortable in our group.

Some people are excluded because they are withdrawn, angry, or defensive, or because they seem different. But these things shouldn't matter. We are to receive fellow believers "just as Christ accepted you, in order to bring praise to God" (v. 7).　　—DE

## When Jesus Grieved

*When Jesus landed and saw a large
crowd, he had compassion on them and
healed their sick.* —MATTHEW 14:14

Many years ago, a Florida mother received news that her son had been killed in the war. Shortly thereafter, she was seen hoeing in her garden.

"It just isn't fitting," chided a neighbor who thought it was inappropriate to be gardening instead of grieving.

"Friend," said the bereaved mom, "I know you mean well, but Jim rejoiced to see green things growing because it meant that his mother and the young ones would be eating. This is his hoe, and when I'm hoeing I can almost feel his big, strong hands under mine and hear his voice saying, 'That's good, Mom, that's good.' Working is the only headstone I can give him."

Jesus also suffered the pain of grief when He was told of the death of John the Baptist, but it didn't deter Him from His work. After a brief period of solitude (Matthew 14:13), His great compassion led Him to heal the sick and to feed 5,000 people.

Is your heart broken today? Does life seem empty? Do you feel like giving up? Remember how Jesus handled His sorrow; He'll strengthen you to do the same.                                                              —DD

## Our Needs and God's Riches

*My God will meet all your needs*
*according to the riches of his glory in*
*Christ Jesus.* —PHILIPPIANS 4:19

A young mother was struggling financially after her husband's death. It was wintertime, and her problem intensified one day when her little boy came in shivering from the cold. "Mommy," he asked, "why can't I have a warm cap like the other kids at school?" The woman had no money but bravely said, "We'll see what we can do."

Later, she knelt in her bedroom and wept in sheer desolation before God, pleading with Him to provide. Great peace flooded her soul, and she knew that somehow her petition would be answered.

Soon a neighbor came to see her. After a brief stay she said, "You know, my son died last fall. Just before he went to heaven I bought him a cap. After his death I put it away and thought I could never part with it. But this morning I opened that drawer, and the Lord impressed upon me that I should give it to your son. Would you take it?" Tearfully, the widow told her neighbor of her earnest prayer. Both gave gratitude to God for His gracious care.

Our real needs will always be supplied from God's riches. Let's fully trust Him.                    —HB

## Good and Bad Laughter

*There is a time for everything, and a season
for every activity under the heavens: . . . a time
to weep and a time to laugh, a time to mourn
and a time to dance.* —ECCLESIASTES 3:1, 4

The Bible says that "a cheerful heart is good medicine" (Proverbs 17:22).

But the Scriptures distinguish between good and bad laughter. The author of Ecclesiastes declared that the laughter of people who have no place for God in their lives has no more value than the noise of crackling thorns in a fire (Ecclesiastes 7:6). God disapproves of any humor that belittles people or makes light of immorality. Sin is never a laughing matter.

Joe E. Brown was a top-notch movie and Broadway comedian of the World War II era. When entertaining American troops in the South Pacific, he was asked by a soldier to tell some "dirty jokes." He responded, "Son, a comedian like me lives for applause and laughter. . . . But if telling a dirty story is the price I must pay for your laughter, then I'm not interested. I've never done an act that I couldn't perform before my mother, and I never will." The soldiers rocked the jungle with their cheers.

*Lord, give us a merry heart. And help us be discerning so we will laugh for the right reasons and about the right things.*                    —HVL

## Honor Your Parents

*"Honor your father and your mother, so
that you may live long in the land the LORD
your God is giving you."* —EXODUS 20:12

It was a sad, unsigned letter from an elderly mother.
"I have an only son," she wrote, "who does all sorts
of things for other people but hates to do anything
for me. He rarely visits me although I live only eight
minutes away. He seldom even calls me."

God puts a high priority on family relationships
throughout life—so says the fifth commandment. On
the surface this seems directed exclusively to children,
but parents must set the example. Children learn to
honor, respect, and obey their parents when they see
Mom and Dad honoring one another, when they feel
respected, affirmed, and loved by their parents, and
when they observe their obedience to God. This commandment to children actually touches us all.

Although we've broken this commandment, our
guilt has been removed by Jesus's death on the cross.
He gives the courage to ask forgiveness of our children and our parents. And if they are not living, we
can show the sincerity of our repentance by strengthening our other family relationships.

We honor our Father when we honor our parents.
                                                              —DD

## In Search of Silence

*I have calmed and quieted myself, I am*
*like a weaned child with its mother; like a*
*weaned child I am content.* —PSALM 131:2

"My next record should be forty-five minutes of silence," said singer Meg Hutchinson, "because that's
what we're missing most in society."

Silence is indeed hard to find. There seems to be
no escape from loud music, loud machines, and loud
voices. But the kind of noise that endangers our spiritual well-being is not the noise we can't escape but
the noise we invite into our lives. Some of us use noise
as a way of shutting out loneliness: voices of TV and
radio personalities give us the illusion of compan-
ionship. Some of us use it as a way of shutting out
our own thoughts: noise keeps us from having to
think for ourselves. We can even use noise as a way
of shutting out the voice of God—keeping us from
hearing what God has to say.

But Jesus, even during His busiest times, made
a point of seeking out places of solitude where He
could carry on a conversation with God (Mark 1:35).
Even if we can't find a place that is perfectly quiet, we
need to find a place to quiet our souls (Psalm 131:2),
a place where God has our full attention.      —JAL

## Honey and Stingers

*I have learned the secret of being content
in any and every situation, whether well
fed or hungry, whether living in plenty
or in want.* —PHILIPPIANS 4:12

A young boy was playing in the yard outside his house when a bee sank its stinger into his pudgy little hand. He ran screaming to his mother shouting, "I hate bees!"

She did what she could to ease his pain and then gave him some bread and honey. As he ate, the mother said, "You really like that, don't you?" He replied, "Oh, yes, I love it!" She then explained that the same little bee that sometimes stings also produces the sweet honey we enjoy.

No Christian can hope to reap the good that comes from a God-directed life without also feeling the sharp barbs of God's discipline in our lives. Along with the sweet parts of life, we must also take the stings. The key is in calling on God for the grace to be content with what He allows into our lives.

Paul said, "I have learned to be content whatever the circumstances," and "I can do all this through him who gives me strength" (Philippians 4:11, 13).

Let's check our attitudes. Are we crabby and complaining, or contented and Christlike? It's a difference of attitude, not circumstances.                    —HB

## Caught by What You Chase

*"Do not store up for yourselves treasures
on earth. . . . But store up for yourselves
treasures in heaven."* —MATTHEW 6:19–20

A man entered the business world with only a few
dollars and a fierce determination to become wealthy.
After much hard work, he was a success—the richest
man in town. But his unscrupulous business methods
left him with no genuine friends. Later, when he went
to the hospital with a terminal illness, he had few
visitors. His money couldn't gain for him the close
relationships for which he longed. He died a lonely
man with little hope for eternity because he chased
money alone.

Pastor Donald Ewing told a very different story.
His mother had accepted Christ in her youth and
had made God's will her delight. When she was
ninety-one, she went to the hospital with a number of
physical problems. A doctor tried to cheer her up by
saying, "Now, don't worry, you're going to be home
in a few days." She replied brightly, "Oh, I know that.
I just don't know which home." Throughout her lifetime she chased heavenly riches and had been so captured by them that she eagerly anticipated going to
be with her Lord.

What are you chasing?        —HVL

## A Century-Old Woman

*They will still bear fruit in old age, they
will stay fresh and green, proclaiming, "The
LORD is upright; he is my Rock, and there is
no wickedness in him." —PSALM 92:14–15*

Behind her were nearly 102 years of life on earth;
before her were the endless reaches of eternity. Dena
had outlived her peers.

I wanted to visit her again, perhaps for the last
time. She had been my neighbor when I was growing
up. She had known my parents, remembered when I
was born, and told great stories about my family. But
I also wanted to ask Dena one question: "After living
more than 100 years, what is the most important
lesson you've learned in life?" So I asked her.

Dena paused, then answered with certainty,
"Everything is from the Lord. 'Nothing in my hand
I bring, simply to Thy cross I cling.'"

Any other response, no matter how significant,
wouldn't have carried the weight of those words. A
century-old woman was still bearing fruit in old age.
By declaring the goodness and righteousness of the
Lord, she had encouraged my faith.

We must never devalue our elderly by overvaluing
youth. We need to listen to those who can look back
over 70, 80, or 90 years or more and affirm without
hesitation God's unfailing love in Christ.     —DD

## Believing without Seeing

*Then Jesus told him, "Because you have seen me,*
*you have believed; blessed are those who have*
*not seen and yet have believed." —*JOHN 20:29

Nearly 2,000 years ago the apostle Peter had a dramatic visit from a heavenly messenger. Even today some people tell of receiving help from angels.

A young child named Pat lost her leg in an accident and bled profusely. At the hospital she overheard a doctor tell her mother, "She won't last until morning." A short time later, Pat felt a gentle hand on her forehead and heard someone say, "Go to sleep, Pat. When you wake up, you'll be better."

Her mother, only a few feet from the bed, heard and saw nothing. But that night Pat slept soundly, and the next morning she was much better. Pat is convinced that it was an angel who touched her and spoke to her that night.

I believe that angels do minister to God's people, because the Bible says they do (Hebrews 1:14). But we don't require such events to believe; God has made himself real to us through His Word.

Jesus's words to Thomas in John 20:29 apply, I believe, to those who trust the Bible even though they have had no dramatic encounters. There is a promised blessing for those who believe without seeing.

—HVL

## Snickering and Suffering

*Praise be to the God and Father of our Lord*
*Jesus Christ, the Father of compassion and the*
*God of all comfort.* —2 CORINTHIANS 1:3

Does the existence of suffering in the world disprove the existence of God? To some, the answer is yes.

When Christian writer Terry Muck attended a convention of humanists in Buffalo, he knew he would hear a life-view opposed to his own. One speaker asked, "Why does God allow children to die, earthquakes to destroy cities, and famine to ravage villages?" The assembled humanists snickered, knowing they could not reconcile these stark realities with a good and all-powerful God. They reasoned that if there were such a Being, there would be no suffering. And since there is suffering, there is no such Being.

As Christians, we need to ask ourselves how we can reconcile suffering and God's existence in our finiteness. We cannot think the thoughts of an infinite God. And we must not be so presumptuous as to say that a loving God could never allow the forces of nature to cause suffering.

We can find peace in our dilemma by opening our hearts to the comfort God gives when we suffer. If we trust Him, He will make real to us His presence and power—and remind us that He is with us in our suffering.                                    —DB

## Thanks for Being You

*Enter his gates with thanksgiving.* —PSALM 100:4

When I served as my mom's live-in caregiver at a cancer center, I got to know Lori, another caregiver who lived down the hallway from us with her husband, Frank. I would chat, laugh, vent, cry, and pray with Lori in the shared living areas. We enjoyed supporting each other as we cared for our loved ones.

One day, I missed the free shuttle that took residents to buy groceries. Lori offered to drive me to the store later that evening. With grateful tears, I accepted her offer. "Thanks for being you," I said. I truly appreciated her for who she was as a person, not just for what she did for me as a friend.

Psalm 100 demonstrates an appreciation of God for who He is, not simply for all He does. The psalmist invites "all the earth" (v. 1) to "worship the LORD with gladness" (v. 2), being confident in knowing "the LORD is God" (v. 3). Our Maker invites us into His presence to "give thanks to him and praise his name" (v. 4). Yes, the Lord remains worthy of our ongoing thankfulness because He "is good," His "love endures forever," and His "faithfulness continues through all generations" (v. 5).

God will always be the Creator and Sustainer of the universe and our intimately loving Father. He deserves our genuine joy-filled gratitude.          —XD

## You Can't Buy It

*Peter answered: "May your money perish
with you, because you thought you could buy
the gift of God with money!"* —ACTS 8:20

A missionary to the Philippines was trying to explain salvation to a wealthy woman, but the woman didn't understand that she couldn't pay for it.

So the missionary used this illustration: "If you wanted to give your daughter a mansion as a gift, how would you feel if she said, 'Mother, you must let me help you pay for the gift. You know I don't make much money, but I think I can squeeze out eight dollars a month.'"

She went on: "That's what you are saying to God. You want to help pay for what Jesus has already paid for."

Many devout, well-meaning people—rich, poor, and in-between—struggle to understand that Jesus paid it all. Convinced that they have to do something to earn God's favor, they attempt to pay for salvation.

We need to understand that when God gave His Son Jesus as a sacrifice, the bill for our sin was paid. For us to try to pay for God's gift is insulting to Him. Genuine trust is believing that God has already taken care of the payment. We can't buy something that has already been purchased with Jesus's death on the cross.                                             —DB

## So Much More!

*From this time many of his disciples turned
back and no longer followed him.* —JOHN 6:66

In a recent year, friends and I prayed for healing for
three women battling cancer. We knew God had the
power. We had seen Him work in the past and believed He could do it again. There were days in each
one's battle when healing looked like it was a reality,
and we rejoiced. But they all died that fall. The loss
hurt deeply. We wanted Him to heal them all—here
and now—but no miracle came.

Some people followed Jesus for the miracles He
performed and to get their needs met (John 6:2, 26).
Some simply saw Him as the carpenter's son (Matthew 13:55–58), and others expected Him to be their
political leader (Luke 19:37–38). Some thought of
Him as a great teacher (Matthew 7:28–29), while
others quit following Him because His teaching was
hard to understand (John 6:66).

Jesus still doesn't always meet our expectations.
Yet He is so much more than we can imagine! He's
the provider of eternal life (vv. 47–48). He is good
and wise; and He loves, forgives, and brings us comfort. May we find rest in Jesus and keep following
Him.                                              —AC

# Through Eyes of Love

*Love is patient, love is kind. It does not envy, it does not boast, it is not proud. It does not dishonor others, it is not self-seeking.* —1 CORINTHIANS 13:4–5

Years ago, an article appeared in the newspaper about a young boy who went to the lingerie department of a store to purchase a gift for his mother. Bashfully he told the clerk that he wanted to buy a slip for his mom, but he didn't know her size. The lady explained that it would help if he could describe her—was she thin, fat, short, tall, or what? "Well," replied the youngster, "she's just about perfect." So the clerk sent him home with a size that turned out to be about twenty sizes too small. That didn't matter, because to the boy, his mom was perfect.

Isn't that the way we should see people—not measured by some cultural standard, but by who God created them to be?

In 1 Corinthians 13 we read that love thinks no evil. This doesn't mean it's blind to the sins of others. But it looks beyond others' weaknesses, accenting the best qualities in people.

Let's examine our response to others in the light of 1 Corinthians 13. We should ask God to help us see others through eyes of love.                    —DD

# A Transforming Resident

*If anyone is in Christ, the new creation
has come: The old has gone, the new
is here!* —2 CORINTHIANS 5:17

When a young man left home for his freshman year of college, his mother was concerned how he would care for his dorm room. So when she visited him at Thanksgiving, she was not surprised to find his room in total disarray. But what shocked her the most were the racy pictures hanging on the walls.

At Christmas time she sent her son a box of presents, including a portrait of Jesus. Later, when she visited the school again, her son was eager for her to see his room. Upon entering, she found on the best wall space the picture of Christ. All the other pictures were gone.

"Jack, there's something different about your room," she said. "It seems that you had more pictures before." "Yes, I did, Mother, but those other pictures all seemed out of place after that one of Jesus came into the room."

If an artist's portrait of Jesus could make that much difference, think of the change Jesus himself can make when He comes into a person's heart. By receiving Christ, we are made brand-new, and this transforming Resident will keep on changing us.

—PVG

## The Teacher as a Midwife

*My dear children, for whom I am again*
*in the pains of childbirth until Christ is*
*formed in you.* —GALATIANS 4:19

The mother of the ancient Greek philosopher Socrates was a midwife. Socrates grew up observing that she assisted women in bringing new life into the world. This experience later influenced his teaching method. Socrates said, "My art of midwifery is in general like theirs; . . . my concern is not with the body but with the soul that is in travail of birth."

Instead of just passing information on to his students, Socrates used the sometimes-painful process of asking probing questions to help them arrive at their own conclusions. Teaching them to think seemed at times like the travail of childbirth.

Paul expressed a similar idea in discipling believers in the faith when he said, "My dear children, for whom I am again in the pains of childbirth until Christ is formed in you" (Galatians 4:19). Paul was concerned that each believer grows to spiritual maturity in Christlikeness (Ephesians 4:13).

Becoming like Christ is a lifelong experience. All of us will have challenges and disappointments along the way. But if we put our trust in Him, we'll grow spiritually and have character qualities that will radiate new life.      —DF

## A Family Reunion

*Instead, we were like young children among
you. Just as a nursing mother cares for
her children.* —1 THESSALONIANS 2:7

For over three decades, the annual Celebration of Life reunion in Colorado Springs has brought together members of a unique family. The festive gathering reunites doctors, nurses, and staff from UCHealth Memorial Hospital Central with former patients from its neonatal intensive care unit. Their parents have come with their children to say thank you to those who saved their lives and gave them a second chance. Dr. Bob Kiley commented, "Both professionally and personally, for all the staff, this solidifies why we're in this job."

I wonder if in heaven there will be many such times when spiritual caregivers and those they helped as "babes in Christ" will reunite to share stories and give praise to God. The New Testament describes how Paul, Silvanus, and Timothy worked among the young believers in Thessalonica with gentleness, "just as a nursing mother cares for her children" (1 Thessalonians 2:7), and with comfort and encouragement, "as a father deals with his own children" (v. 11).

Helping new believers at a critical stage in their faith is a labor of love that will be cause for great rejoicing at the "family" reunion in heaven. —DM

## Praise for Pressure

*The LORD examines the righteous, but
the wicked, those who love violence, he
hates with a passion.* —PSALM 11:5

A young boy was fascinated to see the stirrings of life
in a cocoon. The moth inside was struggling to free
itself, but the process was slow and tedious. Thinking
he would help the moth, he slit the cocoon with his
pocketknife, and the insect emerged freely. But it had
none of the expected color, it couldn't fly, and it soon
died. The boy later learned that a moth's struggle to
free itself is a necessary part of its development and
that the process stimulates body fluids that give luster
to its wings.

For the Christian, life's difficulties can also produce positive results.

Most of us must confess that we find it difficult to
endure times of suffering and trial patiently. Yet, once
we understand that God has a reason for either or-
dering or allowing our difficulties, we will be able to
accept them with gratitude. Bitter disappointments,
painful suffering, and shattering sorrow, if received in
faith, can be a means of strengthening our character.

What peace is ours when we learn to praise the
Lord for pressure!                              —PVG

## One Day at a Time

*Therefore do not worry about tomorrow, for tomorrow will worry about itself. Each day has enough trouble of its own.* —MATTHEW 6:34

The story is told about a man whose store was destroyed by fire. To make matters worse, he had failed to renew his fire insurance. Later that day, a friend asked how he was coping with the shocking loss. "I'm getting along just fine," he said. "I had breakfast this morning, and it isn't time to eat again."

Not only was he taking one day at a time as he faced the seemingly impossible task of starting all over, but he was also taking one hour at a time.

Jesus said, "Do not worry about tomorrow" (Matthew 6:34). He doesn't want us to be burdened with the needless weight of anxiety about the future. We have enough to do to deal with the present.

When I was diagnosed with Parkinson's disease, I had to face serious questions about the future. It would be natural, even expected, for me to worry in a situation like this. But when we know the Lord and place our confidence firmly in Him, we can experience a deep, settled peace that helps us not fret about things we can't control. Then we can rejoice in God's sustaining grace—one day at a time.            —RD

## Take the Time

*"Whoever welcomes one of these little children in my name welcomes me; and whoever welcomes me does not welcome me but the one who sent me."* —MARK 9:37

A legend is told about a rabbi from a small Jewish town. The people had gathered in the synagogue on the eve of Yom Kippur (Day of Atonement), but when the time came for the most important service of the Jewish year to begin, the rabbi was absent.

During the delay, a young mother went home to check on her little daughter, whom she had left sleeping. To her surprise, she saw the rabbi sitting quietly in a chair, holding the child in his arms. He had been walking by on the way to the synagogue when he heard the infant crying and stopped to help. He held the little one until she fell asleep.

There's a lesson for us in this rabbi's example and in Jesus's love for people (Matthew 9:18–26). In our hectic and busy lives, we tend to lose our sense of compassion for others. We must take time to observe and respond to individuals.

Somewhere amid all the demands on your life, take the time to hold the hand of an aging believer, to comfort a tired mother, or to cradle a child until she sleeps.                                   —DE

## Love's Checklist

*Love is patient, love is kind. It does
not envy, it does not boast, it is not
proud.* —1 CORINTHIANS 13:4

A woman named Nancy uses verses from 1 Corinthians 13 to help her cope with the frustrations of a busy family life. She calls verses 4 to 7 "Love's Checklist" and refers to it when anger wells up within her.

Nancy gave an example of how she uses her checklist. She was running errands one morning before she and her family were to leave on vacation. Her husband, Bill, was at home. When she arrived home after stopping at the grocery store, her mother's house, the post office, the bank, and the hospital to visit a friend, she found that all he had accomplished was to wash and polish his car—which they weren't even taking on the trip!

Nancy was angry and said some harsh things to Bill. Then the words of Love's Checklist came to mind: "Love is patient, love is kind." She prayed, then she apologized to her husband for her angry outburst. He said he was sorry too, and they left that afternoon for their vacation—just a little late.

When we're tempted to say angry, bitter things, let's remember Love's Checklist in 1 Corinthians 13.
—DE

# "I'll Take Him"

*Though my father and mother forsake me,
the LORD will receive me.* —PSALM 27:10

When I was in college, I developed a friendship with a fellow student who had suffered a terrible loss. His child had died and his wife had left him because she couldn't deal with the pain.

One day, as my friend and I were walking down the street, we found ourselves behind a disheveled mother with a grubby little boy in hand. She was angry at the child and was walking much too fast for his little legs.

Soon, we watched as the child's hand slipped out of his mother's grasp. She turned around, spat out a curse, and trudged on. The little boy sat on the curb and burst into tears. Immediately, my friend sat down next to him and gathered the little guy in his arms.

The woman turned and, looking at the child, began to curse again. My friend said softly, "Lady, if you don't want him, I'll take him."

So it is with our Father in heaven. He too has known great loss and loves us tenderly. Even if our friends and family forsake us, our God never will (Psalm 27:10). We are ever in His care.          —DR

## Draining or Replenishing?

*They made Him a supper; and Martha
served. . . . Then Mary . . . anointed the
feet of Jesus.* —JOHN 12:2–3 NKJV

If someone spent the whole day with me, how would
he feel at the end of the day—worn out or built up?
That's the kind of question I began to think about as
I listened to Clark Hutchinson talk about relationships. He said he has noticed three kinds: draining,
neutral, and replenishing.

Hutchinson pointed out that Jesus experienced all
three kinds of relationships. Those that exhausted
His energy were perhaps the most common in our
Lord's earthly experience, for He spent much of
His time giving. He healed the sick, encouraged the
downtrodden, and taught the masses. We know that
sometimes He must have been worn out by these
experiences. He often went away to pray and renew
himself (Matthew 14:23; Luke 5:16).

Some of His relationships were probably just casual contacts. But the replenishing ones encouraged
Jesus. They were relationships with people such as
Mary, Martha, and Lazarus, whose love and presence
uplifted the Lord.

How do we relate to others? We can add to their
lives a measure of happiness by giving them a chance
to talk, encouraging them, and suggesting life's
brighter side.

Do we leave people drained or replenished? —DB

## When Trials Become Triumphs

*Indeed, we felt we had received the sentence
of death. But this happened that we might
not rely on ourselves but on God, who
raises the dead.* —2 CORINTHIANS 1:9

The Lord often allows us to go through difficulties so we'll realize how much we need Him.

The mother of a brain-injured child wrote these words: "We would have called our daughter's handicap the greatest tragedy of our lives if it were not for the fact that through it we came to know the Lord better. Words cannot express our disappointment when our little girl failed to experience normal mental development. Yet this made us understand just a bit how our dear Savior must feel when His children do not mature spiritually. The Lord knows that heartaches, if properly accepted, will enrich our lives in a way that could not happen otherwise. Strengthened in the inner man, we come out of our trials better Christians and with a brighter testimony."

Our adversity should not lead to rebellion. Self-pity, murmuring, and bitterness stunt our spiritual development and render us ineffective in the Lord's service. Praise, joyous submission, and a vibrant faith in His loving purposes, however, will stimulate our growth in grace.

If we let the Lord enlarge our soul's capacities through distress, burdens will become blessings and trials will become triumphs.                    —HB

## Farsighted Faith

*I know that my redeemer lives, and that*
*in the end he will stand on the earth. And*
*after my skin has been destroyed, yet in*
*my flesh I will see God.* —JOB 19:25–26

A skilled surgeon has lost his idealism. Again and again he has corrected serious problems through surgery, only to see his patients die later from other ailments. He felt he was just postponing the inevitable.

Faith, however, looks beyond this life to eternity. I thought of this when visiting a thirty-two-year-old mother who had leukemia. She didn't like to think of the possibility of leaving behind a husband and small children. She prayed for a remission or a cure. Her loved ones and friends prayed with her. We didn't know what God would do. She told me she could be happy because she knew that nothing really bad could happen to her. She saw beyond death to the resurrection of the body, reunion with her loved ones, and a home in heaven. Hers was not a shortsighted idealism but a farsighted faith.

The thought of suffering and death can be frightening. Even Job expressed negative sentiments about death. At other times, however, he saw that beyond the grave he would be vindicated and rewarded by God. And he never let go of that confidence.

Farsighted faith always focuses on God.   —HVL

## Set in Concrete

*Start children off on the way they should
go, and even when they are old they will
not turn from it.* —PROVERBS 22:6

A young mother in Kansas made an unusual request of a workman who was smoothing out the freshly poured concrete of a new sidewalk. She asked if she could press her baby's feet onto the concrete. When the man said yes, she stood the child on the wet cement and pointed his toes in the direction of a nearby church. She apparently wanted to make a permanent impression that would influence the future direction of her little boy's life.

This unusual expression of commitment should reflect the desire of all Christian parents for their children's spiritual welfare. We must position our young ones on the right way and recognize the importance of the church in their lives. Our children's spiritual training must begin early. We have the responsibility to encourage them to receive Jesus as their Savior as soon as they are old enough to understand salvation. Then we can cultivate in them a respect for the church and instill in their hearts a love for God and His Word.

By our teaching, our example, and our prayers, let's make sure that we set our children's feet in the right direction.                              —RD

# "Who Made God?"

*Before the mountains were born or you brought forth the whole world, from everlasting to everlasting you are God.* —PSALM 90:2

A mother was approached by her young son, who asked, "Mommy, did God make himself?" She dropped what she was doing and sat down with her youngster for a little talk. Pointing to her wedding band, she said, "This is a 'love ring,' which your daddy gave me when we were married. Look at it closely and tell me where it begins and where it ends."

The youngster examined it carefully and then said, "There's no starting place and no stopping place to a ring." The mother replied, "That's the way it is with God. He had no beginning and has no end, yet He encircles our lives with His presence. Nobody ever made God—He always was!"

Finite humans cannot hope to comprehend fully a Being who always was, who is, and who always will be; yet Scripture tells us that He is "from everlasting to everlasting" (Psalm 90:2).

Although we cannot understand His eternal being, what He imparts to us through the merits of Christ is an everlasting salvation based on His unfailing love and His unchanging truth. And that's the basis for everlasting joy.                                    —HB

## Heirlooms

*I am reminded of your sincere faith, which first lived in your grandmother Lois and in your mother Eunice and, I am persuaded, now lives in you also.* —2 TIMOTHY 1:5

"My great-grandfather owned this rifle," the man said proudly. In his hand was a mint-condition rifle from the days when the pioneers were moving across the American West. I admired its beautiful walnut stock and shiny brass fittings. "It's been in the family more than one hundred years. I'm going to give it to my son when he turns twenty-five."

We give a lot of thought to what we pass on to our children. My wife Shirley cherishes the crystal and chinaware that belonged to her grandmother. It may be something different in your home: a roll top desk, a handmade quilt, or an old family Bible. Heirlooms are important to us.

Other things we can pass on to our children are even more important—things like honorable character or a good name. Second Timothy talks about the best gift of all—the example of faith in Jesus Christ. Timothy's grandmother Lois and his mother Eunice believed on Christ; then Timothy too placed his trust in Him.

As you think about what you want to pass on to your children, don't forget the example of your faith in Christ. It is the most valuable "heirloom" of all.

—DE

## Looking Out for Others

*Not looking to your own interests*
*but each of you to the interests of*
*the others.* —PHILIPPIANS 2:4

Billy, age nine, loved his dog. One day the dog gave him a great big lick on the face. Billy responded by kissing the dog on the tip of his cold, wet nose. The boy's mother, seeing what had happened, was taken aback. Billy noticed her expression and commented, "Don't worry, Mom, I won't give the dog my cold. I'm all over it." Billy never gave a thought to the germs he might get from his pet. His concern was focused entirely on his dog.

That's a far cry from today's popular "me first, others last" philosophy. We are told, "Your own happiness is the important thing. Look out for number one—you!"

Christ never displayed such a self-centered attitude. Paul said in Philippians 2 that Jesus took the form of a servant and became "obedient to death—even death on a cross" (v. 8). He was willing to leave the glories of heaven and pay sin's awful price at Calvary—all because of His deep love for us.

May we strive to be more like Christ by looking out not only for our own interests but also "to the interests of the others" (Philippians 2:4).          —RD

## Like a Little Child

*"Truly I tell you, unless you change and
become like little children, you will never enter
the kingdom of heaven."* —MATTHEW 18:3

One evening many years ago, after saying a good-night prayer with our two-year-old daughter, my wife was surprised by a question. "Mommy, where is Jesus?"

Luann replied, "Jesus is in heaven and He's everywhere, right here with us. And He can be in your heart if you ask Him to come in."

"I want Jesus to be in my heart."

"One of these days you can ask Him."

"I want to ask Him to be in my heart *now*."

So our little girl said, "Jesus, please come into my heart and be with me." And that started her faith journey with Him.

When Jesus's disciples asked Him who was the greatest in the kingdom of heaven, He called a little child to come and join them (Matthew 18:1–2). "Unless you turn from your sins and become like little children," Jesus said, "you will never get into the Kingdom of Heaven" (vv. 3–5 NLT).

Through the eyes of Jesus we can see a trusting child as our example of faith. "Let the little children come to me," Jesus said. "Do not hinder them, for the kingdom of heaven belongs to such as these" (19:14).

—DM

# Paid!

*When he had received the drink, Jesus said,
"It is finished." With that, he bowed his
head and gave up his spirit.* —JOHN 19:30

The purpose for which our Lord came into the world, "to seek and to save that which was lost," reached its climax when He bowed His head on the cross and gave up His spirit. John recorded Jesus's expression in those final moments with the one Greek word *teleo*, which means, "It is finished."

Archeologists have repeatedly found its Latin equivalent, *consummatum est*, scrawled across tax receipts used in those days, indicating it also meant "paid." With sin's account settled on the cross, our debt of guilt was indeed wiped out!

A young fellow once came forward in a gospel meeting, earnestly asking, "What can I do to be saved?" The Christian worker replied, "You're too late!" "Oh, don't say that," the seeker exclaimed, "I'd do anything or go anywhere to obtain it." "I'm sorry," replied the other, "you're too late for that. You can't *do* anything. Your salvation was completed at Calvary. It's a finished work! All you have to do is simply receive Christ. The seeker found peace by looking to the Savior and resting completely on the grace of God."                                                          —HB

## The Pursuit of Happiness

*"Blessed are the poor in spirit. . . .*
*Blessed are those who mourn. . . . Blessed*
*are the meek."* — MATTHEW 5:3–5

Everyone wants to be happy, and people follow many avenues trying to achieve it. Buying fancy cars and luxurious homes. Taking self-improvement programs. Getting involved in a cause. The list goes on.

But that's the wrong list. The right one is found in Matthew 5. Jesus describes the way to deep and lasting happiness. He said we are blessed, or happy, when we are:

- Poor in spirit—recognizing our spiritual bankruptcy without God.
- Mourning—realizing the awfulness of sin and being genuinely sorry for it.
- Meek—demonstrating self-control, even when we are mistreated.
- Hungry and thirsty for righteousness—longing to be holy and pure.
- Merciful—showing mercy to others, just as God shows mercy to us.
- Pure in heart—being single-minded and sincere in our devotion to Christ.
- Peacemakers—sharing the peace Christ offers, and promoting peace with one another.
- Persecuted—being willing to suffer for Jesus's sake.

Pursuing happiness? Do it Jesus's way.          —DB

## Where Saintliness Begins

*Each one of you also must love his wife as he loves himself, and the wife must respect her husband. . . . Children, obey your parents in the Lord, for this is right.* —EPHESIANS 5:33; 6:1

Five-year-old Brian was impressed by the story of Simon the Stylite, a fifth-century Syrian hermit. This man was admired as a saint because he lived for more than thirty-five years on a platform atop a high pillar. Determined to follow Simon's example, Brian put the kitchen stool on the table and started his perilous climb. When his mother saw what he was doing, she shouted, "Brian! Get down before you break your neck!" As he obeyed, he muttered, "You can't even become a saint in your own house."

Of course, Brian was not aware of the true meaning of the word—everyone who trusts Jesus as Savior is already a saint (see Romans 1:7 NKJV), a person set apart for God. Yet his complaint does remind us that it's difficult to be saintly at home. When we're in public, we try to appear pleasant and attractive because we desire approval, but at home we figure that our family will love us no matter what. So we are not always saintly.

The Psalm 128 picture of a happy, harmonious home represents one of life's greatest delights. Do you want a home like that? Then remember that saintliness starts at home.　　　　　　　　　　　—HVL

## A New Heart

*Therefore, if anyone is in Christ, the new
creation has come: The old has gone, the
new is here!* —2 CORINTHIANS 5:17

There's an old Indian fable about a mouse who was afraid of cats. A wizard felt sorry for him and offered to help him lose his fear. So with the mouse's approval, the wizard turned him into a cat. The cat, however, was afraid of dogs. So the wizard turned the cat into a dog. But the dog was afraid of tigers. So the wizard turned the dog into a tiger. When the wizard discovered that the tiger was afraid of hunters, he exclaimed in disgust, "You're hopeless. What you needed was a change of heart! And that I cannot give you."

People too need a new heart. Everyone must be completely changed on the inside to overcome all of the sin-related fears.

This inner change occurs when we admit our sinfulness and place our trust in Christ for salvation. By God's Spirit we are born again, and we become a "new creation" (2 Corinthians 5:17). We are at peace with God, and as we live in obedience to Him we experience the peace of God.

Have you experienced the miracle of the new birth? We all need a new start with a new heart.

—RD

## The Power of God's Music

*Let the message of Christ dwell among you
richly as you teach and admonish one another
with all wisdom through psalms, hymns, and
songs from the Spirit, singing to God with
gratitude in your hearts.* —COLOSSIANS 3:16

When *The Sound of Music* was released in 1965, it won many accolades—including five Academy Awards—as it captured the hearts of people worldwide. Still today people attend special showings of the film where viewers come dressed as their favorite character.

Music is deeply rooted in our souls. And for followers of Jesus, it is a powerful means of encouraging each other along the journey of faith. Paul urged the believers in Colossae, "Let the message about Christ, in all its richness, fill your lives. Teach and counsel each other with all the wisdom he gives. Sing psalms and hymns and spiritual songs to God with thankful hearts" (Colossians 3:16 NLT).

Singing together to the Lord embeds the message of His love in our minds and encourages our souls. Whether our hearts cry out, "Create in me a pure heart, O God" (Psalm 51:10), or joyfully shout, "And he will reign forever and ever" (Revelation 11:15), the power of God-honoring music lifts our spirits and grants us peace.

Let us sing to the Lord today.                    —DM

## The Tattered Rug

*Children are a heritage from the LORD,*
*offspring a reward from him.*
—PSALM 127:3

A preacher tells of being entertained by a couple who had two teenage boys. He said that when he entered the house he immediately sensed it was a warm and loving home. During the course of his stay, he noticed that the carpet in the living room was tattered, and he wondered about it.

Before he left, the mother related a story that accounted for its condition. One day several boys from the neighborhood were having a good time in the living room. She preferred that they play elsewhere, so she asked them to leave. But her son's friends all claimed that their moms wouldn't want them messing up their houses.

The mother sensed that her home was the only one where the boys felt free to come and have fun. From then on they were always welcome. "After hearing that," said the preacher, "the tattered rug seemed almost beautiful—it was worn out in helping make those boys good."

A feeling of being loved and accepted is more important than a little wear and tear in the house. A "tattered rug" may be more a badge of honor than an eyesore!           —HB

## Let's Take a Break

*[Jesus] said to them, "Come with me
by yourselves to a quiet place and
get some rest."* —MARK 6:31

According to tradition, when the apostle John was overseer in Ephesus, his hobby was raising pigeons. It is said that on one occasion another elder passed his house as he returned from hunting and saw John playing with one of his birds. The man gently chided him for spending his time so frivolously. John looked at the hunter's bow and remarked that the string was loose. "Yes," said the elder, "I always loosen the string of my bow when it's not in use. If it stayed tight, it would lose its resilience and fail me in the hunt." John responded, "And I am now relaxing the bow of my mind."

We cannot do our best work while being constantly under pressure. When Jesus's disciples returned from a strenuous preaching mission, their Master recognized their need for rest in a quiet place.

Hobbies, vacations, and wholesome recreation are vital to a well-balanced, godly life. We lose our effectiveness by keeping our lives so tightly strung that we are always on edge. If it seems we can't relax, Jesus may be inviting us to take a break—to "get some rest."                                    —DB

## Sleepless Nights

*I will praise the Lord, who counsels me; even
at night my heart instructs me.* —PSALM 16:7

The psalmist David had his dark, lonely nights when
everything seemed out of control. Doubts and fears
assailed him, and there was no escape from his problems. He tossed and turned just as we do, but then he
turned to his Shepherd (Psalm 23:1) and reminded
himself of the Lord's presence. That brought peace
to his anxious, troubled soul. With God "at my right
hand," David said, "I will not be shaken" (16:8).

We too have occasions of wakefulness when anxious thoughts jostle one another for attention, when
we curse the darkness, and when we long for sleep.
But we mustn't fret, for darkness can be our friend.
God is present in it, visiting us, counseling us, in-
structing us in the night. Perhaps on our beds, as
nowhere else, we may hear God's voice. We can listen
to His thoughts and meditate on His Word.

We can talk to the Lord about every concern, casting our care on Him (1 Peter 5:7). That's what can set
us apart from ordinary insomniacs. That's the secret
of quiet rest.                                    —DR

# The Future Glory

*I consider that our present sufferings are
not worth comparing with the glory that
will be revealed in us.* —ROMANS 8:18

I recall the day my father, Dr. M. R. DeHaan, the
founder of this ministry, died. As the sun was sinking beneath the western horizon, Dad took a deep
breath and slipped into the presence of the One he
had loved and served so faithfully. During his final
days, he experienced unbearable physical distress. He
could say in a special way with Paul, "we ourselves
groan within ourselves, waiting for the adoption, to
wit, the redemption of our body" (Romans 8:23 KJV).

After Dad's death, my mother was leafing through
an old copy of *Our Daily Bread* and noticed these
words: "The only way left is UP, Mother! Now all I
need is patience! Dad" (December 6, 1965). Exactly a
week later, he was gone. In that same issue my father
had folded over the corner of the article, "The Way
Out Is Always Up" and had underlined this: "For our
light affliction, which is but for a moment, worketh
for us a far more exceeding and eternal weight of
glory" (2 Corinthians 4:17 KJV).

If you are suffering today, look up—and look
ahead! The comfort that sustained my father can also
be yours.                                   —RD

## The Listening Prayer

*Teach me your way, LORD, that I may rely
on your faithfulness; give me an undivided
heart, that I may fear your name.* —PSALM 86:11

How do you feel when you talk with someone who
isn't listening to you? It can happen with a friend who
has his own plans for how a conversation should go.

Now think about this in regard to your prayer-life.
Could it be that the way we talk to God is a one-sided
conversation dominated by us? Notice the observa-
tion of William Barclay in *The Plain Man's Book of
Prayers*: "It may be that one of our great faults in
prayer is that we talk too much and listen too little.
When prayer is at its highest, we wait in silence for
God's voice to us."

We might call this "the listening prayer," and it's a
practice we need to develop. We need to find a way
to get alone with God in quiet, to speak to Him in
earnest, taking time to listen to the urgings of the
Spirit and the instruction of His Word. We must say,
"Teach me your way, LORD, that I may rely on your
faithfulness" (Psalm 86:11).

We all need to learn the art of the listening prayer.
—DB

## The Faith of a Child

*"Whoever welcomes one of these little
children in my name welcomes me; and
whoever welcomes me does not welcome me
but the one who sent me."* —MARK 9:37

Lottie Kaulfield testified to the power of a child's witness in her life. When she and her husband were younger, they were not churchgoers. But their daughter began attending Sunday school when she was five or six years old. Soon she was singing to her mother the songs she had learned. She also started telling her the Bible stories she heard. The little girl loved going to Sunday school so much that she wanted to attend every week.

When the family made other plans, she would always be deeply disappointed. Finally, after seeing her daughter's love for Sunday school, Lottie began attending with her. It wasn't long before she trusted Jesus Christ as her Savior. One by one, the entire family came to know the Lord. As Lottie concluded her testimony, she observed that a little child had led her family to the best thing that ever happened to them—believing in the Lord Jesus and making the church an important part of their lives.

The faith of a little child can change a life.  —DE

## Times of Silence

*The LORD is good to those whose hope
is in him, to the one who seeks him; it is
good to wait quietly for the salvation of
the LORD.* —LAMENTATIONS 3:25–26

I remember several occasions when I stepped outside
in the stillness of a cold winter morning and gazed
upon fields and buildings coated with dazzling frost
or covered with sparkling snow. What an unforgettable experience! During the night, the silvery frost
had come silently, its unseen fingers deftly touching
the landscape. Or the feathery snowflakes had de-
scended without awakening a single soul. The silence
of such a moment would often bring the words of
Psalm 46:10 to mind: "Be still, and know that I am
God." I would also think of Habakkuk 2:20: "The
LORD is in his holy temple; let all the earth be silent
before him."

There are other times of silence when God speaks
to us. Sooner or later we lie sleepless as a result of illness, grief, or anxiety. These can be precious moments
of peaceful solitude when we tell the Lord we love
Him and want Him to speak to us. In the stillness we
can learn lessons we'd learn in no other way. Let's
set aside some time today to be silent before God.

—HVL

## Learning to Rest

*"Take my yoke upon you and learn from me,
for I am gentle and humble in heart, and you
will find rest for your souls."* —MATTHEW 11:29

Many Christians are anxious and troubled. Although they are experiencing the "rest" of salvation that accompanies the forgiveness of sins and are looking forward to the eternal "rest" of heaven, their souls are still in turmoil.

A closer look at their anxiety can reveal the reason for their distress. Having never learned to rest in the Lord, they fail to experience the "quietness and trust" (Isaiah 30:15) that comes to those who daily fellowship with Him through Bible study and prayer.

Don't let yourself become a victim of fruitless fretting. If you do, you'll lose the peace and joy that is your rightful heritage. Instead, set aside part of each day to talk with God, thanking Him for who He is and what He has done for you. Then, by reading His Word and believing His comforting promises, your faith will grow stronger and a supernatural peace will flood your soul.

Jesus said, "Come to me, . . . and I will give you rest" (Matthew 11:28). Have you learned to rest in Him?                                              —HB

## Where's the Baby?

*The Lord himself will give you a sign: The*
*virgin will conceive and give birth to a son,*
*and will call him Immanuel.* —ISAIAH 7:14

Two well-dressed women were having lunch together
in an exclusive restaurant. A friend saw them and
greeted them.

"What's the special occasion?" she asked. One of
the women said, "We're having a birthday party for the
baby in our family. He's two years old today." "Where's
the baby?" the friend asked. The child's mother answered, "Oh, I dropped him off at my mother's house.
She's taking care of him until the party's over. It
wouldn't have been any fun with him along."

How ridiculous—a birthday celebration for a child
who wasn't welcome at his own party! Yet, when you
stop to think about it, that's no more foolish than
going through the Christmas season, with all of its
festivities, without remembering the One whose birth
we are supposed to be honoring.

And that's the way many people celebrate Christmas.
In all the busyness—the party-going, gift-shopping,
and family gatherings—the One whose birthday they
are commemorating is almost completely forgotten.

At Christmastime, in all of your good times with
family and friends, make sure you don't leave out the
Lord Jesus. Give Him the honor He deserves. —RD

## Job Opening

*Be joyful in hope, patient in affliction,*
*faithful in prayer.* —ROMANS 12:12

A few years ago, just over a week before Christmas, my mother-in-law, Lenore Tuttle, died at the age of eighty-five. When she went home to be with Jesus, she left a void not only in our family but also in her church. One of its most faithful prayer warriors was gone.

At Mother Tuttle's funeral, the presiding pastor showed the congregation her prayer box. It contained dozens of prayer cards on which she had written the names of people she prayed for every day, including one that mentioned the pastor's gall bladder surgery. On top of that prayer box was this verse: "But without faith it is impossible to please Him, for he who comes to God must believe that He is, and that He is a rewarder of those who diligently seek Him" (Hebrews 11:6 NKJV). She was a true prayer warrior who diligently sought the Lord.

Each day, many older saints who have continued steadfastly in prayer (Romans 12:12) move on to heaven. This creates a "job opening" for people who will commit themselves to praying faithfully. Many of these positions remain unfilled. How can we help?
—DB

## The Smells of the Stable

*"The virgin will conceive and give birth to a son, and they will call him Immanuel" (which means "God with us").* —MATTHEW 1:23

A stable? What a place to give birth to the Messiah! The smells and sounds of a barnyard were our Savior's first human experience. Like other babies, He may even have cried at the sounds of the animals and the strangers parading around His temporary crib.

If so, they would have been the first of many tears. Jesus would come to know human loss and sorrow, the doubts his brothers and family had about Him, and the pain His mother experienced as she saw Him tortured and killed.

Yet from His very first moments, Jesus was "God with us" (Matthew 1:23), and He knew what it meant to be human. This would continue for over three decades, ending at His death on the cross.

Because of His love for you and me, Jesus became fully human. And being human allows Him to identify with us. Never again can we say that no one understands us. Jesus does.

May the Light that entered the world that night cast its brilliance into the deepest corners of our souls, giving us the peace on earth of which the angels spoke so long ago.                              —RK

# Where's the Peace?

*"Glory to God in the highest heaven, and
on earth peace to those on whom
his favor rests."* —LUKE 2:14

For many people, Christmas is the best day of the year. It's a time to celebrate the birth of the Prince of Peace (Isaiah 9:6).

But for some, there is no peace at Christmas. Tom Rademacher of *The Grand Rapids Press* kept track of police reports for Christmas Eve and Christmas Day one year. Here's what he found: A man threatened to kill his eighteen-year-old girlfriend. A thief snatched a woman's purse after she pulled into her garage. Thugs robbed a man of his Christmas presents in a store parking lot. A fifteen-year-old was arrested at three o'clock Christmas morning for toting a gun. That's just the tip of the iceberg. Think of all the police reports in the large cities of the US.

What does all this say about the coming of the Prince of Peace? The peace that was promised at His coming is an individual quietness of soul, which is experienced only by those who accept His gift of salvation. Universal peace awaits Christ's return as King.

Let's thank God for sending Jesus to bring the peace of sins forgiven.                              —DB

## The Prince of Peace

*Peace I leave with you; my peace I give
you. I do not give to you as the world
gives. Do not let your hearts be troubled
and do not be afraid.* —JOHN 14:27

I've always wondered about the promise of peace
the angelic host made to the shepherds in the fields
outside Bethlehem. For the last 2,000 years, peace
on our planet has been a rare commodity. Wars continue to ravage innocent lives, domestic violence is a
growing calamity, divorce rates soar, churches split,
and peace in our restless and wayward hearts seems
to be an elusive dream.

Where is the promised peace? Actually, on reflection, we can see that Jesus brought all that is needed
for peace in our world. He taught the principles of
peace, calling for people to love their neighbors as
they love themselves. And Jesus promised, "Peace I
leave with you; my peace I give you" (John 14:27).
He told us to turn the other cheek, go the extra mile,
forgive offenses, reject greed, tolerate each other's
weaknesses, live to serve and love one another as He
has loved us.

In large part, peace is up to us. Paul verifies this
in Romans 12:18, "As far as it depends on you, live
at peace with everyone." Let's make peace our gift to
the world as we reflect the Prince of Peace.　　　—JS

## A Personal Story

*Though my father and mother forsake me,
the LORD will receive me.* —PSALM 27:10

A baby just hours old was left in a manger in a Christmas nativity outside a church. A young, desperate mother had wrapped him warmly and placed him where he would be discovered. We can be thankful this baby was given a chance in life.

This gets personal for me. As an adopted child myself, I have no idea about the circumstances surrounding my birth. But I have never felt abandoned. Of this much I am certain: I have two moms who wanted me to have a chance in life. One gave life to me; the other invested her life in me.

In Exodus we read about a loving mother in a desperate situation. Pharaoh had ordered the murder of all baby boys born to the Jewish people (1:22). So, Moses's mother hid him as long as she could. When Moses was three months old, she put him in a watertight basket and placed the basket in the Nile River—where he was rescued.

When a desperate mother gives her child a chance, God can take it from there. He has a habit of doing that—in the most creative ways imaginable.   —TG

## Significant Surrender

*Humble yourselves, therefore, under
God's mighty hand, that he may lift
you up in due time.* —1 PETER 5:6

Throughout history, Mary the mother of Jesus has been held in high esteem. And rightly so! She was singled out by God to deliver the long-awaited Messiah.

But before we get lost in the significance of her life, let's take a look at what it meant for her to surrender to the assignment. Living in a small backwater Galilean village where everyone knew everyone else's business, she would have to live with the perceived shame of her premarital pregnancy. Explaining to her mother the visits of the angel and the Holy Spirit probably didn't calm things down. To say nothing of the devastating interruption that her pregnancy would bring to her plans to marry Joseph.

In that light, her response to the angel who told her the news about her role as Jesus's mother is amazing: "Behold, the maidservant of the Lord! Let it be to me according to your word" (Luke 1:38 NKJV). A life of significance is most often preceded by a heart eager to surrender to God's will regardless of the cost.

What significant experience does God have in store for you? It starts with surrender to Him.  —JS

## Mary's Christmas

*Mary treasured up all these things and
pondered them in her heart.* —LUKE 2:19

It was anything but an idyllic, silent night on that
cool Bethlehem evening when a scared teenager gave
birth to the King of kings. Mary endured the pain of
her baby's arrival without the aid of anything more
than the carpentry-roughened hands of Joseph, her
betrothed. Shepherds may have been serenaded in
nearby fields by angels singing praises to the Baby,
but all Mary and Joseph heard were the sounds of
animals, birth agony, and the first cries of God in
baby form.

As Joseph laid the infant in Mary's arms, a combination of wonder, pain, fear, and joy must have
coursed through her heart. She knew, because of
an angel's promise, that this tiny bundle was "the
Son of the Most High" (Luke 1:32). As she peered
through the semidarkness into His eyes and then into
Joseph's, she must have wondered how she was going
to mother this One whose kingdom would never end.

Mary had much to ponder in her heart on that
special night. Now, over 2,000 years later, each of us
needs to consider the importance of Jesus's birth and
His subsequent death, resurrection, and promise to
return.                                              —DB

## Take Time to Ponder

*Mary treasured up all these things and*
*pondered them in her heart.* —LUKE 2:19

Parents love to remember the developmental milestones of their children. They will record in a baby book when their little ones first roll over, then crawl, and take their first steps. Often they will take photographs and save baby clothing to bring back the memories of those precious experiences.

According to Luke 2:19, Mary, the mother of Jesus, kept a baby book of sorts—in her heart. She treasured the promises that had been given about her Son and "pondered them." Mary had heard of great things concerning her Son from angels and shepherds (1:32; 2:17–18), and she would think deeply about them.

Our faith will be strengthened and we will be encouraged when we meditate on what the Scriptures say about God and compare it with the way He works in our own lives (John 14:21). He is a God who answers prayer (1 John 5:14–15), comforts us in our suffering (2 Corinthians 1:3–4), and provides for our needs (Philippians 4:19).

When we take time to ponder, we will see the faithfulness of our great God.                          —DF

## Parent Care

*When Jesus saw his mother there, and the disciple*
*whom he loved standing nearby, he said to her,*
*"Woman, here is your son," and to the disciple,*
*"Here is your mother." From that time on, this*
*disciple took her into his home.* —JOHN 19:26–27

An elderly mother lives in a retirement home in Michigan. Her three grown sons live in other states. Each month they take turns and fly back to be with their mother and to look after her affairs. They started doing this years ago, even before their father died. "It's because the love is there," their mother told me.

When Jesus was bearing our sins on the cross and suffering intense agony, His heart was filled with loving care for His mother. Seeing her anguish, He fulfilled His duty to provide for her after His death. He entrusted her to the care of John, the disciple He loved. He would take her into his own home, and they would be a comfort to each other.

Jesus showed by His example that no matter how great our own burden of responsibility, it is always the Father's will that we extend loving concern to our parents. The fifth commandment (Exodus 20:12) is as up-to-date as it was when Jesus fulfilled it just moments before He died on the cross.

Children, behold your parents!                     —DD

## Finding Rest

*He refreshes my soul. He guides me along the*
*right paths for his name's sake.* —PSALM 23:3

A vacation can be good for body and soul. But many people don't have the luxury of time away from work and daily responsibilities. What can we do when we must remain in demanding circumstances?

Psalm 23 paints a beautiful word picture of a caring shepherd, secure sheep, and a tranquil scene of quiet meadows and still waters. But it is the Lord, our shepherd, who gives rest, not the green grass or the flowing stream. "He refreshes my soul. He guides me along the right paths for his name's sake" (v. 3).

Rest is a place of peace that our spirits find in God. Neither the presence of those who oppose us nor the dark valley of death can keep us from what hymnwriter Cleland McAfee called "a place of quiet rest, near to the heart of God." Through prayer and meditation on His Word, we can commune with Him. In the Lord's presence we can experience the rest and renewal we so desperately need.                    —DM

## Quiet, Please

*After the earthquake came a fire, but the
LORD was not in the fire. And after the fire
came a gentle whisper.* —1 KINGS 19:12

The spread of personal digital music players has
resulted in concerns about hearing loss. Long-term
exposure to music at a high volume has been shown
to cause serious hearing impairment. In a sense, too
much hearing can result in an inability to hear.

In the midst of this cacophony of sound, it's easy
to miss the one voice that matters most.

Elijah had listened to Jezebel's threats and the
voice of his own fear, so he fled to a cave to hide.
In the cave he was confronted with the overwhelming noise of wind, an earthquake, and fire (1 Kings
19:11–12). Then the cave grew silent and the voice
of the Lord—the only sound that mattered—broke
through as "a still small voice" (v. 12 NKJV).

If we are to hear God speaking to our hearts
through His Word, we need to pull away from the
noise. Only when we learn to be quiet can we really
understand what it means to commune with the God
who cares for us.

In our "quiet time" today, let's make an effort to
listen for the voice of God.                    —BC

## The Quiet Road

*Because so many people were coming and going that they did not even have a chance to eat, he said to them, "Come with me by yourselves to a quiet place and get some rest."* —MARK 6:31

Fifty miles west of Asheville, North Carolina, I turned off the busy highway and drove the remaining distance to the city on the scenic Blue Ridge Parkway. On that late fall afternoon I drove slowly, stopping often to savor the mountain vistas and the last of the brilliant autumn leaves. The journey was effective in restoring my soul.

The experience caused me to ask, "How often do I travel the quiet road with Jesus?"

After Jesus's disciples completed a demanding period of ministry, He said to them, "Come with me by yourselves to a quiet place and get some rest" (Mark 6:31). Instead of a long vacation, they had only a short boat ride together before being thronged by the crowd. The disciples witnessed the compassion of the Lord and participated with Him in meeting the needs of the multitudes (vv. 33–43). When the long day finally ended, Jesus sought renewal in prayer with His heavenly Father (v. 46).

There is great value in taking time each day to walk the quiet road with our Lord.                —DM

# "I Did Not Know It"

*Then Jacob awoke from his sleep and said,*
*"Surely the LORD is in this place, and I*
*did not know it." —GENESIS 28:16 NKJV*

As Jacob did in Genesis 28, I like to remind myself
each morning when I awaken that God is here, "in
this place," present with me (v. 16). As I spend time
with Him each morning, reading His Word and responding in prayer, it reinforces my sense of His presence—that He is near.

We take the Lord's presence with us all through
the day, blending work and play with prayer. He is
our teacher, our philosopher, our companion—our
gentle, kind, and very best friend.

God is with us wherever we go. He is in the com-
monplace, whether we know it or not. "Surely the
LORD is in this place," Jacob said of a most unlikely
spot, "and I did not know it" (Genesis 28:16 NKJV).
We may not realize He is close by. We may feel lonely
and sad. Our day may seem bleak and dreary without
a visible ray of hope—yet He is present.

Amid all the clamor and din of this visible and
audible world, listen carefully for God's quiet voice.
Seek Him. He is with you wherever you go!     —DR

# Writers

**JAMES BANKS** (JB) is pastor of Peace Church in Durham, North Carolina. Dr. Banks has written several books, including *Praying Together* and *Prayers for Prodigals*. He and his wife, Cari, have two adult children.

**HENRY BOSCH** (HB) (1914–1995) was the founder of the devotional booklet *Our Daily Bread* and its first editor. Throughout his life, he battled illness but turned his weaknesses into spiritual encouragement for others through his devotional writing.

**MONICA BRANDS** (MB) has a master of theological studies from Calvin Seminary in Grand Rapids, Michigan. She has worked with children with special needs. Monica grew up in Minnesota in a family with eight children. She began writing for *Our Daily Bread* in 2017.

**DAVE BRANON** (DB) is a senior editor with Discovery House. Dave has been involved with the devotional *Our Daily Bread* since the 1980s. He has written seventeen books, including three for Discovery House: *Beyond the Valley*, *Stand Firm*, and *Living the Psalms Life*.

**ANNE CETAS** (AC) became a follower of Jesus in her late teens. At nineteen, she was given a copy of *Our Daily Bread* by a friend. Several years later, she joined the editorial staff of *Our Daily Bread* as a proofreader. Anne began writing for the devotional booklet in September 2004 and is senior content editor for the publication.

**POH FANG CHIA** (PFC) trusted Jesus Christ as Savior as a teenager. She is an editor and a part of the Chinese editorial review committee serving in the Our Daily Bread Ministries Singapore office.

**BILL CROWDER** (BC), a former pastor, is vice president of ministry content for Our Daily Bread Ministries. Bill travels extensively as a Bible conference teacher, sharing God's truths with fellow believers in Malaysia and Singapore and other places where ODB Ministries has international offices. His many published books include *Seeing the Heart of Christ* and *For This He Came: Jesus' Journey to the Cross*.

**LAWRENCE DARMANI** (LD) is a noted novelist and publisher in Ghana, West Africa. Lawrence is editor of *Step* magazine and CEO of Step Publishers. He and his family live in Accra, Ghana. His book *Grief Child*, earned him the Commonwealth Writers' Prize as best first book by a writer in Africa.

**DENNIS DEHAAN** (DD) (1932–2014) became the second managing editor of *Our Daily Bread* upon the retirement of Henry Bosch in 1981. A former pastor, he loved preaching and teaching the Word of God.

**MART DEHAAN** (MD), former president of Our Daily Bread Ministries, followed in the footsteps of his grandfather M. R. and his dad Richard in that capacity. Mart, who was associated with *Day of Discovery* as host from Israel for many years, is now senior content advisor for Our Daily Bread Ministries. He can be heard weekdays on the radio program *Discover the Word*.

**M. R. DEHAAN** (MRD) (1891–1965) founded this ministry in 1938 when his radio program went out over the air in Detroit, Michigan, and eventually Radio Bible Class was begun. He was president of the ministry in 1956 when *Our Daily Bread* was first published.

**RICHARD DEHAAN** (RD) (1923–2002), son of the founder of Our Daily Bread Ministries, Dr. M. R. DeHaan, was responsible for the ministry's entrance into television. Under his leadership, *Day of Discovery* television made its debut in 1968. The program was on the air continuously until 2016.

**XOCHITL** (soh-cheel) **DIXON** (XD) equips and encourages readers to embrace God's grace and grow deeper in their personal relationships with Christ and others. Serving as an author, speaker, and blogger at xedixon.com, she enjoys singing, reading, motherhood, and being married to her best friend, Dr. W. Alan Dixon Sr.

**DAVID EGNER** (DE), a retired Our Daily Bread Ministries editor and longtime *Our Daily Bread* writer, was also a college professor during his working career. In fact, he was a writing instructor for *Our Daily Bread* writers Anne Cetas and Julie Ackerman Link at Cornerstone University in Grand Rapids, Michigan.

**ESTERA PIROSCA ESCOBAR** (EPE) is a Romanian with a heart for the world. After coming to the US as a college student, she experienced the Christian community's love for internationals. She is now National Field Director for International Friendships, Inc. (IFI). Estera and her Chilean-born husband, Francisco, live in Grand Rapids, Michigan.

**DENNIS FISHER** (DF) was for many years a senior research editor at Our Daily Bread Ministries—using his theological training to guarantee biblical accuracy. He is also an expert in C. S. Lewis studies. He and his wife, Janet, a former university professor, have retired to Northern California.

**VERNON GROUNDS** (VG) (1914–2010) was a long-time college president (Denver Seminary) and board member for Our Daily Bread Ministries. Vernon's life story was told in the book *Transformed by Love*.

**TIM GUSTAFSON** (TG) writes for *Our Daily Bread* and serves as an editor for Discovery Series. As the son of missionaries to Ghana, Tim has an unusual perspective on life in the West. He and his wife, Leisa, are the parents of one daughter and seven sons.

**HIA CHEK PHANG** (CPH) and his wife, Lin Choo, reside in the island nation of Singapore in Southeast Asia. C. P. came to faith in Jesus Christ at the age of thirteen. He is special assistant to the president of Our Daily Bread Ministries, and he helps with translating resources for the ministry. He and his wife have a son, daughter-in-law, grandson, and granddaughter.

**KIRSTEN HOLMBERG** (KH) has been a part of the *Our Daily Bread* writing team since March 2017. She lives in the northwest part of the United States, and in addition to her writing, she has a ministry of speaking to various church, business, and community groups. She is the author of *Advent with the Word: Approaching Christmas through the Inspired Language of God*.

**ADAM HOLTZ** (AH) is senior associate editor of Focus on the Family's media review website *Plugged In*. He has written a Bible study, *Beating Busyness*, and his first *Our Daily Bread* articles appeared in January 2018. He and his wife, Jennifer, have three children.

**ARTHUR JACKSON** (AJ) grew up in Kansas City, and he later returned home after spending nearly three decades in pastoral ministry in Chicago. He began writing for *Our Daily Bread* in 2017. He serves as director of two ministries—one that cares for pastors and one that seeks to plant churches worldwide. He and his wife, Shirley, have five grandsons.

**CINDY HESS KASPER** (CHK) served for more than forty years at Our Daily Bread Ministries. An experienced writer, she penned youth devotional articles for more than a decade. She is a daughter of longtime senior editor Clair Hess, from whom she learned a love for singing and working with words.

**ALYSON KIEDA** (AK) has been an editor for Our Daily Bread Ministries for over a decade and has more than thirty-five years of editing experience. Alyson has loved writing since she was a child and is thrilled to be writing for *Our Daily Bread*. She feels blessed to be following in her mother's footsteps—she wrote articles many years ago for another devotional.

**RANDY KILGORE** (RK) spent most of his twenty-plus years in business as a senior human resource manager before returning to seminary. Since finishing his Master of Divinity in 2000, he has served as a writer and workplace chaplain in Massachusetts. A collection of his devotionals appears in the book *Made to Matter: Devotions for Working Christians*.

**LESLIE KOH** (LK) was born and raised in Singapore, where he spent more than fifteen years as a journalist for a local newspaper, *The Straits Times*, before moving to Our Daily Bread Ministries. He has found moving from bad news to good news most rewarding, and he still believes that nothing reaches out to people better than a good, compelling story.

**ALBERT LEE** (AL) was director of international ministries for Our Daily Bread Ministries for many years, and he lives in Singapore. Albert's passion, vision, and energy expanded the work of the ministry around the world. Albert grew up in Singapore, and he took a variety of courses from Singapore Bible College, as well as served with Singapore Youth for Christ from 1971–1999.

**JULIE ACKERMAN LINK** (JAL) (1950–2015) A book editor by profession, Julie began writing for *Our Daily Bread* in 2000, and also published the books *Above All, Love; 100 Prayers Inspired by the Psalms;*

and *Hope for All Seasons*. Julie lost her long battle with cancer in April 2015.

**DAVID MCCASLAND** (DM) lives in Colorado, where he enjoys the beauty of God's grandeur as displayed in the Rocky Mountains. An accomplished biographer, David has written several books, including the award-winning *Oswald Chambers: Abandoned to God* and *Eric Liddell: Pure Gold*.

**ELISA MORGAN** (EM) has authored over fifteen books on mothering, spiritual formation, and evangelism, including *The NIV Mom's Devotional Bible* and *Hello, Beauty Full: Seeing Yourself as God Sees You*. She currently authors a blog under the title, *Really* (elisamorgan.com). For twenty years, Elisa served as CEO of MOPS International. Elisa is married to Evan (longtime senior vice president of global ministry efforts for Our Daily Bread Ministries), and they live in Denver, Colorado.

**KEILA OCHOA** (KO) teaches in an international school and assists with Media Associates International, a group that trains writers around the world to write about faith. She and her husband have two young children.

**AMY PETERSON** (AP) works with the honors program at Taylor University. She has a BA in English Literature from Texas A&M and an MA in Intercultural Studies from Wheaton College. Amy taught ESL for two years in Southeast Asia before returning stateside to teach. She is the author of the book *Dangerous Territory: My Misguided Quest to Save the World*.

**AMY BOUCHER PYE** (ABP) is a writer, editor, and speaker. The author of *Finding Myself in Britain: Our Search for Faith, Home, and True Identity*, she runs the Woman Alive book club in the UK and enjoys life with her family in their English vicarage.

**HADDON ROBINSON** (HR) (1931–2017), a renowned expert on preaching, served many years as a seminary professor. He wrote numerous books and hundreds of magazine articles. For a number of years he was a panelist on Our Daily Bread Ministries' radio program *Discover the Word*. Dr. Robinson went home to his eternal reward on July 22, 2017.

**LAUREN RODEHEAVER** (LR) resides in Grand Rapids, Michigan, with her husband and five young children. She earned her BA in Psychology from Taylor University and a Master's in Counseling Psychology at Seattle School of Theology. Since then, she has taught writing to homeschool students and practiced counseling/spiritual direction.

**DAVID ROPER** (DR) lives in Idaho, where he takes advantage of the natural beauty of his state. He has been writing for *Our Daily Bread* since 2000, and he has published several successful books, including *Out of the Ordinary* and *Teach Us to Number Our Days*.

**LISA SAMRA** (LS) was born and raised in Texas. She graduated with a BA in journalism from the University of Texas and earned a Master of Biblical Studies degree from Dallas Theological Seminary. Lisa now lives in Grand Rapids, Michigan, with her husband, Jim, and their four children.

**JENNIFER BENSON SCHULDT** (JBS) writes from the perspective of a mom of a growing family. She has written for *Our Daily Bread* since 2010. For several years, she also penned articles for another Our Daily Bread Ministries publication: *Our Daily Journey*.

**JOE STOWELL** (JS) is president of Cornerstone University where he stays connected to today's young adults in a leadership role. A popular speaker and a former pastor, Joe has written a number of books over the years, including *Strength for the Journey* and *Jesus Nation*.

**HERB VANDER LUGT** (HVL) (1920–2006) was senior research editor at Our Daily Bread Ministries for many years, responsible for checking the biblical accuracy of the literature published by the ministry. A World War II veteran, Herb spent several years as a pastor before his ODB tenure began.

**PAUL VAN GORDER** (PVG) (1921–2009) A writer for *Our Daily Bread* in the 1980s and 1990s, Paul was a noted pastor and Bible teacher—both in the Atlanta area where he lived and through the *Day of Discovery* TV program.

**LINDA WASHINGTON** (LW) received a BA in English/Writing from Northwestern University in Evanston, Illinois, and an MFA from Vermont College of Fine Arts in Montpelier, Vermont. She has authored or coauthored fiction and nonfiction books for kids, teens, and adults, including *God and Me* and *The Soul of C.S. Lewis*.

**MARVIN WILLIAMS** (MW) is senior teaching pastor at a church in Lansing, Michigan. His foray into Our Daily Bread Ministries came as a writer for *Our Daily Journey.* In 2007, he penned his first *Our Daily Bread* article.

**KAREN WOLFE** (KW) was originally from Jamaica but now lives in Tennessee with her husband Joey. She became a Christian as an adult, and she later received theological training at New Orleans Baptist Theological Seminary. Her debut article in *Our Daily Bread* appeared in August 2017.

**JOANIE YODER** (JY) (1934–2004) was a beloved *Our Daily Bread* writer for ten years. In addition, she published the book *God Alone*.

# Help us get the word out!

Our Daily Bread Publishing exists to feed the soul with the Word of God.

### If you appreciated this book, please let others know.

- Pick up another copy to give as a gift.
- Share a link to the book or mention it on social media.
- Write a review on your blog, on a bookseller's website, or at our own site (ourdailybreadpublishing.org).
- Recommend this book for your church, book club, or small group.

### Connect with us:

 @ourdailybread

@ourdailybread

@ourdailybread

Our Daily Bread Publishing
PO Box 3566
Grand Rapids, Michigan 49501 USA

✉ books@odb.org

# MORE GREAT DEVOTIONALS FOR WOMEN

*from*
## Our Daily Bread